I0752677

THE SECRET GENESIS OF
AREA 51

THE SECRET GENESIS OF AREA 51

TD BARNES

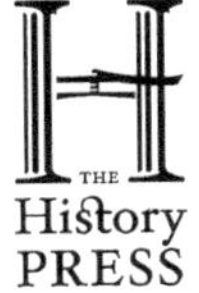

Published by The History Press
Charleston, SC
www.historypress.net

First published 2017

ISBN 978-1-5402-2645-7

Library of Congress Control Number: 2017940927

Notice: The information in this book is true and complete to the best of our knowledge. It is offered without guarantee on the part of the author or The History Press. The author and The History Press disclaim all liability in connection with the use of this book.

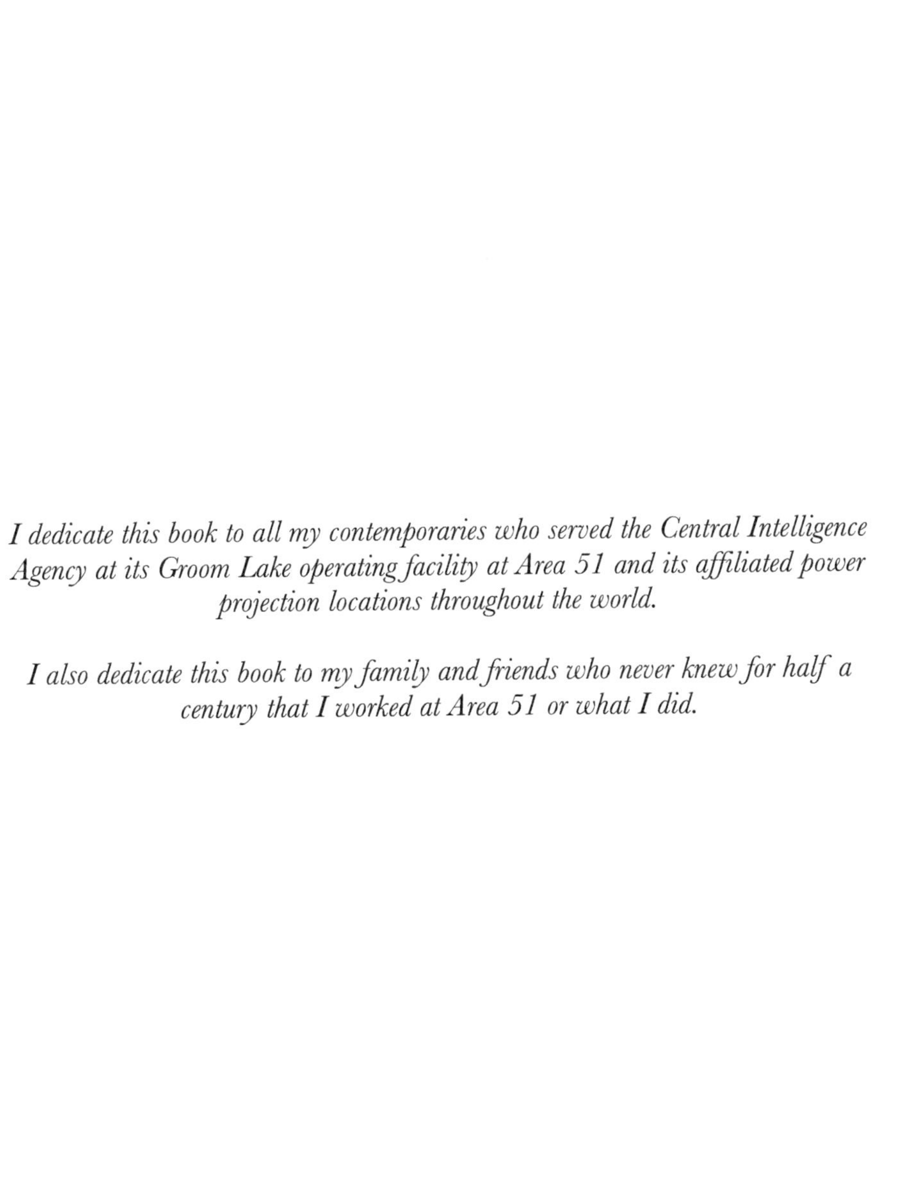

I dedicate this book to all my contemporaries who served the Central Intelligence Agency at its Groom Lake operating facility at Area 51 and its affiliated power projection locations throughout the world.

I also dedicate this book to my family and friends who never knew for half a century that I worked at Area 51 or what I did.

For it is the lot of some men to be assigned duties about which they may not speak. Such work is not for every man. But, those who accept the burdens implicit in this silent labor realize a camaraderie and sense of value known to few. Nothing can steal or erase these memories. They will last always, untarnished, ever better.

—former Area 51 commander Colonel Larry McClain

CONTENTS

Acknowledgements 11
Introduction 13

1. An Uneasy Truce 19
2. The War that Wasn't 27
3. A Young Agency versus the Old Guard 43
4. Scouting for Area 51 61
5. Organizing in Secrecy 85
6. We Can't Tell You the Assignment, Gentlemen 109
7. Flying the Angel 119
8. Watertown Goes Operational 133
9. The Overflight Missions 145
10. Back at the Ranch 163

Epilogue 175
Glossary 179
Bibliography 181
Index 185
About the Author 191

ACKNOWLEDGEMENTS

I first acknowledge my wife, Doris, and my two daughters, Deborah and Tamera. Doris didn't know until 2009 where I worked or for whom during all the years she dropped me off in a secured area at Nellis AFB to catch a plane on Monday morning and picked me up when I returned Friday evening. She learned from Director Michael Hayden at Langley that I was at Area 51 working for the Central Intelligence Agency (CIA) on black projects. Our daughters knew where I worked because they, too, worked in the black world after I left it. They did not know until Doris did what my work was because it was still classified top secret up to that point. Neither Doris nor I know what they did because what they did is still classified.

I especially acknowledge my Area 51 CIA contemporaries, known as the Roadrunners, for whom I have been honored to serve as the alumni president for years. These are the CIA, Air Force and contractors working at or directly affiliated with the CIA projects at Area 51, many of them identified in this book.

I acknowledge the following individuals for their contributions to the CIA's era at Area 51:

Dr. David Robarge, PhD, the CIA's chief historian and author of *Archangel: CIA's Supersonic A-12 Reconnaissance Aircraft.*

The Honorable Gene Poteat, retired CIA, for his technical contributions to Area 51. Poteat fathered information warfare. With Project PALLADIUM, he forever changed the course of U.S. aerial reconnaissance.

Helen H. Kleyla, who compiled the report declassified by the CIA and herein referenced by me. The declassified report documents the political turmoil leading to the Central Intelligence Agency establishing Area 51. Kleyla served the CIA for thirty years, much of it as the assistant to CIA's Dick Bissell. Kleyla was the first woman to set foot at the CIA facility in Area 51.

Richard Mervin Bissell Jr., the Central Intelligence Agency officer responsible for the U-2 spy plane. Bissell and Herbert Miller, another CIA officer, chose Area 51 as the CIA's test facility. As the CIA's DD/P (deputy director of plans), Bissell also oversaw the early stages of Project OXCART, the development of the Lockheed A-12.

Dr. Albert D. "Bud" Wheelon, PhD, the first CIA deputy director of science and technology, for his support of Project OXCART. I acknowledge Wheelon's friendship and support of my oral history endeavors.

CIA Area 51 commanders Richard Newton, Werner Weiss and Richard A "Dick" Sampson for their leadership that made Area 51 what it is today.

CIA's John Parangosky, project manager for OXCART, for developing America's first stealth plane that today remains the world's fastest and highest-flying manned air-breathing aircraft ever.

Lockheed's Kelly Johnson and all the other corporate management and employees supporting the CIA at Area 51.

In this acknowledgment, I include the historians, writers and aviation enthusiasts whose research and support brought to light the rich and historical legacy of the CIA at Area 51.

Lastly, I acknowledge all my contemporaries who served at or supported those serving at Area 51. These include the unnamed agency, military and civilians whose participation remains buried or lost beneath the shroud of compartmentalized secrecy. Many remain unknown and are destined never to receive the acknowledgment deserved.

INTRODUCTION

World War II ended with Europe devastated. Vast swaths of Europe and Asia lay in ruins, with the world population of 2 billion reduced by 4 percent, 80 million people killed (670,846 of them servicemen and women) and 30,314 missing. The front lines in Europe were silent, but for how long?

The world's largest country, the Communist Russia Federation—better known as the Soviet Union or the USSR (the Union of Soviet Socialist Republics)—France, England and the United States divided the Allied-occupied Germany. However, the Soviet Union, a union of various subnational republics, wanted more; it wanted revenge for over twenty-seven million of its people killed during World War II. The two colonialist allies, France and England, wanted to regain their colonies occupied by the enemy during the war. They all expected the United States to foot the bill to rebuild Europe even though the United States was still waging war against Japan in the Pacific.

In April 1945, following the death of U.S. president Franklin D. Roosevelt, the new U.S. president, Harry S. Truman, rather than using "get along" diplomacy as Roosevelt did, berated Soviet foreign minister Vyacheslav Molotov over his spread of communism. At the same time, the United States was financially supporting rebuilding its colonialist allies, England and France, and their liberated colonies to prevent them falling to the Soviet communist movement. The United States extended $400 million in military aid to Greece and Turkey, signaling its intent to contain communism in the Mediterranean.

After providing nearly $11 billion in aid to several European countries between 1945 and 1947 through the United Nations Relief and Recovery Administration, the Truman administration announced the Marshall Plan in June 1947 to provide aid to sixteen nations. The Soviet Union took an increasingly hostile view of the Marshall Plan, refusing East Bloc participation and calling it an "imperialist ploy" for the enslavement of Europe. In September 1947, the Soviets founded the Communist Information Bureau, which ordered party members to mobilize against the Marshall Plan. French and Italian communists responded by staging strikes and intensive propaganda campaigns.

Thus, it came to be that the Soviet Union returned to its Red Army ways of rebuilding by occupying the liberated countries, forcefully spreading communism throughout Eastern Europe.

In the war against Japan, Major General Curtis LeMay's Twentieth Air Force B-29s had conducted an unprecedented five-month fire blitz using four B-29 groups operating from India, staging through China to spew incendiaries within the maximum range of southern Japan. The hellish low-level aerial incendiary firebombing of Japan from the air in night attacks had Tokyo burning following the single most destructive attack on a city in the history of warfare, killing some 250,000 civilians and maiming many more. One raid, the Meetinghouse raid, indiscriminately killed more people than the atomic bombings of Hiroshima or Nagasaki that supposedly ended the war with Japan. Only ten cities larger than 100,000 people escaped the attacks, which were so extensive that they resorted to bombing towns of 30,000 people or fewer.

By May 1945, the Japanese had lost the war in the Pacific and were making requests for peace. On August 3, 1945, Japan offered to surrender but withdrew the offer because the Potsdam Conference called for an unconditional surrender, exposing many of Japan's top government officials to face war crimes trials like those ongoing against Germany's leaders in Europe.

On August 9, 1945, exactly three months after the surrender of Germany and between the August 6 American atomic bombing of Hiroshima and the bombing of Nagasaki on August 9, 1945, the massive and battle-hardened Red Army steamrolled into Manchuria. The Soviet invasion of Manchuria, known as the Manchurian Strategic Offensive Operation or Operation August Storm, played a significant part in the Japanese government's decision to surrender unconditionally on August 15, 1945.

Soviet troops brushed aside scattered Japanese resistance and sliced through what had once been an elite Japanese army, only stopping when they ran out of gas, to occupy Manchuria, where about 700,000 troops looted and terrorized the people of Mukden in three days of rape and pillage. Many Japanese settlers chose mass suicide over the approaching Soviet army. Mothers killed their children before killing themselves or being mercy-killed by the Japanese forces.

The decisive Soviet invasion, in a single stroke, evaporated all of Japan's strategic and diplomatic options. While the invasion of Manchuria contributed to the surrender of Japan and the end of World War II, it also provided an opportunity for the Soviets to occupy Manchuria and the northern portions of the Korean peninsula under the control of communist-backed regimes.

For President Truman, the Soviet invasion made ending the war extremely time sensitive. He needed the atomic bomb to win the war before the Russians, who had done in four days what the United States was unable to do in four years. Giving the Russians credit for winning the war would give the perception of Soviet military power and enhance communism.

Japan had no allies, the war had destroyed its fleet, its islands were under a naval blockade and its cities were burning from months of concentrated firebomb air attacks when, on August 6, 1945, the B-29 bomber *Enola Gay* dropped the first atomic bomb (nicknamed "Little Boy") on Hiroshima. Two days later, the United States dropped the second bomb on Nagasaki.

Dictator Joseph Vissarionovich Stalin, the general secretary of the central committee of the Soviet Union, saw the dropping of the bomb as the United States intimidating the Soviet Union, using its atomic advantage for imperialism.

The United States Sought Intelligence Too Little and Too Late

In July 1941, Roosevelt had appointed William Joseph Donovan, a United States soldier, lawyer, intelligence officer and diplomat, as the coordinator of information, the nation's first peacetime, non-departmental intelligence organization. However, this appointment occurred too late for Donovan to develop the knowledge to prevent the Japanese sneak attack on Pearl Harbor. Only after the surprise attack by Japan did the president form the Office of Strategic Services (OSS)

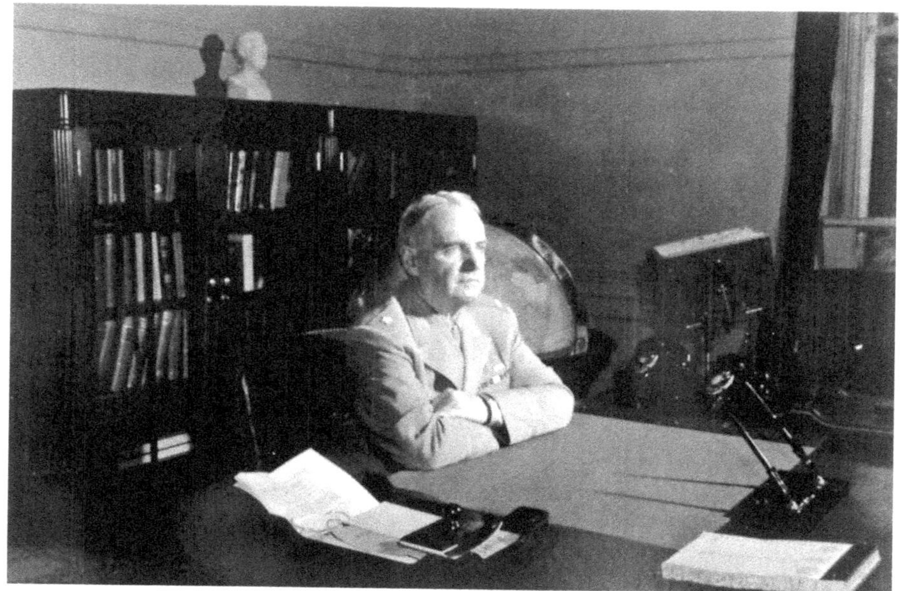

William J. "Wild Bill" Donovan, the father of American intelligence and director of the Office of Strategic Services (OSS), the precursor to the Central Intelligence Agency, was an American soldier, lawyer, intelligence officer and diplomat during World War II. *Wikipedia.*

to collect and analyze the strategic information required by the joint chiefs of staff. Even then, the Office of Strategic Services only conducted special operations not assigned to other agencies.

The forming of the Office of Strategic Services shaped a lasting U.S. intelligence hierarchy in the United States; the office shared jurisdiction over foreign intelligence activities with the Federal Bureau of Investigation but left the military branches to conduct intelligence operations in their areas of responsibility.

One could argue that Truman's treatment of the Russian leader, Stalin, merely inflamed him and changed the course of history. One could also wonder the motives for dropping the two atomic bombs on a defeated nation willing to surrender.

Regardless of the reasons, the use of the atomic bomb alienated Stalin. Russia next invaded Japanese Sakhalin and the Kuril Islands. But then the giant bear, Russia, spread its communist dominance by occupying the countries it liberated from the Japanese. The Red Army remained in liberated Korea north of the thirty-eighth parallel, dividing the Korean peninsula into Soviet and U.S. occupation zones along that line.

History has shown that the end of World War II brought a sentiment throughout the United States of returning to normalcy. Unfortunately, the leaders considered normalcy as demobilizing wartime agencies. The Soviet Union was still occupying North Korea and threatening to do the same with South Korea, making it one Korea—a communist Korea. Nonetheless, President Truman withdrew American troops from South Korea, and a month following the surrender of Japan, he signed Executive Order 9621, terminating the Office of Strategic Services. He said it was because Donovan's civilian and military rivals feared the man they called "Wild Bill Donovan" creating a peacetime intelligence service modeled on the Office of Strategic Services.

Why? Was this the reason, or was it to squash any questions about how the war with Japan ended?

Declassification

In March 2016, the Central Intelligence Agency declassified and released a report titled "CIA, Directorate of Science and Technology (DST), History of the Office of Special Activities (OSA) from Inception to 1969." This report officially confirmed that the CIA was responsible for developing the mythical, highly classified Area 51 in Nevada. The author, an Area 51 veteran, could now respond to these two issues and many others that this declassification released for the telling. This book answers five questions: who, what, where, when and why. However, it does not venture into the still classified post-CIA era at Area 51.

CHAPTER 1

AN UNEASY TRUCE

Allies and Communists

The United States and its allies had much more to fear than the American president's and the military services' fear of Donovan and each of them protecting their turf. They quickly learned that more war was the normalcy for the Russians. Soviet amphibious forces were landing in Korea even while the Soviet Union was invading Manchuria, and shortly afterward, the French Far East Expeditionary Corps of the Provisional Government of the French Republic entered Vietnam to restore colonial rule.

Where diplomacy might have prevented another war, Russia was not the only one alienated by President Truman. At this point, Ho Chi Minh did not have the communist label that came later for political reasons. Where Roosevelt opposed the French resuming their colonization of Indochina, Truman did the opposite.

When Truman pulled the plug on the Office of Strategic Services, the OSS's Special Operations Team Number 13, code-named the "Deer Team," was in French Indochina training Viet Minh guerrillas, gathering intelligence in the waning days of World War II and collaborating with Ho Chi Minh for his coming to power.

With the surrender of Japan, Vietnam was for the first time in two thousand years free of occupation. With Roosevelt dead, Ho Chi Minh pleaded with President Truman to keep the French from returning to rule his country. President Truman ignored his request and, instead, insulted Ho Chi Minh by giving him a small number of Colt .45 semi-automatic pistols to show that "Ho had the support of the United States."

A lost opportunity for the United States, it pulled the Office of Strategic Services team out of Vietnam and opposed Ho Chi Minh's attempt for the independence of the Democratic Republic of Vietnam by supporting the French resuming their colonialism. This lack of aid forced Ho to seek the assistance of communist Russia to keep the French out. Consequently, Vietnam emerged from World War II as the Viet Minh—a communist and nationalist liberation movement under the Marxist-Leninist revolutionary Ho Chi Minh. The resulting First Indochina War would last until July 1954, with the United States paying 80 percent of the cost of a war that France would lose and the United States would continue until April 1975—an inevitable war to contain Soviet-sponsored communism.

By early 1946, Truman had realized that his disbanding the Office of Strategic Services had blinded the United States to what the Russians were doing militarily. He realized the lack of vital intelligence on Soviet Union activities coming from the rivalry that existed among the military services having independent information-gathering means. To avoid exacerbating these rivalries, the president first established the Central Intelligence Group in 1946. He ultimately created the Central Intelligence Agency in 1947 to provide U.S. leaders with a strategic warning of an attack by the Soviet Union.

Also, in 1947, two years after the end of World War II, President Truman's fear of communism was such that he created the Truman Doctrine as an American foreign policy to counter the Soviet geopolitical spread during the Cold War. He fueled the political and military tension with the Soviet Union by providing aid to Greece and Turkey to prevent them from falling into the Soviet sphere. The doctrine further pledged aid to all nations threatened by Soviet expansionism. This difference in policy brought the Cold War to a head. The USSR saw no way to defend its borders except to extend them as it continued its consolidating control over the Eastern Bloc states. The United States countered this with a strategy of global containment to challenge Soviet power by extending military and financial aid to the countries of Western Europe. Truman signed the Marshall Plan into effect, costing the United States $12.4 billion.

The Soviet Union refused an offer to participate in Truman's Marshall Plan and blocked the benefits to the Eastern Bloc countries, East Germany and Poland. Soviet premier Joseph Stalin ordered the blockade of all land routes from West Germany to Berlin to starve out the French, British and American forces from the city. He wanted it all. The Soviet Union severed all land and water connections to halt all rail and barge traffic to and from Berlin with the intent of starving the German people. The three Western powers responded by launching the Berlin airlift to supply the citizens of Berlin. The airlift lasted for more than a year, during which time hundreds of American, British and French cargo planes ferried 2.3 million tons of provisions from Western Europe. A plane took off or landed in West Berlin every thirty seconds, making nearly 300,000 flights in all.

Meanwhile, Russia remained entrenched in the Far East, where the Soviet's Communist Information Bureau was calling for the withdrawal of foreign soldiers from Korea and calling for free elections in each of the two administrations and unification of the peninsula.

The Formation of the CIA

In 1947, when the Central Intelligence Agency came into existence to replace the Central Intelligence Group, little did it realize that in less than a decade, it would undertake overhead reconnaissance over the Soviet Union, modeling after the Nazis with their brutal military conquests against their neighboring countries.

Twenty months after the January 1946 forming of the Central Intelligence Group, under the National Security Act of 1947, the Soviet Union posed a greater threat to the United States than ever. Paranoia about the Soviet threat deepened in June 1947 when a United States Air Force Project Mogul balloon crashed on a ranch near Roswell, New Mexico. The location of the wreckage created a sequence of events triggered when the public information officer at Roswell Army Air Field issued a press release stating that personnel from the field's 509th Operations Group had recovered a "flying disc" and that a UFO (unidentified flying object) had crashed on a ranch near Roswell.

Paranoia erupted as UFO sightings occurred throughout the world. Ordinary American citizens saw flying saucers and feared the Russians had joined with extraterrestrial invaders. The incident went viral when early on Tuesday, July 8, the Roswell Army Air Force issued a press release that was immediately picked up by numerous news outlets. The release stated:

> *The many rumors regarding the flying disc became a reality yesterday when the intelligence office of the 509th Bomb group of the Eighth Air Force, Roswell Army Air Field, was fortunate enough to gain possession of a disc through the cooperation of one of the local ranchers and the sheriff's office of Chaves County. The flying object landed on a ranch near Roswell sometime last week. Not having phone facilities, the rancher stored the disc until he could contact the sheriff's office, who in turn notified Maj. Jesse A. Marcel of the 509th Bomb Group Intelligence Office. The action was immediately taken, and the disc was picked up at the rancher's home. It was inspected at the Roswell Army Air Field and subsequently loaned by Major Marcel to higher headquarters.*

The unidentified flying object paranoia extended all the way to President Truman, who almost immediately ordered the United States Air Force separated from the Army Air Corps. The Roswell incident remains today the world's most famous, most exhaustively investigated and most thoroughly debunked UFO claim ever.

The United States and its allies had much more to fear: the spread of communism and the growing Soviet Union threat. But first, Truman had his internal political battles to contend with, which were brought on by his disbanding the National Intelligence Authority and the Central Intelligence Group. When he signed the National Security Act of 1947 to establish the National Security Council (NSC), he reactivated the old World War II Office of Strategic Services to become the modern-day Central Intelligence Agency.

Secretary of State James Byrnes took the position that an organization such as the Central Intelligence Agency should be responsible to him—that he should be in control of all intelligence. The army and the navy, on the other hand, strongly objected, each maintaining that every department required its independent intelligence. They considered a central intelligence organization a threat to their prerogatives and a competitor for resources. They wanted the CIA's role to be to pool information that each agency contributed to it. That was not to be.

The National Security Act provided new offices that included the secretary of defense, Department of the Army, Department of the Navy and Department of the Air Force, along with other departments and agencies of the government concerned with national security. The president feared Donovan might foster a movement to establish a super body controlling all intelligence. Thus, he fought against the organized information of the Office of Strategic Services when the United States most needed the knowledge it provided. Nonetheless, he shouldered the CIA with the nation's survival when he asked the CIA to focus on Russia to determine the kind and number of strategic weapons the Soviet Union had. It meant them having to know how the Soviet Union intended to use them.

The Communist Scare

The CIA saw the entire world in turmoil. On August 29, 1949, the Soviet Union added to the world's fear of communism when it tested its first atomic bomb, known to Americans as Joe 1. Suddenly, the communist Soviet Union ranked as the world's second nuclear power and an adversarial contender against the United States in a nuclear arms race. The minute hand of the symbolic Doomsday Clock had inched closer to midnight in its countdown to a global catastrophe as the world moved closer to a nuclear war.

In the United States, the Red Scare ran rabid, with Senator Joseph McCarthy naming numerous American celebrities as members of the Communist Party. He relentlessly pushed through and became the chairman of the Government Committee on Operations of the Senate as he widened his scope to investigate dissenters. He continued for over two years, relentlessly questioning numerous government departments to the point that McCarthyism caused panic with his witch hunts and fear of communism, exasperated by Mao Zedong declaring the foundation of the People's Republic of China, adding a quarter of the world's population to the communist camp.

One could easily compare the Soviet spread of communism to German's Nazi movement. Any notion of world peace faded and war alliances ceased when the Soviet Union in effect formed an imaginary boundary dividing Europe into two separate areas. The split became the Iron Curtain blocking the Soviet Union and its satellite states from open contact with the West and non-Soviet-controlled areas. The east side of the Iron Curtain contained the countries connected to or influenced by the Soviet Union. On either side of the Iron Curtain, states developed their own international economic and military alliances. The western countries had no idea what was occurring on the Soviet aspect of this imaginary wall that started as a symbolized effort and became watchtowers overlooking a barrier marked by posts and signs, a strip of land with dog patrols. Barbed-wire fences soon appeared, followed by rumors of the Soviet Union's intent to erect an actual wall in Berlin to separate the city.

While the world was watching the Soviet Union in Europe, in 1948, Russian inserted its influence in the Far East by proclaiming the Democratic People's Republic of Korea the legitimate government of all Korea and propping Kim Il-sung up as prime minister. In communist China, the American consul and his staff were virtual hostages in Mukden. The calamitous prospect of war with the Soviet Union now included China.

Amid the war drums, the saber rattling and the swirling clouds of war, the Central Intelligence Agency, only three years old, lacked the resources to gain the intelligence needed as World War III with Russia and China appeared inevitable. Through all of this, the CIA maintained its focus on Moscow while elsewhere, the Republic of China severed diplomatic relations with the United Kingdom and diplomatically recognized Vietnam as independent from France.

Within four years of World War II ending, the Soviet Union had the states of Eastern Europe effectively curtained off from the outside world and was carrying out with utmost secrecy the expansion of all Soviet strategic capabilities—its bomber forces, ballistic missiles, submarine forces and nuclear weapons plants. The Soviet air defense system was unknown for determining U.S. retaliatory policies, rendering the entire panoply of U.S. intelligence tradecraft ineffective against the Soviet Bloc.

The Soviet empire bullied and intimidated its enemies and victims as it sought a proxy war with the United States. Every May Day, the first day of May, it flaunted its increasing strategic capabilities, creating the perception that it vastly overshadowed the United States' role in the military world. The entire U.S. military establishment went on alert in response to the USSR intimidating the world by parading a massive number of troops along with its latest war machines, aircraft and missiles for all to see. The USSR secrecy about its actual strength made it impossible for the United States to establish retaliatory measures.

The Soviet Bloc borders curtailed U.S. HUMINT covert human intelligence activities, costing the CIA the loss of its intelligence gathering by telephone, telegraph and radiotelephone. The CIA found its entire panoply of intelligence tradecraft ineffective at a time when rumors concerning the large bomber forces of the Soviet Union shocked Washington. At almost all levels, the U.S. government realized the need to seek information on Soviet strategic forces and their strategic capabilities.

The Cold War continued, with the Soviet Union at every chance opposing the United States, whether as a proxy enemy combatant or as an adversary at the United Nations. Whatever the United States wanted or did, the Soviet Union opposed. When the Soviet Union acquired the atomic bomb in 1949, President Harry S. Truman responded by establishing a nationwide emergency radio broadcast alert system to warn the citizens of an invasion and to prevent enemy planes using radio transmitters as navigation aids for direction finding in a real attack.

The government established nuclear bunkers for high-ranking public officials, and critical military facilities began operating inside mountains. Throughout America, citizens built fallout shelters in their cities and their backyards. The shelters were identified by ominous placarded yellow and black trefoil radiation warning signs. American cities conducted civil air raid drills to the warbling sounds of civil defense klaxons. American schools performed duck and cover drills, where students took cover beneath their school desks in prone-like positions with eyes protected from the blinding light of the nuclear fireball.

President Truman was focused on the Soviet Union in Europe when he announced his intent to withdraw all remaining American forces from South Korea by June 1949. Stalin was waiting in the shadows when the commander of KMAG (Korean Military Advisory Group), General William Lynn Roberts, voiced utmost confidence in the ROK (Republic of Korea) army when he boasted of defending against a North Korean invasion as mere "target practice."

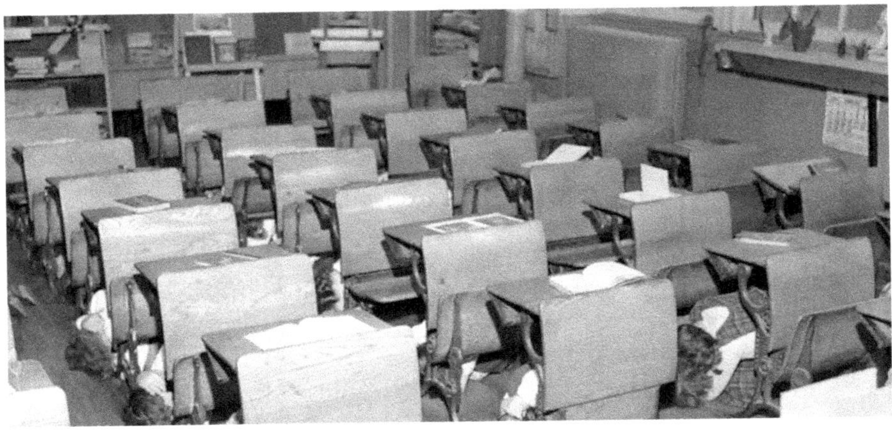

American schoolchildren practicing a duck and cover drill for protection from a feared Soviet atomic bomb attack. *Wikipedia.*

Stalin saw the situation differently. Once the Americans left, he could take South Korea without getting the Soviet Union embroiled in a war with the United States. Less than a year later, Secretary of State Dean Acheson confirmed Stalin's view when Acheson failed to include Korea in his outline of the strategic Asian Defense Perimeter. The American soldiers were entirely withdrawn from Korea, showing the American military strategists focusing more on Europe and the Soviet Union than East Asia.

Military deception, using strategic, political and diplomatic means, was a critical element of Russia's geopolitical ambitions. The Soviet doctrine was never admitting your true intentions and denying your activities. Use all means, both political and military, to maintain an edge of a surprise for the Soviet Union military forces. The Soviets kept the Americans guessing through the repertoire of deceit, disguise and psychological warfare doctrine the Soviet Union used in the Battle of Stalingrad. While the United States focused on what the Soviets were hiding behind the Iron Curtain, the Red Army was eyeing the American weakness in the Far East.

Thus, the nation's Central Intelligence was still in its infancy when in 1951, two years later, the United States was back at war, another shooting war. Some called it the Korean War, an undeclared war with North Korea and China.

CHAPTER 2

THE WAR THAT WASN'T

Getting Through the Iron Curtain

The Korean War was a proxy war with the Soviet Union that confirmed America's fear of the United States being on Russia's list of countries to conquer. Rather than call it a war with Russia, American president Harry Truman called the war a police action.

The Soviets were right about the timing and the American military weakness in the Far East. The Americans did not intervene to stop the communist victory in China during the Chinese civil war. Now, in the spring of 1950, President Truman's withdrawal of all American troops from South Korea had left the South Koreans with no tanks, anti-tank weapons or heavy artillery—no means of stopping an attack from the north. The United States wasn't even looking to see what the Soviet Union was doing north of the thirty-eighth parallel. When the United States did exclude Korea from its outline of the strategic Asian Defense Perimeter, Stalin saw this as the Americans discarding South Korea—as a signal of the United States having no will to fight in the Far East.

Consequently, on Sunday, June 25, 1950, the Soviet Union and China ignited the inevitable proxy war with the pro-western Republic when the communist North Korean People's Forces, supported by Soviet-supplied tanks, heavy artillery and aircraft, poured seventy-five thousand strong across the thirty-eighth parallel to invade the Republic of South Korea.

For the second time, a surprise Pearl Harbor–like attack had caught the United States unprepared. However, this time, the action occurred in Korea, with North Korean soldiers doing the fighting. President Truman had his second war and the Central Intelligence Agency its first.

When Secretary of State Dean Acheson notified President Harry Truman at his home in Independence, Missouri, of the invasion, Truman reacted by instructing Acheson to contact the United Nations to seek a resolution condemning the attack and offering aid to assist South Korea. Meanwhile, two days later, the South Korean forces sacked Seoul. In five days, the South Korean forces of ninety-five thousand men were down to fewer than twenty-two thousand.

The Korean War Intelligence Controversy

By all appearances, the North Korean attack caught the Truman administration, the U.S. Army's Far East Command under General Douglas A. MacArthur and the fledgling CIA by surprise. The surprise attack sparked a persistent controversy about whether the agency warned U.S. policymakers that North Korea would attack its southern neighbor. Despite the agency having encountered insurmountable obstacles as the army, navy, Atomic Energy Commission and others refused to share information that they considered exclusive prerogatives and usurped responsibilities, the CIA would have to dispel widely held assertions that it had committed a serious intelligence breach.

The new CIA had only five thousand employees worldwide, counting at the time of the invasion the components it inherited from the Central Intelligence Group. Only one thousand of them were analysts, and only three were employed as operations officers in Korea. In the three years before the Korean War, the Joint Research and Development Board formed by the secretaries of war and the navy had stymied and blocked attempts to staff the Central Intelligence Agency, which prevented the agency obtaining any useful intelligence.

Nonetheless, contrary to what historians would write for many decades, CIA analysts frequently reported happenings in Korea during the prewar years. Admittedly, the CIA reports were from a perspective that highlighted the Soviet Union's involvement rather than local Korean events. Through all the Soviet smokescreens of deceit, the CIA saw anything beyond routine as Soviet mischief-making and proxy-sponsored "tests" of American resolve.

The CIA analysts never counted on the Soviet Union, still recovering from World War II, orchestrating a monolithic communist movement worldwide to stamp out freedom. Thus, the CIA never expected the invasion of South Korea that marked the first military action of the Cold War. Barring a Soviet decision for global war, such action did not make sense. Nonetheless, three years after its creation, the CIA found itself unexpectedly involved and had to scramble to find and train personnel to conduct an array of espionage and covert operations unilaterally and in support of U.S. Armed Forces taking part in the UN coalition.

Stalin had stated his intent to Truman and the Allies even before they withdrew America's support of South Korea, yet the CIA received the blame for the lack of intelligence causing the war. The Truman administration and critics of the CIA conveniently forgot how only six months earlier, Secretary of State Dean Acheson had failed to include Korea in his outline of the strategic Asian Defense Perimeter. Nor did they give the agency's Office of Research and Reports credit for dire predictions about the possibility of some regional crises from 1947 through 1950. Understandably, in a world menaced by communists everywhere, the CIA's reporting on Korea did not stand out either in intelligence publications or the minds of policymakers. All eyes focused on Moscow, the Kremlin, East Germany—wherever there was a spread of communism.

At the time, America viewed the communist movements around the world as Kremlin-controlled. Therefore, events in Korea seemed to be just one of many fronts in the Cold War. North Korean activity was closely interrelated with other Soviet-induced crises but not of any greater or lesser importance. Everyone was, at the time, focused on the security of Europe against the Soviet Union. The Soviet strategy of deceit worked.

In all fairness to the agency, starting in 1949, the CIA reporting on the potential for war in Korea was more explicit. When President Truman sought military proposals for withdrawing U.S. forces from the peninsula, the CIA warned that removing U.S. troops would likely lead to war. Nevertheless, the critics did not fault President Truman for withdrawing all American soldiers from Korea. In doing so, he all but waved a flag to signal the Soviet bear to come and get South Korea.

Almost from the moment of the last U.S. military personnel departure, North Korea began a continuing southward movement of the expanding North Korean People's Army toward the thirty-eighth parallel. The CIA saw the acquisition of heavy equipment and armor. However, recognizing "the present program of propaganda, infiltration, sabotage, subversion and guerrilla operations against southern Korea," the agency did not see an invasion as imminent.

No one blamed President Truman for disbanding the Office of Strategic Services, which could have probably foreseen the surprise attack across the thirty-eighth parallel. Instead, critics of the CIA before and after the Korean invasion focused on the CIA's relatively few references to Korea in intelligence reporting. They noted the lack of any predictive estimated or other "actionable" warning information to allow U.S. policymakers to anticipate Korean events before they reached the crisis stage. The critics rated it an intelligence failure of the highest magnitude. The administration feared the war quickly widening into another world war should the Chinese or Soviets decide to get involved as well. The critics were wrong, and the president was right. Regardless, during the next two years, the agency underwent significant organizational changes and hired additional personnel to remedy any real or alleged deficiencies, resulting in a larger CIA and a new Directorate of Intelligence created in early 1952.

In some ways, the United States invited the war by not including South Korea in the strategic Asian Defense Perimeter. Officially, the United States never declared it a war. President Truman described it as a "police action." It became the "Forgotten War" or the "Unknown War" from the lack of public attention it received both during and after the action.

To the CIA, this was the second U.S. war to occur from the lack of prior intelligence to foresee the invasion—another Pearl Harbor. The CIA vowed it would never allow a sneak attack to happen again.

The United States entered the Korean War flying propeller-engine bombers and fighters virtually unopposed. The Soviet Union showed up with the MiG-15. Suddenly, there was a MiG Alley, where American pilots found themselves clashing with Soviet-piloted MiG-15s over North Korea. The Soviet Union extended its air defense policy even more during its proxy war against the United States during the Korean War, downing a twin-engine U.S. Navy Neptune bomber near Vladivostok in 1951 and an RB-29 in the Sea of Japan on June 13, 1952.

Regardless of its name, lost in the war were 5 million soldiers and civilians: 36,574 Americans died, 7,984 of them still missing in action and 4,714 still listed as prisoners of war, many of these believed taken to the Soviet Union. Nonetheless, the Korean War failed to receive the same media attention in the United States as had World War II. The television series *M*A*S*H*, a comedy set in a field hospital in South Korea, became the most famous representation of the war. The final episode became the most watched in television history up to that time.

The United States emerged from the Korean War, where American pilots faced the Soviet MiG-15, urgently needing strategic intelligence on the Soviet Union and its satellite states. At significant risk, U.S. Air Force and Navy aircraft began long-range aerial reconnaissance on peripheral flights using oblique photography to penetrate the veil of secrecy around military activities in the Soviet interior. These shallow penetration reconnaissance flights covered only the Soviet Union west of the Urals and west of the Volga River, and only a few of the important regions for which they paid a high price in lives lost and increased international tension. The United States lost ten RB-47 planes with seventy-five crew members and pilots to Russian antiaircraft guns.

They found that only an electronic reconnaissance mission, however, could provide signal data on the existence of Soviet radar. They began actual intrusions into Soviet territory, seeking to photograph targets impossible to image from the periphery. The RB-47s found gaps in the Soviet air warning network, looking for weaknesses where they could dart in with a penetration photography flight to photograph what they could. At best, the U.S. intelligence gained fragmentary bits of SENSINT (sensitive intelligence).

However, this information came at a high cost of lives. The Soviet air defenses aggressively attacked the existing reconnaissance aircraft, primarily bombers converted for reconnaissance duty such as the Boeing RB-47, making them vulnerable to antiaircraft artillery, missiles and fighters. In Operation Home Run, six crews flew RB-47 reconnaissance aircraft to penetrate the northern area of Russia without making it public for discussion. The United States kept this secret because it did not want to admit to these operations. The Soviet Union kept it a secret because it did not want to acknowledge that the United States could overfly the Soviet Union with such ease. Nonetheless, avoiding the navy and air force aircrew losses called for a spy plane with a camera that the Soviet Union could not shoot down.

President Harry Truman wanted to develop such a plane; however, the United States Air Force chief, General Curtis LeMay, refused to build an aircraft that did not shoot guns or drop bombs. He protected his turf by opposing anyone other than the U.S. Air Force doing any such flying.

Faced with a stalemate with the air force, and wishing to use civilian aircrews and nonmilitary planes, the president turned to the Central Intelligence Agency to secretly build such a plane. But first, the CIA had to battle both the U.S. Air Force and the politicians in Washington to do so. These political battles would continue through twelve directors of Central Intelligence and several presidents occupying the Oval Office.

Project LINCOLN—The BEACON HILL Report

On June 15, 1952, a group met concerning the loss of lives while conducting reconnaissance flights over the Soviet Union. The group of experts became known as Project LINCOLN and their report the BEACON HILL Report, a study of Air Force Intelligence prepared at a secretarial school on Beacon Hill in Boston to research aerial reconnaissance.

Physicist Carl Overhage, working on the development of Technicolor at Kodak, chaired the study group of experts in aerodynamics, propulsion, optics and a broad spectrum of fields. The group included Saville Davis from the *Christian Science Monitor*, Allen Donovan from the Cornell Aeronautical Laboratory, Peter Goldmark from Columbia Broadcasting System Laboratories, Stewart Miller of Bell Laboratories and Louis Ridenour of Ridenour Associates, Inc.

One of the group was Edward M. Purcell, a physicist who won a Nobel Prize in 1954 for his work in nuclear resonance. He had served on advisory bodies that included the USAF Scientific Advisory Committee and Edwin Land's Technological Capabilities Panel study group.

Another of the group was James G. Baker, a Harvard astronomer and lens designer who was a leading designer of high-acuity aerial lenses during World War II and continued this work after the war. He also headed the Air Force Intelligence Systems Panel and served on the Technological Capabilities Panel's Project Three committee that urged the development of the U-2 aircraft. Baker designed the lenses for the U-2's cameras.

Committee member Richard Perkin, the president of the Perkin-Elmer Corporation, was a close friend of James Baker and was also a member of several advisory panels, including the BEACON HILL project. He would later help Baker decide what cameras to use in the first U-2 aircraft.

Edwin Land was an incredibly talented inventor famous for the development of polarizing filters and the instant-film camera. He also devoted considerable time and energy to voluntary government service. During World War II, Land worked for the Radiation Laboratories, and after the war, he served on numerous air force advisory panels. As the head of the Technological Capabilities Panel's study group investigating U.S. intelligence-gathering capabilities, Land became a strong advocate of the development of a high-altitude reconnaissance aircraft (the CL-282) under civilian rather than air force control. Land and James Killian persuaded President Eisenhower to approve the U-2 project and, later, the first photo satellite project. Land also served on the President's Board of Consultants for Foreign Intelligence Activities.

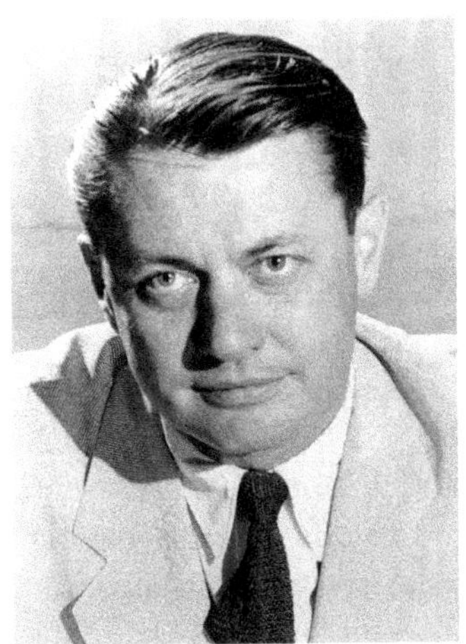

Lieutenant Colonel Richard Leghorn, an MIT graduate in physics, served as recon pilot in World War II and was recalled from Kodak during the Korean War to develop the overflight concept. He headed the Scientific Engineering Institute, working on reducing the U-2's vulnerability to radar detection. *Wikipedia.*

Lieutenant Colonel Richard Leghorn, the Wright Air Development Command liaison officer on the committee, was an MIT (Massachusetts Institute of Technology) graduate in physics. He joined the army air force in 1942 and went to work for reconnaissance expert Colonel George Goddard. By the time of the invasion of Europe, Leghorn was chief of reconnaissance for the Ninth Tactical Air Force. After the war, he began preaching the need for "pre-D-day" reconnaissance to gather intelligence on the Soviet Bloc. He returned to the air force during the Korean War and later worked in Harold Stassen's Disarmament Office. In 1956, he would become the head of the Scientific Engineering Institute, working on reducing the U-2's vulnerability to radar detection.

The study group spent weekends at various air bases, laboratories and firms where it conducted briefings on the latest technology and projects focusing on aerial reconnaissance. Members discussed new approaches to aerial reconnaissance using high-flying aircraft, camera-carrying balloons and even an "invisible" dirigible, a giant, flat-shaped airship with a blue tint, a nonreflecting coating, that cruised at an altitude of ninety thousand feet at slow speeds while using a large camera lens to photograph targets of interest.

At the Massachusetts Institute of Technology, the panel spent three months detailing ways to improve the amount and quality of intelligence gathered on the Soviet Bloc, advocating radical approaches to obtain national intelligence using radar, radio, photographic surveillance, passive infrared and microwave reconnaissance and the development of high-altitude reconnaissance aircraft.

In March 1953, the need for a reconnaissance plane obtained another believer with William E. Lamar, the chief of the New Developments Office, Bombardment Aircraft Branch, at Wright Air Development Center in Dayton, Ohio. He drew up a proposal calling for high-altitude reconnaissance aircraft.

Shortly afterward, the U.S. Air Force implemented the ideas of the BEACON HILL Report that addressed the concerns of the president and the U.S. political and military leaders regarding the Soviet Union's moving inexorably toward having military parity with the United States. This concern came from the Soviet's displaying alarming progress with nuclear weapons when it detonated a hydrogen bomb manufactured from lithium deuteride. To the United States, this demonstrated a sharp advancement in technology over its heavy water method.

The Soviet Union followed this successful hydrogen bomb test two months later with an aggressive incident where Soviet troops crushed an uprising in East Berlin. Officials such as Secretary of State John Foster Dulles saw the Soviet Union as a threat to future peace. A top-secret study by RAND Corporation, an American nonprofit global think tank originally formed by Douglas Aircraft Company, pointed out the vulnerability of the U.S. bases to a surprise attack by Soviet long-range bombers.

Even without the RAND Corporation study, the U.S. Air Force feared the Soviet bomber force surpassing the U.S. fleet. The fear was for an excellent reason: the capability of the Soviet Union to launch a surprise attack on the United States might destroy 85 percent of the Strategic Air Command (SAC) bomber force.

No one wanted another MiG surprise. The Soviet Union escalation of the war in the Far East combined with the RAND Corporation's study prompted the U.S. Air Force to establish the Intelligence Systems Panel (ISP). Through this new advisory group, the U.S. Air Force sought ways of implementing the construction of high-flying aircraft and high-acuity cameras.

The experts—Land, Overhage, Donovan and Miller—used the BEACON HILL Study Group's report for recommendations. The CIA contributed Edward L. Allen of the Office of Research and Reports (ORR) and Philip Strong of the Office of Scientific Intelligence (OSI) to the group.

The U.S. military expressed its desire for better strategic aerial reconnaissance to help determine Soviet capabilities and intentions. Thus, when the Intelligence Systems Panel first met at Boston University on August 3, 1953, Strong emphasized the poor state of U.S. knowledge of the Soviet Union. He informed the others that the best intelligence available on the Soviet Union's interior dated back to the German Luftwaffe during World War II. Worse yet, the German photography covered only the Soviet Union west of the Urals, west of the Volga River and only a few of the important regions.

On July 27, 1953, the Korean War formally ended with the signing of an armistice where North and South Korea remained separated and occupied almost the same territory they had when the war began. The proxy war with the Soviet Union ended with General Curtis E. LeMay, the commander in chief of the Strategic Air Command (CINSAC), still facing the question of what the Soviet Union was doing behind its closed borders and what Russia and the Soviet Bloc intended to do next. Compounding the general's lack of knowledge about the Soviet's war capability was his receiving a scathing review following Strategic Air Command's performance. His bombers recently had performed dismally during simulated bomb runs against American cities. Consequently, he didn't trust the air force's bombing radar guidance system's bomb-on-target accuracy required for delivery of the first-generation twenty-kiloton atomic bombs available at the time.

The failing Strategic Air Command bombing evaluations highlighted the nation's concern about the Soviet Union now being a nuclear threat. Military commanders worldwide questioned to what extent the Soviets had developed their nuclear weapons and the magnitude of the Soviet military buildup in Eastern Europe.

President Dwight Eisenhower had earlier proposed to Soviet premier Nikita Khrushchev to allow unfettered overflights by both nations to photograph military installations to stabilize the situation. Khrushchev refused the open skies proposal.

Following Khrushchev's refusal, Eisenhower decided to give the green light for the development of a reconnaissance aircraft capable of overflights of the Soviet Union above the range of Soviet countermeasures. Eisenhower acknowledged the country's need for this kind of information. At the same time, he feared the enemy eventually catching the planes and this being a problem. His fear was well grounded.

Earlier, in 1952, the U.S. Air Force at Cape Canaveral in Florida used the SRC-584 radar before transferring it to NASA for use at Beatty and Ely, Nevada, on the NACA (National Advisory Committee on Aeronautics)/ NASA High Range corridor extending from Wendover, Nevada, to

Dryden/Edwards AFB in California. Thus, the U.S. Air Force and CIA realized that NASA had modified the radar's tracking capability. If NASA could do so, so could the Soviet Union. The successful modification proved the need for a new reconnaissance aircraft to overfly the Soviet Union. It showed the United States needed an aircraft capable of escaping detection by the same model radar that Russia used.

In 1953, the Soviet Union's best interceptor, the MiG-17, could barely reach forty-five thousand feet, so many thought an aircraft flying at seventy thousand feet placed it beyond the reach of Soviet fighters, missiles and radar. For early warning, the Soviet Union used an SCR-370 having a range of 120 miles. Though having a greater range, the curvature of the earth limited its track capability to a maximum forty-thousand-foot altitude.

For tracking, the Soviet Union used the early American-built (Signal Corps Radar) SRC-584 radar system that Russia obtained through the World War II Lend-Lease program. The SRC-584 system was microwave-

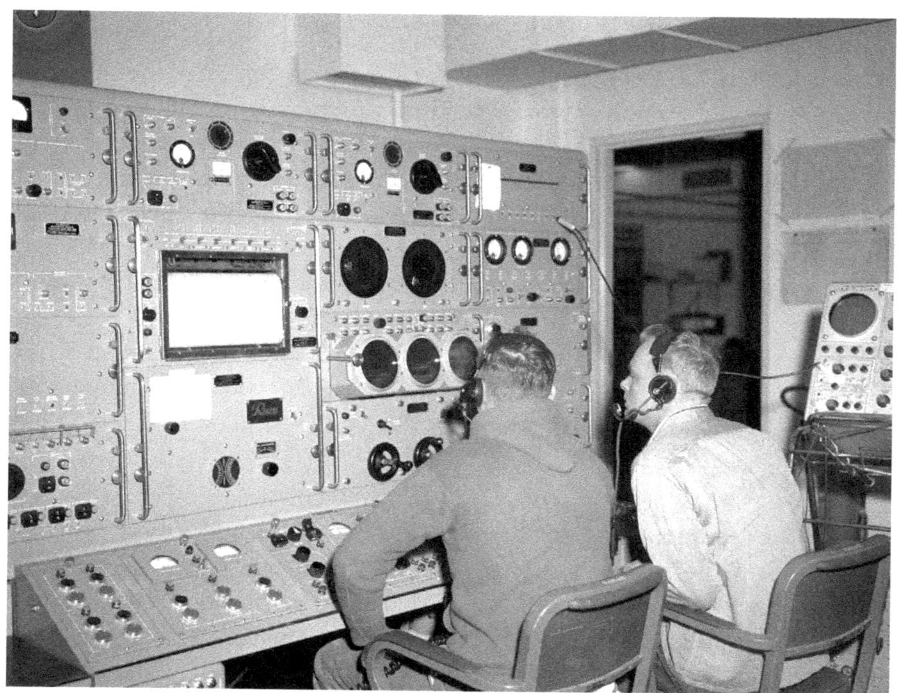

The SCR-584 Mod-II microwave-type radar (Signal Corps Radio #584) built by the MIT Radiation Laboratory was used during World War II for the U.S. Army's primary antiaircraft gun-laying system and provided the Soviet Union without compensation under the March 1941 Lend-Lease Act. The Soviet Union used this radar to track the CIA's U-2 overflights. *NASA*.

type radar designed and built by the MIT Radiation Laboratory as the U.S. Army's antiaircraft gun-laying system during World War II. The SRC-584 tracking radar detected bomber-size targets at a maximum range of only forty miles, tracked them at eighteen miles and up to ninety thousand feet. However, the SRC-584 radar used such high-power consumption that it burned out its cavity magnetron tube (an electron tube for amplifying or generating microwaves, with the flow of electron control by an external magnetic field). Therefore, unless it received a warning from the search radar, the target-tracking radars remained inactive. Consequently, Major John Seaberg and his collaborators based their advocacy of high-altitude photo reconnaissance on the belief that the Soviet Union search radar could not detect an aircraft flying higher than sixty-five thousand feet, and even if it did, its tracking radars would be inactive. The four believed that an aircraft ascending to sixty-five thousand feet before entering the range of the radar could fly undetected by the early warning radar.

John H. "Jack" Carter, now retired from the U.S. Air Force and the assistant director of Lockheed's Advanced Development Program, heard about the competition for a high-flying reconnaissance plane. He dropped by to see Eugene Kiefer, an old friend and colleague from AFDAP (the U.S. Air Force's Office of Development Planning). He then returned to California, where he sought out Lockheed vice president L. Eugene Root, the top civilian official at AFDAP. Carter proposed to Root that Lockheed should submit a design for an aircraft capable of reaching altitudes between sixty-five and seventy thousand feet and a speed near Mach 0.8. He introduced a nonstandard model, one that eliminated the landing gear, disregarded military specifications and had low load factors. He emphasized the need to accelerate development to allow the aircraft to serve a long and useful life.

To save weight and increase altitude, Carter suggested the design eliminate having landing gear and avoid attempting to meet combat load factors for the airframe. The Lockheed Company asked Clarence "Kelly" Johnson to come up with such a design.

Kelly Johnson already rated as one of the world's leading aeronautical engineers. His military and civilian design credits included the P-38, P-80, F-104 and the Constellation. In 1953, he conceived the CL-282 plane to overfly the Soviet missile test facility at Kapustin Yar in the Soviet Union to obtain intelligence that the air force refused to attempt. For the proposal, Johnson based his CL-282 design on the Lockheed XF-104, a plane with long, slender, high-aspect-ratio sailplane wings and a short fuselage.

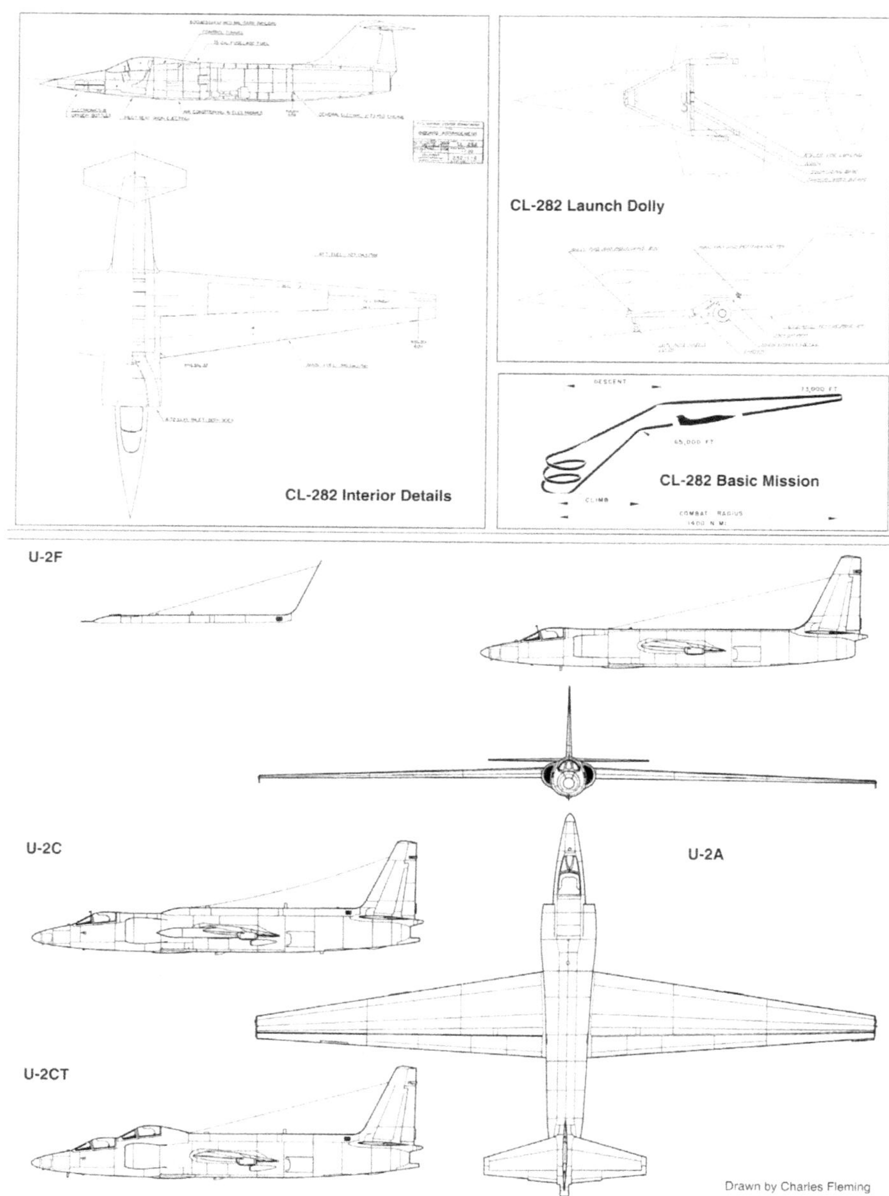

CL-282 (U-2) details. *From Jay Miller's* Lockheed's Skunk Works, the First Fifty Years.

Johnson had earned a reputation for completing projects ahead of schedule while working in a separate division of the company, informally called the Skunk Works. This reputation helped Lockheed earn admission to the competition in the fall of 1953. Lockheed approved Carter's proposal and, by early 1954, had its best aircraft designer, Kelly Johnson, working on the CL-282, which later became the U-2.

His concept saved weight and increased the aircraft's altitude by limiting the stress to the airframe to only 2.5 g. He selected the General Electric J73/GE-3, the same non-afterburning turbojet engine chosen for the F-104, and adapted many of the CL-282's design features from gliders. He ended up with a design having detachable wings and tail, a plane that landed on its reinforced belly instead of landing gear, making it a jet-propelled glider.

The three firms—Bell Aircraft Corporation of Buffalo, New York; the Fairchild Engine and Airplane Corporation of Hagerstown, Maryland; and the Lockheed Skunk Works of Burbank, California—submitted their proposals in January 1954, with Bell proposing the model 57, later known as the X-16, a twin-engine craft with a maximum altitude of 69,500 feet. Fairchild entered the M-195, a single-engine plane with a maximum potential altitude of 67,200 feet, and Glenn L. Martin Aircraft Company of Baltimore submitted a large wing design version of the B-17 called the Model 294 with a height of 64,000 feet.

Kelly Johnson sent the CL-282 design to Brigadier General Bernard Schriever's Office of Development Planning in early March 1954. On the recommendation of Kiefer and Charles F. "Bud" Wienberg, General Schriever asked Lockheed to submit a specific proposal. Lockheed did so the following month, with Johnson following with a plan for Lockheed to construct and maintain thirty aircraft.

Johnson submitted the proposal to a group of senior Pentagon officials that included Schriever's superior, Lieutenant General Donald L. Putt, deputy chief of staff for Development, and Trevor N. Gardner, special assistant for the Research and Development to the secretary of the U.S. Air Force. Johnson's proposal interested the civilian officials. However, it failed to interest the generals. Kiefer, Wienberg and Burton Klein from the Office of Development Planning presented the CL-282 design to the commander of the Strategic Air Command, General Curtis E. LeMay, in early April 1954. General LeMay stood up halfway through the briefing, took his cigar out of his mouth and told the briefer that if he wanted high-altitude photographs, he would put cameras on his B-36 bombers.

He added that he lacked any interest in a plane with no wheels or guns. The general left the room, remarking the whole business a waste of his time. (Note: General LeMay felt the same concerning the later SR-71, saying, in effect, that he did not want anything that did not shoot guns or drop bombs.)

Seaberg recommended the adoption of both the Martin and Bell proposals while expressing a preference to Martin's version as an interim project. The U.S. Air Force approved Martin's proposal to modify the B-17, seeing this as providing a rapid completion and deployment potential.

In mid-May, Seaberg and his colleagues evaluated the Lockheed submission and rejected it in early June. Rather than the unproven General Electric J73 engine proposed by Johnson, the engineers at Wright Field preferred the Pratt & Whitney J57 engine. The designs from Fairchild, Martin and Bell all incorporated this engine.

The U.S. Air Force, preferring multiengine aircraft to the single-engine design proposed by Lockheed, did nothing different to reduce the loss of camera-carrying bombers conducting ferret flights over Soviet military installations. The Strategic Air Command continued flying Reflex Alert deployments of Convair B-36 and B-47 Stratojet long-range nuclear bombers to overseas bases such as Nouasseur Air Base in French Morocco. The intent was to place them within striking range of Moscow with enough fuel to escape. As one might expect, the original concept of using a light plane met rejection. It was not a combat aircraft.

The U.S. Air Force also felt two engines better than one, embracing the theory that if one engine failed, the other engine could bring the plane back to a base. Unfortunately, the U.S. Air Force's concept required excess weight that made high-altitude flying impossible. Nonetheless, General Curtis LeMay, "Old Iron Pants," had no interest in the air force flying a specially powered, single-engine glider that would fly at seventy thousand feet, at a speed of five hundred knots, to a range of 3,000 nautical miles with only a lone pilot. Instead of carrying bombs or guns, it would use a camera with a long focal length to photograph man-sized targets within a strip 200 miles wide and 2,500 miles long.

Setting aside the two engines, guns and bombs rhetoric, LeMay and his like-minded staff, the U.S. Air Force rejected Lockheed's CL-282 proposal simply because it had only one engine and its design was too unusual. Meanwhile, despite the U.S. Air Force rejection, Lockheed continued working on the CL-282 while the company sought new sources of support for the aircraft.

Aviation records and history revealed single-engine aircraft more reliable than multi-engine planes. The U.S. Air Force failed to realize a high-altitude reconnaissance aircraft deep in enemy territory would have little chance of returning to a friendly base should an engine fail. Such a failure would force the plane to descend to an altitude reachable by enemy planes or missiles.

Following the Berlin Airlift, the United States and the Soviet Union faced each other in the air hundreds of times. The bloodiest period started in 1950, during the Korean War, when Soviet fighters shot down over twenty United States Navy and Air Force planes, mainly reconnaissance aircraft, in one-sided fights with Russian MiGs.

Dimitri Volkogonov, co-chairman of a Russian-U.S. commission formed to investigate the fate of Americans missing from and since the Korean War, claimed Americans imprisoned in the Soviet Union included more than 730 pilots and other airmen who either made "forced landings on Soviet territory" or were shot down on Cold War spy flights. Volkogonov was not specific on their fate but spoke about prisoners interned in labor camps, some executed and others eventually forced to renounce their U.S. citizenship.

CHAPTER 3

A YOUNG AGENCY VERSUS THE OLD GUARD

A New Kind of Warfare

Eisenhower categorically refused the possibility of letting someone from the U.S. Air Force fly one of the aircraft. Eisenhower stated, "If the Soviet Union shoots down such an aircraft while flying over the Soviet Union, I'd prefer it to be a nonmilitary aircraft with a civilian pilot. The provocation would then be slightly less in the eyes of the Communists."

Sharing this concern was Major John Seaberg, an aeronautical engineer for the Chance Vought Corporation recalled to active duty during the Korean War. With the Korean War ended, the U.S. Air Force teamed him with German aeronautical experts Woldemar Voigt and Richard Vogt to develop a new aircraft that combined the high-altitude performance of the latest turbojet engines and high-efficiency wings to reach ultra-high altitudes. Seaberg, being military, wanted both an aircraft weapons system and an aircraft with an operational radius of 1,500 nautical miles with the capability of conducting pre- and post-strike reconnaissance missions. To obtain an optimum subsonic cruise speed at altitudes of seventy thousand feet, he calculated a payload of up to seven hundred pounds of observation equipment and with a crew of one.

President Eisenhower had ruled out military intervention in Eastern Europe early in his administration, despite his campaign rhetoric about rolling back world communism. He feared provoking a war with the Soviet

Union and quickly made it known his dissatisfaction with the quality of the intelligence estimation of Soviet strategic capabilities. He was dismayed at the paucity of reconnaissance on the Soviet Bloc and, when he pledged presidential support to Seaberg, Leghorn, Wienberg and Kiefer, believed that the United States needed a high-flying reconnaissance plane.

The committee members met at MIT on April 15, 1954, and again in November, at which time the panel proposed that the CIA proceed with the project that Kelly Johnson, head of the Lockheed Skunk Works, had proposed earlier to the air force. The panel suggested that the CIA combine the technological version of Johnson with the strategic version of Richard S. Leghorn, who had commanded the army air force's Sixty-Seventh Reconnaissance Group in Europe during World War II.

Leghorn had worked with several optical scientists and engineers before receiving pilot training and becoming the commander of the Thirtieth Photographic Reconnaissance Squadron flying missions over northern France. He had photographed German forces, transport networks and communications facilities in preparation for the D-day invasion.

Following his 1951 recall to active duty with the U.S. Air Force during the Korean War, he became the head of the Reconnaissance Systems Branch of the Wright Air Development Command in Dayton, Ohio. There, he strived for an aerial surveillance aircraft capable of exceeding sixty thousand feet, altitudes above those of any Soviet plane. Thus, Leghorn realized the need for high-altitude aerial reconnaissance when he transferred in early 1952 to the Pentagon, where he planned the U.S. Air Force's reconnaissance required for the next decade.

There, Leghorn worked for Colonel Bernard A. Schriever, assistant for development planning to the U.S. Air Force's deputy chief of staff for Development. In his new position, he worked with Charles F. "Bud" Wienberg, a colleague while at Wright Field, and Eugene P. Kiefer, a Notre Dame graduate in aeronautical engineering. Kiefer designed reconnaissance aircraft at the Wright Air Development Center during World War II. Leghorn felt his having three reconnaissance experts working together placed emphasis on his solution enough to involve the U.S. Air Force in high-altitude photo reconnaissance. He was the first to articulate a vision of how to meet the intelligence demands of this new postwar era. Unfortunately, General LeMay felt otherwise.

The U.S. Air Force agencies listened to Leghorn and awarded Martin Aircraft Company a contract from the Air Research and Development Command to examine modifying the B-57. The U.S. Air Force picked the

B-57 for its long, high-lift wings and the American version of the new Rolls-Royce Avon-109 engine to give it high-altitude potential. Meanwhile, the Wright Air Development Command (WADC) in Dayton, Ohio, joined in seeking ways to achieve sustained flight at high altitudes.

The USAF solicited designs from Bell Aircraft Corporation of Buffalo, New York; Fairchild Engine and Airplane Corporation of Hagerstown, Maryland; and Glenn L. Martin Company of Baltimore thinking three smaller aircraft companies would gain it more priority and a better aircraft than Boeing, Convair, North American, Douglas or Lockheed. However, only Bell and Fairchild were asked to submit bids on a new plane. Martin was asked to examine the possibility of improving the height of the altitude performance of the B-57 already in use.

However, even without Martin's specifications or drawings, BEACON HILL committee member Allen F. Donovan from the Cornell Aeronautical Laboratory knew alterations to the B-57 by Martin Aircraft Company would not solve the air force's reconnaissance requirements addressed in the BEACON HILL Report. He made this known at the next Intelligence Systems Panel meeting scheduled for May 24 and 25 at Boston University. In this session, he represented Polaroid Corporation Panel and the Cornell Aeronautical Laboratory as they evaluated the changes made to the B-57 by Martin Aircraft Company.

Donovan explained to the panel how adding weight made any multi-engine aircraft built per military specifications impossible for high flight. He told the group that the B-57 was vulnerable to Soviet interception. He explained, "Safe was a penetrating aircraft flying above 70,000 feet for the entire mission."

Donovan mentioned to the panel what Philip Strong of the CIA had told him concerning the Lockheed Aircraft Corporation's designing a lightweight, high-flying aircraft. The thought impressed Chairman Baker of the Intelligence Systems Panel, who urged Donovan to evaluate the Lockheed design. He asked him also to gather ideas from other aircraft manufacturers concerning high-altitude aircraft.

Donovan could not make the trip to Lockheed until late summer. What he saw made him realize that this was exactly the type of plane sought by the other Intelligence Systems Panel members and him.

He met with an old air force acquaintance, Lockheed vice president L. Eugene Root, and learned about the U.S. Air Force's competition for a high-altitude reconnaissance plane. Kelly Johnson revealed to him what he planned for Lockheed's unsuccessful entry. Donovan, a lifelong sailplane enthusiast, recognized the CL-282 design being a jet-propel glider. He knew it could attain the altitude necessary for carrying out reconnaissance of the Soviet Union.

Donovan returned on August 8 and contacted James Baker to suggest an urgent meeting of the Intelligence Systems Panel. Other commitments of the members, however, prevented the panel from hearing Donovan's report until September 24, 1954, at the Cornell Aeronautical Laboratory.

Several members, including Edwin H. Land and Strong, could not attend. It upset those who did to learn of the U.S. Air Force funding a close competition for a tactical reconnaissance plane without informing them. They forgot their annoyance and listened once Donovan began describing Kelly Johnson's rejected design.

Donovan maintained his insistence on high-altitude reconnaissance aircraft flying above seventy thousand feet to escape interception. He stressed what he considered the three essential requirements for a high-altitude spy plane: a single engine, a sailplane wing and small structural load factors.

Donovan favored single-engine aircraft because it lightened the plane and made a more reliable plane than a multi-engine aircraft. He again explained how an aircraft could return to base on one engine. He, however, stipulated this would happen only at an altitude of thirty-four thousand feet. At this altitude, the Soviets shooting them down became a certainty.

Donovan felt they needed a sailplane wing to take maximum advantage of the thrust of a jet engine operating in the rarefied atmosphere of extreme altitude. Engineers estimated the power curve of a jet engine lowering to 6 percent of its sea level thrust in the thin atmosphere above seventy thousand feet.

Most of all, he stressed the need for low structural load factors and strengthening the wings and the wing root area, the part of the wing on a fixed-wing aircraft close to the fuselage. Withstanding the high speeds and sharply turned mandate by the standard military airworthiness rules added too much weight to the airframe, negating the efficiency of the sailplane wind.

Donovan insisted that only Kelly Johnson's CL-282 met those requirements. He described the CL-282 as a sailplane not having to meet combat aircraft specification. Thus, it flew above Soviet fighters.

Donovan convinced the Intelligence Systems Panel of the merits of the CL-282 proposal. This panel reported to the U.S. Air Force, which had already rejected the CL-282 in favor of the B-57 the air force was using for specialized "Sneaky Pete" reconnaissance missions in the Far East.

While the U.S. Air Force's uniformed hierarchy favored the Bell and Martin aircraft, some high-level civilian officials continued to support the Lockheed design. One of the civilians was Trevor Gardner, special assistant for Research and Development to air force secretary Harold E. Talbott.

Gardner shared his preference with some prominent West Coast proponents of the Lockheed proposal. Most of them he knew from his once heading the Hycon Manufacturing Company, producing aerial cameras in Pasadena, California.

Gardner recalled Kelly Johnson's presentation on the CL-282 in early April 1954. He believed the design illustrated the most promise for reconnaissance over the USSR. It helped that Gardner's special assistant, Frederick Ayer Jr., and Garrison Norton, an adviser to Secretary Talbott, believed as he did.

Most of the civilian officials, including Gardner, were more positive about the CL-282. They preferred its higher potential altitude and smaller radar cross-section. Gardner tried to win Strategic Air Command commander LeMay over to collecting strategic rather than tactical intelligence. General LeMay, however, remained uninterested in an unarmed aircraft. His lack of interest left Gardner, Ayer and Norton with little choice when they approached Philip G. Strong, the CIA chief of the operations staff in the Office of Scientific Intelligence.

At the time, the CIA depended on the military for overflights. General LeMay wasn't interested in changing to a plane such as the CL-282. Even the director of Central Intelligence, Allen Dulles, was opposed to the idea, favoring human over technical intelligence-gathering methods. Thus, it seemed that only the civilians in the photography field and aerial intelligence were sold on high-flight reconnaissance. Their concern was for a good cause. Neither the air force nor the CIA was producing any usable information from the bomber flights.

Marine Corps Reserve Colonel Strong, who later advanced to the rank of brigadier general, served on several air force advisory boards that kept him well informed regarding developments involving reconnaissance aircraft. He met with Gardner, Norton and Ayer in the Pentagon on May 12, 1954, six days before the Wright Air Development Command began its evaluation of the Lockheed proposal.

From Gardner's enthusiasm for the CL-282, Strong at first thought the U.S. Air Force officials supported the Lockheed design. He soon learned of the U.S. Air Force choosing the modified version of the Martin B-57 and the new Bell X-16 to meet future reconnaissance needs.

Despite Lockheed's CL-282 having support by September 1954, the members of the Intelligence Systems Panel and high-ranking air force civilians such as Trevor Gardner still reported to the U.S. Air Force. The U.S. Air Force's commitment to the Martin R-57 and the Bell X-16 prevented it from offering funds to Lockheed to pursue the CL-282 concept. Therefore, Lockheed needed additional support from outside the U.S. Air Force if it wanted to give life to the CL-282 project. Moreover, this support could only come from scientists serving on the high-level advisory committees.

In late December 1954, the Land Group spent more than an hour driving around in a committee member's year-old Ford while discussing which of the high-altitude aircraft proposals to recommend to the president. Choosing between Bell, Martin, Fairchild or Lockheed, committee member Allen Donovan favored going with the Lockheed aircraft to fill the needs of the intelligence community.

The CIA saw that the air force's brute force methods were no match for the Soviet radar system. The air force's failure to produce the needed intelligence on the Soviet Union's intentions and capabilities came at a time when HUMINT-gathering activity by the CIA in the Soviet-denied territory remained virtually nil while international tensions increased around the world.

With the air force's aerial reconnaissance and the CIA's HUMINT capabilities stifled, the CIA saw the solution as its having the ability to defeat radar detection. Rather than the air force's traditional targeting and damage assessment, the agency's new philosophy of reconnaissance became looking for warning indicators, force levels and an enemy's capability to launch an attack. Thus, the CIA added technology to its covert means of gathering intelligence. The prime objective for the CIA became the acquisition of the Soviet Union's technical capabilities.

The CIA changed its intelligence-gathering methods, bringing in people knowledgeable in such things as pulse duration, pulse repetition and the frequencies used in the Soviet Union's electronic warfare operations. To collect this intelligence, the CIA became the aggressor, devising methods of frightening or threatening the Soviets into turning on their radar systems for the CIA to evaluate and exploit.

During the Korean War, President Truman had obtained the passage of the CIA Act, NSC 5412, the National Security Council Directive on Covert Operations, which stipulated the classification of the CIA's activities and its budget. The act enabled any other government agency to transfer funds to the CIA "without regard to any provisions of law." A part of this act stipulated the U.S. government would have to plausibly disclaim responsibility and deny any exposed CIA actions or activities.

Also during the Truman presidency, the administration's concern over Soviet "psychological warfare" prompted the new National Security Council to authorize the launching of peacetime covert action operations. The NSC made the director of Central Intelligence responsible for psychological warfare. He established at the same time the principle that covert action was an exclusive function of the executive branch. The CIA certainly was a natural choice for Truman to assign this function, at least in part because the agency operated with unvouchered funds under its control to provide minimal risk of exposure in Washington.

During the Korean conflict, the agency's covert operations had grown quickly. However, peacetime covert activities were new to the United States. Wartime commitments and other missions soon made covert engagements the most expensive and bureaucratically prominent of the CIA's activities. The Departments of State and Defense feared the CIA alone having this power might cause the military to create a new rival covert action office in the Pentagon.

These concerns were warranted. Now under the Eisenhower administration, the first civilian director of Central Intelligence, Allen Dulles, had formerly served with the Office of Strategic Services. The CIA director's brother, John Foster Dulles, was the secretary of state during the Eisenhower administration; his sister was a diplomat; his maternal grandfather was the secretary of state under Benjamin Harrison; and his uncle by marriage was the secretary of state under Woodrow Wilson. He, a diplomat and a corporate lawyer, did not keep the White House and the Pentagon informed of precisely what the CIA was doing in clandestine operations overseas to the point that Eisenhower concluded in 1960, at the end of his presidency, that American intelligence was in shambles.

The Eisenhower administration on March 15, 1954, reaffirmed the Central Intelligence Agency's responsibility for conducting covert actions abroad. However, the CIA had to advise in advance the representatives of the secretary of state, the secretary of defense and the president before initiating any major covert action programs. President Eisenhower designated a Planning Coordination Group as the body responsible for coordinating covert operations. This "Special Group" emerged as the executive body to review and approve covert action programs initiated by the CIA.

The covert actions oversight group changed its name to the 303 Committee, the name coming from the National Security Action

Memorandum No. 303, dated June 2, 1964. McGeorge Bundy, National Security advisor, became the chairman of the committee.

The National Security Council directed the CIA to conduct "covert" rather than merely "psychological" operations. The NSC defined these operations as "all activities planned and executed that any U.S. Government responsibility for them was not evident to unauthorized persons. If uncovered, the U.S. Government could plausibly deny any responsibility for them. Such operations shall not include armed conflict by recognizing military forces, espionage, and counter-espionage, nor cover and deception for military operations." Under Dulles's direction, the CIA created MK-Ultra, a top-secret mind control research project managed by Sidney Gottlieb, and Dulles, who had in 1950 led the agency's covert operations as deputy director for plans, also personally oversaw Operation Mockingbird, a program that influenced foreign and domestic media companies.

At the time, Senator Joseph McCarthy was issuing subpoenas against the CIA in a series of investigations into potential communist subversion of the agency. Although none of the investigations revealed any wrongdoing, the hearings were potentially damaging, not only to the CIA's reputation but also to the security of sensitive information. To discredit him and stop his investigation of communist infiltration of the CIA, the CIA, under Dulles's orders, broke into McCarthy's Senate office and fed disinformation to him.

Johnson could not have timed it better to get Lockheed into the equation on coming up with a high-flying reconnaissance plane. The CIA had become more enamored of the idea of using Lockheed's proposal for national security needs after noting the air force's dismal results of obtaining the desperately needed intelligence to verify what the Soviet Union was up to. The CIA liked Kelly Johnson's motto: "Be quick, be quiet, be on time." The CIA remembered this when it started receiving intel from numerous sources that the Soviet Union was moving ahead quickly with a family of liquid-fueled, nuclear warhead–equipped intercontinental ballistic missiles.

The U-2 Program: Too Secret to Explain

On November 26, 1954, the day after Thanksgiving, Richard M. "Dick" Bissell Jr., an economist who had taught at both Yale and MIT and was currently a special assistant to Allen Dulles, first learned about President Eisenhower approving a secret program that Dulles wanted him to take

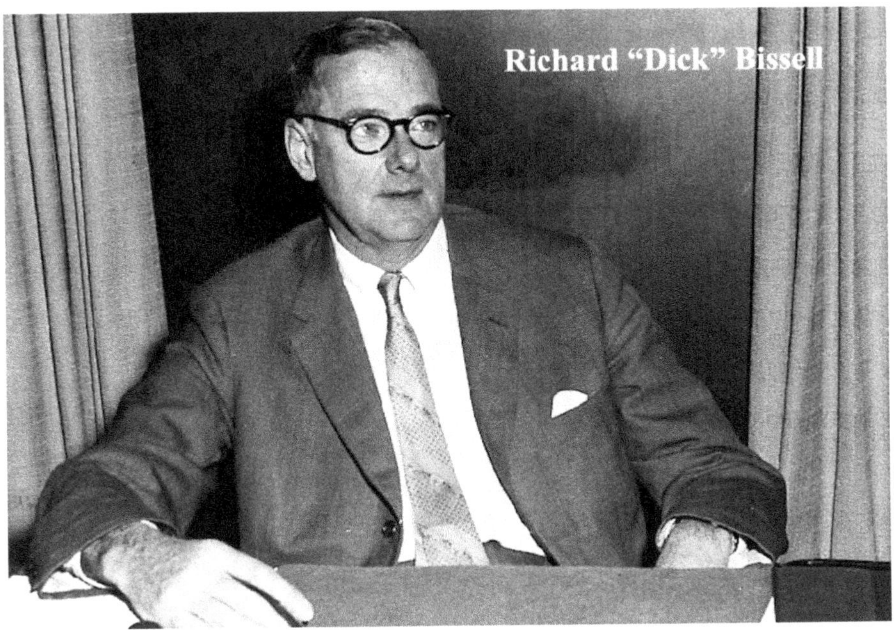

Richard M. Bissell Jr., an economist who had taught at both Yale and MIT and was special assistant to Allen Dulles, was the Central Intelligence Agency officer responsible for the U-2 spy plane and the Bay of Pigs invasion. *Wikipedia.*

charge of. Dulles described the project as too secret for him to explain and gave Bissell a packet of documents to acquaint himself.

Bissell, a former economics professor at MIT and a high official of the Marshall Plan, had become Allen W. Dulles's special assistant for planning and coordination in January 1954. He received responsibility for the new U-2 project at the end of that year and would head all CIA overhead reconnaissance programs from 1954 until 1962.

Bissell had long known in general terms of the proposal to build a high-altitude reconnaissance aircraft. Now, he was learning the details concerning the proposed project of sending aircraft over the Soviet Union.

The following day, late on the morning of December 2, 1954, Dulles sent Bissell to the Pentagon to represent the CIA at an organizational meeting for the U-2 project. Herbert I. Miller, chief of the Office of Scientific Intelligence's Nuclear Energy Division, and soon to become the executive officer of the overflight project, accompanied Bissell to the meeting.

Bissell and Miller arrived at the Pentagon the following afternoon to meet with a group of key air force officials that included Trevor Gardner and Lieutenant General Donald L. Putt. Bissell attended the meeting with neither Dulles nor him knowing of the president having tasked the agency with running a project that the director of Central Intelligence (DCI), following the meeting, instructed Bissell to "work it out." This project, too secret to explain, became more highly classified than the Manhattan Project that produced the atomic bomb.

Allen Dulles, who favored the classical agent form of espionage rather than technology, lacked enthusiasm concerning the CIA's taking a military role. The participants spent little time delineating air force and agency responsibilities in the project, taking for granted the CIA's handling the security matters. It concerned them that the air force had a separate contract for Pratt & Whitney J57 engines that might jeopardize the project's security. Much of the discussion centered on methods to divert air force materiel to the program.

The U.S. Air Force promised to turn over several J57 engines in production for B-52s, KC-135s, F-100s and RB-57s. When Bissell asked who was paying for the airframes built by Lockheed, the others greeted his query with silence. Everyone present expected the CIA to come up with the funds. The meeting adjourned with Bissell volunteering to consider it, advising Dulles afterward that the money for the project would have to originate from the Contingency Reserve Fund.

This fund, according to the director of Central Intelligence, with the president and the director of the budget's approval, was supposed to be for paying the costs of the Central Intelligence Agency's covert activities. Nonetheless, Dulles told Bissell to draft a memorandum for the president for funding the overflight program and for putting together a staff for Project AQUATONE, the project's new code name. The CIA assigned the cryptonym "AQUATONE" to the project, with the USAF using the name "OILSTONE" for its support to the CIA.

The project staff grew slowly, with many of the individuals working on overhead reconnaissance also remaining on the rolls of other agency components. To achieve maximum security, Bissell made the project staff self-sufficient, with Project AQUATONE having contract management, administrative, financial, logistics, communications and security personnel. He, thus, avoided having to turn to the CIA directorates for assistance. Bissell funded the developing Project AQUATONE separate from other agency components, paying its personnel and operating costs outside of regular agency accounts.

Meanwhile, at Lockheed, Kelly Johnson and twenty-five engineers redesigned the airplane to provide for a new landing gear, different engine, different camera bay and a means of further improving performance. Eighty-one people, including shop personnel, worked on the plane now known as the U-2.

In December 1954, the CIA ordered twenty aircraft. Kelly promised delivery of the first one in eight months and froze the design on December 10, 1954. He presented the first status of the plane along with a cost letter for $20 million to Washington in mid-December 1954. The government made the first check out to Kelly Johnson personally and sent it to his home to maintain the secrecy of the program.

Lockheed completed the initial wind tunnel tests before Christmas and began tooling on December 27, 1954, producing a production aircraft that differed considerably from the original CL-282.

Forging a CIA–Air Force Partnership

The CIA's U-2 project headquarters concurrently moved forward with procuring the aircraft and equipment. It recruited personnel and planned for the testing and operational phases. Dick Bissell began what he later described as "a rather civilized and amicable battle" with the U.S. Air Force to hammer out a charter for joint USAF/CIA project participation.

At the initial interagency meetings to establish the U-2 program in December 1954, the participants failed to work out a clear delineation of responsibilities between the CIA and the U.S. Air Force. They agreed only with the U.S. Air Force supplying the engines and the CIA paying for the airframes and cameras.

Myriad details remained unsettled. The CIA and air force representatives worked on an interagency agreement to assign specific responsibilities for the program. These negotiations proved difficult.

Dick Bissell experienced his first significant encounter with General Twining on March 7, 1955. In preparation for this meeting, Bissell, on February 25, created a briefing paper. He summarized project developments to date and recommended giving urgent attention to advance preparations for acquiring air force support in the operational phase. The project needed to complete research and planning in the fields of aeromedicine, intelligence requirements, flight planning, meteorology and logistics. The project required selecting and completing an organizational structure to recruit and train Lockheed test pilots and air force personnel holding important positions.

The briefing paper passed to General Twining in advance of the meeting recommended designating a single officer responsible for all the activities of the U.S. Air Force in support of and as a participant in the project. His having this authority and responsibility positioned him to arrange for secret access to the variant resources of the U.S. Air Force on which he hoped to draw. The plan was for him to join with the CIA project officer in developing organizational plans for approval by appropriate authorities in the CIA and the U.S. Air Force. The program positioned him to secure other air force personnel as needed for the project at an early date.

In further preparation for a meeting on March 7, 1955, with the air force chief of staff Nathan Twining, Dick Bissell prepared a background paper for the director and General Cabell. He first warned them of General Twining wanting the operational commands and the Strategic Air Command responsibility for air force supporting AQUATONE. Dick Bissell recommended the director take a general line with the chiefs of staff.

DCI Allen Dulles took up discussions with Twining on this subject following Bissell's meeting earlier that month. Nathan wanted SAC, headed by General Curtis E. LeMay, to run the project once the planes and pilots became ready to fly. Dulles opposed such an arrangement and dragged the CIA-USAF talks on for several months, with Twining remaining determined to have the Strategic Air Command in full control once the aircraft deployed.

Even with General LeMay wanting nothing to do with the U-2, he sent Colonel Douglas T. "Doug" Nelson TDY (temporary duty) from Strategic Air Command Headquarters to monitor the program and report to him.

Nelson, who later retired as a major general, had earned his student pilot's license before he was old enough to get a permit to drive a car. He flew his first plane in 1930 at the age of nine. For five dollars, Nelson flew an old Waco, taking off on the beach in Seaside, Oregon. He soloed on his sixteenth birthday in an E-2 Taylor Cub on a rainy day over a grass strip, also in Oregon. His early military service took him to the Middle East desert, Alaska and the China-Burma Theater of Operations. During the war, he flew 590 combat hours, primarily in C-46s.

In 1946, after a tour of duty as a fighter aircraft instructor pilot, Nelson separated from the U.S. Army Air Force to become a commercial airline pilot, flying DC-3s with West Coast Airlines until November 1947, when he received a regular commission and returned to active duty. He received an assignment to Strategic Air Command, where he served in the Thirty-Third Fighter Group before attending Air Tactical School in Florida.

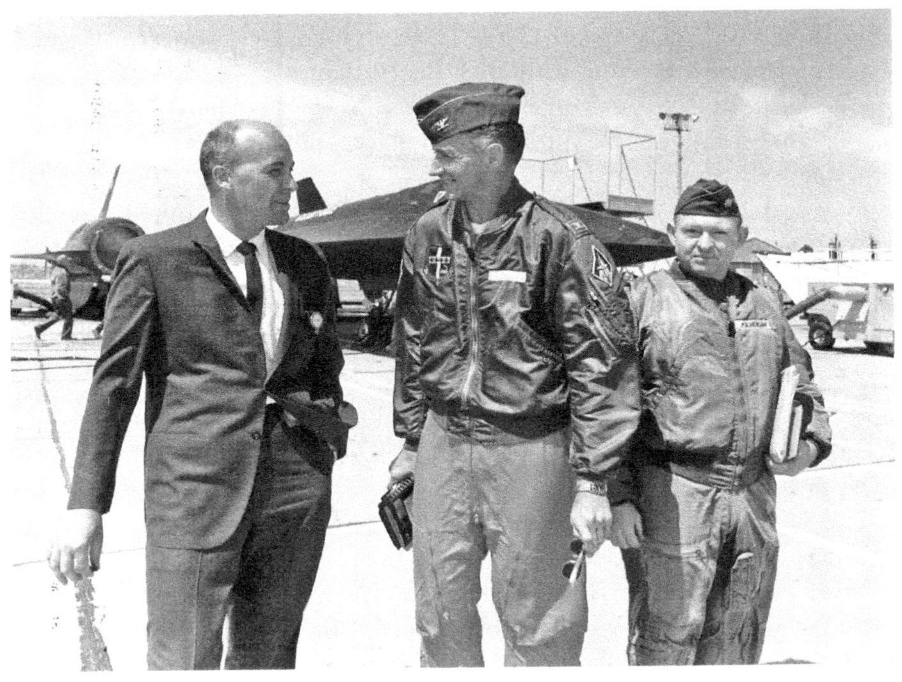

Lockheed's Bob Murphy, Colonel Doug Nelson and Lieutenant Colonel Peterson at Area 51. Murphy and Nelson were with both the U-2 program and the A-12 successor. *Bob Murphy.*

Nelson had spent October 1948 to March 1949 in Palestine as part of the United Nations Truce Force. While there, he sometimes relied on camels as his mode of transportation with the Syrian Camel Corps. He then returned to the States and became a B-29 lead crew aircraft commander at Walker Air Force Base in New Mexico.

Nelson was serving at Strategic Air Command headquarters, Offutt Air Force Base, Nebraska, with the Tactics Branch and Recon Division, Directorate of Operations, when, in 1956, General LeMay appointed him the Strategic Air Command project officer to support the CIA U-2 program.

General LeMay's sending Colonel Nelson to watch what the CIA was doing didn't bother Bissell. Bissell felt it was none of the CIA's business how the U.S. Air Force organized its activities. However, LeMay's sending a senior officer challenged the character of the project. It forced Bissell to impose certain requirements that had a bearing on the organization.

General LeMay could not accept the thought of his air force stepping aside while the CIA flew planes against the nation's enemies. At the same time, the attitude of General Curtis LeMay raised some concern. He had made it clear at a meeting with Dick Bissell that as soon as the CIA paid for the U-2 (the U.S. Air Force designation for the Lockheed CL-282), he planned to take it over. He further stated that he did not expect that date to be too far in the future.

Having LeMay's air force colonel present caused many to perceive the CIA's U-2 project as a clandestine, intelligence-gathering operation based on military pilots flying the missions. Clandestine intelligence gathering was not the case. Bissell wanted the project to have the least amount of military aura possible. It had to be rigorously secure. It had to be a CIA operating facility and not an air force base. It had also to be subject to close and continuous policy control by the senior policymakers of this government. Bissell felt such control much easier to maintain with the CIA's project headquarters in Washington.

The CIA and Bissell were thinking of also having non-Americans fly reconnaissance missions. Bissell made the initial policy decision to proceed based on its conforming to this concept. This way, the CIA avoided describing the project as a military operation conducted by any offensive arm of a regular military establishment.

The CIA saw the project as a power projection operation with a U.S.-based facility operating as the nucleus of a global aerial spy operation. The agency was doing what the U.S. Air Force refused to do: it was building its fleet of reconnaissance planes to overfly the USSR.

Bissell saw the CIA power projection as having the capacity to rapidly and effectively deploy and sustain its aerial reconnaissance. Having power projection meant its U.S. base had to remotely operate from multiple dispersed locations outside the limited bounds of its territory.

Bissell wanted the CIA capable of responding on a global scale. At this stage, this meant deploying anywhere in the world that the Soviet Union or others posed a threat to the United States and its allies. Flying globally meant his having to plan for the logistical difficulties inherent in projecting its U-2 detachments. The U-2 project would have to proceed with even more secrecy than did the Manhattan Project that developed the atomic bomb. Security was such that for several months, Bissell, a tall man, usually wearing tennis shoes, gray-colored trousers and a checkered sports jacket, would show up at the Lockheed Skunk Works known only as "Mr. B." Few ever knew of the CIA involvement in an ultra-secret project ostensibly for weather reconnaissance by the First Weather Reconnaissance Squadron, Provisional.

The vital necessity for security brought with it two implications for the organization. First, it had to limit knowledge of the project to the narrowest possible circle of those with a need to know. This category included only those individuals working on some aspect of AQUATONE and a few top policymakers. Second, it organized the project to give it the best possible cover.

The U.S. Air Force normally operated through a chain of command. It also conducted a policy of routinely rotating its personnel assignments. For this CIA project, the air force had to operate outside its chain of command protocols. It had to focus its responsibility for maintaining security and ensuring close control using special channels rather than the usual chain of command. Both air force SOPs (standard operating procedures) were reasons for choosing the CIA over the air force to manage the U-2 program. The CIA did not follow either of these policies.

Bissell knew that doing this the CIA way would alienate "Old Iron Pants," General LeMay. Nonetheless, he felt the project's character required the air force participants to station its leadership in Washington. Another thing was the air force had to give its representative the authority to deal with the CIA and with other components regarding the project's business. This requirement meant there could not be the typical air force chain of command.

Bissell also wanted a direct channel from the Washington project headquarters to overseas units. The U.S. Air Force balked at the idea of the CIA playing down any connection to the air force's operational command. Bissell insisted on avoiding any identification of the project with the military. He took these requirements up with the air force chief of staff, Nathan Twining.

No substantial agreement came from the meeting. A month later, Dick Bissell fired his second shot. He gave to Generals Everest and Putt for discussion purposes a memorandum addressed to the deputy chief of staff for operations. The opening paragraph began:

> *It was understood the view of the Air Staff that Air Force support for Project AQUATONE in its operational phase should be the responsibility of the Strategic Air Command. Assistance and support during research, development, and procurement will, however, continue as the liability of the Deputy Chief of Staff, Development.*

Accepting this premise, Dick Bissell continued to explain the original concept of the project being a clandestine intelligence-gathering operation. Using the CIA to run the program would minimize the risk of detection and offer plausible attribution to the U.S. government. He indicated the CIA's assumptions regarding the character of project operations.

The CIA would determine the number of aircraft, the equipment and operating facilities. As to specific functions performed by the CIA, it would recruit and administer the civilian pilots. The CIA would furnish maintenance personnel for primary mission aircraft and equipment. It would maintain project security control, project communications and the collection and coordination of requirements and intelligence.

Bissell channeled air force support by suggesting the CIA's viewpoint, which exposed differences of opinion existing between Generals Everest and Putt. Neither accepted the CIA's proposals. Nor did either of them present or put forth an agreed counterproposal of their own.

On June 8, 1955, Colonel George McCafforty informed Bissell concerning Generals Twining, White and Everest's engaging in a controversy over the U.S. Air Force's role in the project. They had instructed the Office of the Deputy Chief of Staff, Personnel, to take no further action on the project's personnel requirements pending a settlement of the issue.

Dick Bissell sought the assistance of Trevor Gardner, who had a letter signed by the secretary of the U.S. Air Force to General Twining urging the chief of staff and his deputies to agree with the CIA as much as possible.

Trevor Gardner had during World War II worked on the Manhattan Project, and later he headed the General Tire and Rubber Company before starting his research and development firm, the Hycon Company, which built aerial cameras. Gardner served as the secretary of the air force's special assistant for Research and Development and then as the assistant secretary for Research and Development during Eisenhower's first term of office. Gardner's concern about the danger of a surprise attack helped lead to the establishment of the Technological Capabilities Panel. Gardner also urged the building of Lockheed's CL-282 aircraft.

The secretary contemplated a joint task force of the CIA and the U.S. Air Force to carry out the operational phase of Project OILSTONE (the U.S. Air Force cryptonym for AOUATONE). Colonel Ritland would head the U.S. Air Force portion and serve as deputy to the senior project officer designated by the director of Central Intelligence for all operational activities.

Bissell sought to hasten an air force decision by drafting a memorandum outlining specific organizational arrangements based on the secretary's formula. He sent copies to Gardner and Generals Everest and Putt as preparation for another meeting in the first week of July. However, the agreement never happened.

Within the agency, the charter for Project AQUATONE had gone through twelve drafts during the first month of planning before submission to the director and approval by him on January 10, 1955. In his refining process, Dick Bissell's comprehensive six-page document that was expected to remain valid for three months remained unaltered for the seven years of its duration.

CHAPTER 4

SCOUTING FOR AREA 51

President Dwight D. Eisenhower, inaugurated four months earlier, sought ideas from the civilian sector for developing and flying high-altitude aircraft for surveillance. He assigned MIT president James R. Killian Jr. to meet with other Scientific Advisory Committee members in the Boston area. The president based his approval on an authorization to the director of Central Intelligence to obligate in the fiscal year 1955 an amount not to exceed $35 million from the reserve for aircraft procurement. The project outline estimated the cost of the airframes, photographic and electronic equipment and some field maintenance equipment at $31.5 million with a margin of error of $2 million, within the $35 million limit.

These estimates assumed the U.S. Air Force was furnishing technical assistance and supervision of all government-furnished equipment (GFE). The assessment included forty jet engines and transportation of materiel and personnel to a yet unspecified testing site. The estimate placed pilot recruitment and training costs at $600,000. If the U.S. Air Force underwrote the flight training, it reduced to $100,000 the charge to the CIA for the initial period.

The estimates in the project outline contained no allowance for the testing program, since it fell within the fiscal year 1956, or any allowances for acquisition or preparation of bases, operational costs or costs to process the photographic and electronic products obtained from overflights.

Using "unvouchered" funds—virtually free from any external oversight or accounting—the CIA wrote checks to finance secret programs, such as the

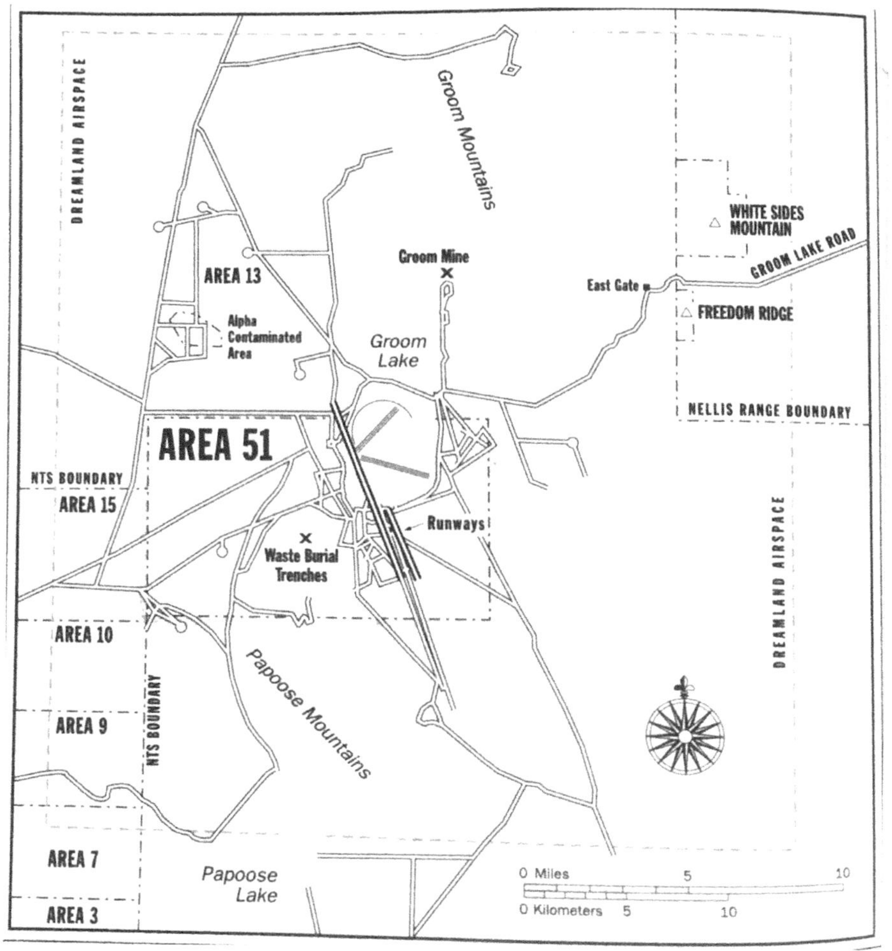

Regional layout of Area 51 in Nevada. *From David Darlington's* Area 51: The Dreamland Chronicles.

U-2. The process went back to Public Law 110, Central Intelligence Agency Act of 1949, approved by the Eighty-First Congress, which designated the director of Central Intelligence as the only government employee allowed to dispense federal money without the use of vouchers.

Using non-vouchered funds made it possible to eliminate competitive bidding and thereby limited the number of parties knowing of a given project. The use of non-vouchered funds sped up the federal procurement cycle. It enabled a general contractor such as Lockheed to purchase much, if not all, of the needed supplies for a project without resorting at each step to the mandatory procedures involving public, competitive bidding,

Allen Dulles, with the approval of President Eisenhower, financed the startup of constructing the U-2 using unvouchered funds from the agency's Contingency Reserve Fund. The "U" referred to the deliberately vague designation "utility" instead of "R" for "reconnaissance," and the U-1 and U-3 aircraft already existed.

Bissell, as head of the project, used this covert funding subject to the guidance of the director and deputy director with authorization to obligate funds in amounts up to $100,000. Any items in excess required the director's approval. Bissell was also required to maintain the closest possible security control over all phases of AQUATONE, a requirement that turned into one of the most difficult and yet unbelievably successful tasks for several years until it grew into a bureaucratic committee with representation from every intelligence agency of the government.

Lockheed's original proposal to the U.S. Air Force in May 1954 amounted to $28 million for twenty U-2s equipped with GE J73 engines. During negotiations with CIA general counsel Lawrence R. Houston, Lockheed changed its proposal to $26 million for twenty airframes plus a two-seat trainer model and shared with the U.S. Air Force furnishing the engines.

On December 22, 1954, the CIA signed a letter contract with Lockheed using the code name Project OARFISH. The CIA proposal gave Lockheed "performance specifications" rather than the more rigid and demanding standard air force "technical specifications."

To finance the U-2 program, President Eisenhower authorized DCI Dulles to use $35 million from the CIA's Contingency Reserve Fund. Houston insisted on the CIA budgeting $22.5 million for the airframes because it needed the balance of the available $35 million for cameras and life-support gear. The two sides agreed on a fixed-price contract with a provision for a review three-fourths of the way through to determine if the costs exceeded the $22.5 million.

With the agency about to sign a contract with Lockheed for $22.5 million to build twenty U-2 aircraft, the company needed a cash infusion to keep the work going. On February 21, 1955, Bissell wrote a check on an agency account for $1.25 million and mailed it to the home of Kelly Johnson.

Johnson's willingness to begin work on the aircraft without a contract illustrated the importance of the use of non-vouchered funds for covert procurement. It paved the way for the CIA to use secret funding for its sensitive projects at Area 51, simplifying both procurement and security procedures. It made the funds non-attributable to the federal government with no public accountability for their use.

In July 1955, the U.S. Air Force was still withholding decisions needed urgently to move the project forward. The director of Central Intelligence, using Bissell's briefing papers, attended a conference at Air Defense Command Headquarters in Colorado, with the U-2 project the number one agenda item. Bissell had outlined proposals advanced to date and recommended the task force responsible for the project have a clear responsibility for both operational planning and the actual conduct of operations. He specifically called for having a clear and direct line of command from headquarters to the field detachments. Within that premise, Bissell saw three feasible alternatives: 1) a CIA-controlled task force drawing on air force personnel and support; 2) the air force being in control and drawing on the CIA for support or control; and 3) drawing on both agencies for support.

Though the USAF and the navy would eventually fly the U-2, the CIA had majority control over the project, code named Project Dragon Lady. Despite SAC chief LeMay's early dismissal of the CL-282, the USAF in 1955 sought to take over the project and put it under SAC until Eisenhower repeated his opposition to military personnel flying the aircraft. Nonetheless, the USAF substantially participated in the project; Bissell described it as a "49 percent" partner. The USAF agreed to select and train pilots and plot missions, while the CIA would handle cameras and project security, process film and arrange foreign bases.

It took a face-to-face meeting of DCI Dulles and the top air force official to bring results with the approval of a joint agreement titled "Organization and Delineation of Responsibilities—Project OILSTONE." It was signed by General Twining for the U.S. Air Force and Dulles for the CIA in August 1955. The agreement gave the responsibility for the general direction and joint control of the project to the DCI and the chief of staff of the USAF. Subject to guidance from higher authority, the CIA appointed a project director and the U.S. Air Force appointed a deputy project manager responsible for the conduct of the project through all its phases.

Per the agreement, the U.S. Air Force Project Group, headed by Colonel Russell A. Berg, acted in the name of the chief of staff of the U.S. Air Force and SAC. The group performed a supporting role with no control in the training and operational phases. Commenting on how this agreement worked in practice, Bissell some years later said:

In the negotiations with the US Air Force, a concept emerged which worked well for five years. The U-2 project was quite explicitly set up as a joint Air Force/the CIA project. Throughout the U-2 phase, the US Air Force was a supporting element. It held precisely 49% of the common stock. Quite aside from interdepartmental clearance obligations of the normal sort, I had to clear every major policy decision with two bosses. They did it, and it did work, and it worked smoothly and well. Whether it could ever work again was something I won't comment on because I don't know.

Eventually, President Eisenhower settled the dispute. "I want this whole thing a civilian operation," the president wrote. "If uniformed personnel of the armed services of the United States flew over Russia, it was an act of war—and I don't want any part of it." With the issue of control over the program settled, the two agencies soon worked out the remaining details.

The OILSTONE pact gave the U.S. Air Force responsibility for pilot selection and training, weather information, mission plotting and operational support. The CIA retained responsibility for cameras, security, contracting film processing and arrangements for foreign bases. Also, the CIA kept a voice in the selection of pilots. All aeronautical aspects of the project, including the construction and testing of the aircraft, remained the exclusive province of Lockheed.

Because of this agreement, the CIA remained in control of the program; Richard Bissell later remarked how the U.S. Air Force became a supporting element and to a major degree wanted a role more than supplying half the government personnel. He said the U.S. Air Force held 49 percent of the common stock.

Lockheed produced the twenty aircraft at a total of $18,977,597 (including $1.9 million in profit), or less than $1 million per plane. It was all on time and under budget, a miracle in today's defense contracting world.

Designing a New Type of Plane

Kelly Johnson pulled together a team of engineers at Lockheed's Advanced Development facility in Burbank, California, known as the Skunk Works, taking them away from Lockheed projects without being able to explain why to their former supervisors. The engineers immediately began to work sixty-five hours a week on the project under a letter contract with Lockheed.

Rather than going with Lockheed's original proposal to the air force in May 1954 that called for twenty U-2s (called "angels" because they flew so high), equipped with GE J73 engines, Lockheed negotiated for twenty airframes plus a two-seat trainer model. The formal contract, No. SP-19 13, was signed on March 2, 1955, and called for the delivery of the first U-2 in July 1955 and the last in November 1956.

Kelly Johnson's approach to prototype development placed his engineers not more than fifty feet from the aircraft assembly line to make them immediately aware of any difficulties in construction.

Although the final product resembled a typical jet aircraft, its construction was unlike any other U.S. military aircraft. The new, 2.5g aircraft was technologically challenging from a design standpoint, with drag and weight the more significant design challenges. The designers kept the weight to four pounds per square foot by going with a bicycle landing gear arrangement with a single strut. Mounted mid-span on each wing to provide balance were the jettisonable pogos, the wheeled struts that supported the fueled wings before takeoff. The tail assembly attached to the main body with just three tension bolts, a sailplane design to save weight. The U-2's two separate wing panels attached to the fuselage sides with tension bolts. The fragile wings had a "gust control" mechanism that set the ailerons and horizontal stabilizers into a position that kept the aircraft in a slightly nose-up attitude, thereby avoiding sudden stresses caused by wind gusts (again, just as in sailplanes).

The U-2 would have a speed of Mach 0.8 or 460 knots at altitude. Its initial maximum altitude would be 70,600 feet, and the ultimate maximum altitude would be 73,100 feet. The new plane would take off at 90 knots, land at 76 knots and glide 244 nautical miles from 70,000 feet. Johnson promised the first test flight would occur on or before August 2, 1955, and the completion of four aircraft by December 1, 1955.

Fuel Problems

As with any new aircraft design, the U-2 encountered problems for Lockheed and other relevant support vendors to resolve. One such problem was fuel control and the propensity of the engine dumping engine oil into the cockpit via the ventilation system. Another was restarting the aircraft, which required descending to thirty-five thousand feet or lower, making it vulnerable to

Soviet interception. Finding this unsatisfactory, Pratt & Whitney developed a high-altitude version of the J57 engine to provide added payload and altitude capability.

The pilots found the aircraft fuel control system very primitive. They referred to it as the "water spigot" because it was either on or off. It didn't have a central control, a crucial consideration with the early U-2 that required to maintain trim as it consumed fuel.

None of the first fifty U-2s had normal fuel gauges. The aircraft contained a complex system of fuel lines and valves draining to a central sump, making it impossible to provide the pilots with an Empty/Full type of fuel gauge. Instead, they used mechanical fuel totalizers/counters.

Before each mission, the ground crew set the counters to indicate the total amount of fuel in the wings. A flow meter then subtracted the gallons of fuel consumed during a flight, which the pilots recorded on a log to compare with estimates made by mission planners for each leg of the flight.

The pilots double-checked the log by keeping track of the fuel consumption by monitoring airspeed and flight time. The planes often ran out of fuel or experienced flame-outs (the flame in the combustion chamber of a jet engine extinguishing), with a resultant loss of power because of the poor fuel control system. During the early part of the program, the pilots averaged seven flame-outs per flight, each time requiring the U-2 operating at a seventy-thousand-foot altitude to descend into the thicker air at twenty to thirty thousand feet to get a restart. One U-2 pilot ran out of fuel and glided over nine hundred miles to an air force base.

The Cameras

Lockheed faced a battle with the U.S. Air Force when it came to photography. The U.S. Air Force reconnaissance experts had all gained their practical experience during World War II in the multi-engine bombers. Aerial reconnaissance at that time required the multi-engine bombers to accommodate the long focal length the cumbersome 240-inch Boston camera needed. The camera's size required partial disassembly of the YC-97 Boeing Stratocruiser carrying it.

By December 1954, Lockheed was at work designing the U-2's airframe, and Pratt & Whitney was already building the J57 jet engine, but no firm plans existed for the special cameras that weren't too bulky and had sufficient resolution for high-altitude reconnaissance. A resolution of fewer than ten feet from altitudes above sixty-eight thousand feet required an aerial camera almost four times as good as any existing.

In the mid-1940s, James G. Baker of Harvard and Richard S. Perkin of the Perkin-Elmer (P-E) Company of Norwalk, Connecticut, had collaborated on designing very-high-acuity lenses for an experimental camera for the army air force. Baker realized that size and weight were the major restraining factors for developing a camera for the U-2 and began working on a radically new system in October 1954, even before the CIA adopted the Lockheed proposal. Baker needed almost a year to produce a working model of such a complex camera. However, Kelly Johnson had promised to have a U-2 in the air within eight months. Baker consulted with his friend and colleague Richard Perkin and came up with the Hycon Manufacturing Company–built air force camera known as the K-38, a twenty-four-inch aerial framing camera that he adapted for the U-2.

Perkin suggested modifying several standard K-38 cameras to reduce their weight to the U-2's 450-pound payload limit. At the same time, Baker made critical adjustments to improve the acuity of existing K-38 lenses. Baker did this in a few weeks to several modified K-38s, now known as A-l cameras. The camera was ready when the first "angel" aircraft took to the air in mid-1955.

The CIA awarded Hycon a contract for the modified K-38 cameras. Hycon, in turn, subcontracted Perkin-Elmer to provide new lenses and to modify the cameras to make them less bulky. In turn, Perkin-Elmer subcontracted to Baker's Spica, Incorporated to rework the existing K-38 lenses and later design an improved lens system known as the A-1 camera system.

The A-1 used two 24-inch K-38 framing cameras, one mounted one vertically and the other resting in a rocking mount. The A1 photographed a 17.2-degree swath beneath the aircraft onto a roll of 9.5-inch film. The rocking mount allowed it to alternately photograph out to 36.5 degrees the left oblique and right oblique onto separate rolls of 9.5-inch film that unwound in opposite directions to minimize their effect on the balance of the aircraft.

The U-2s equipped with the A-1 camera system also carried a Perkin-Elmer tracking camera to make continuous horizon-to-horizon photographs of the terrain passing beneath the plane. The U-2 also carried a backup camera system, a K-17 six-inch three-camera trimetrogon unit using nine-inch film.

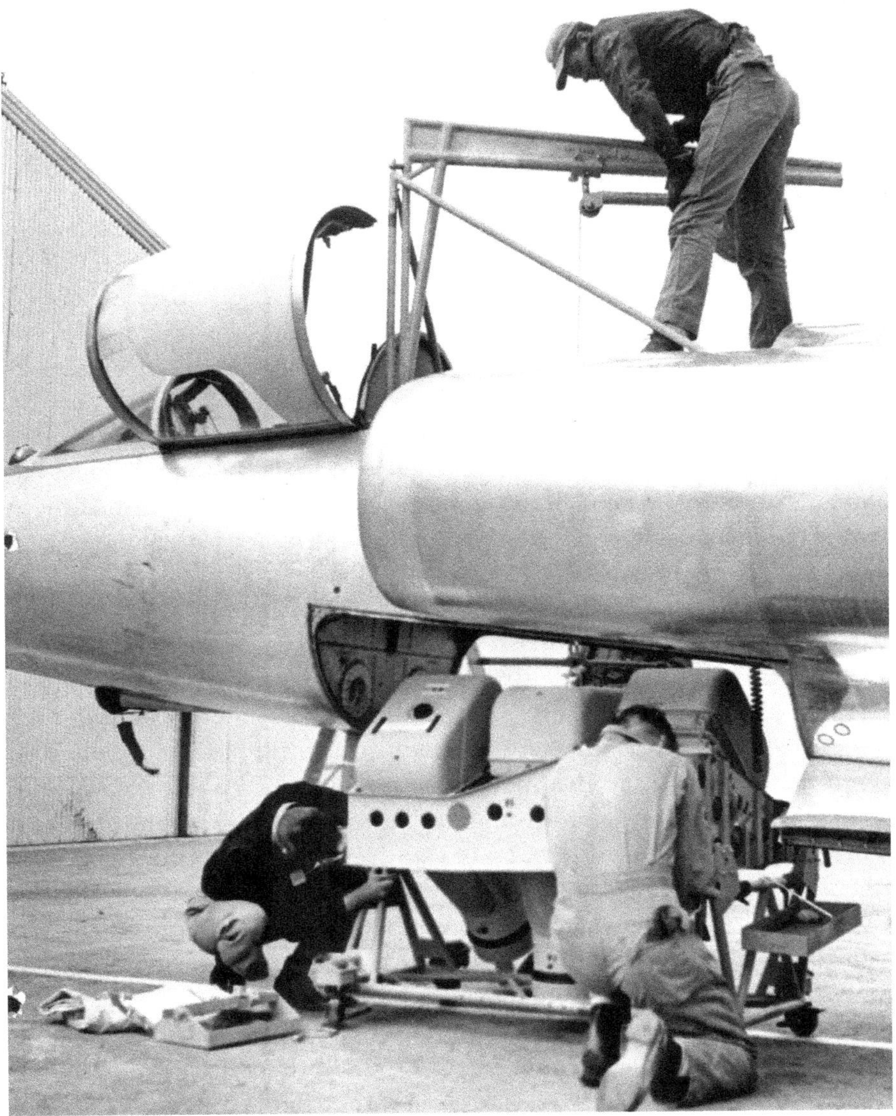

Mounting the Type A camera system in the U-2's Q-bay. *CIA via TD Barnes Collection.*

Problems with the A-1 rocking system required Baker to come up with the new camera system known as the A-2, which returned to a trimetrogon arrangement. The A-2 consisted of three separate K-38 framing cameras and 9.5-inch film magazines. One K-38 filmed the right oblique, another the vertical and a third the left oblique. The A-2 system also included a 3-inch tracking camera and came equipped with the new 24-inch f/8.0 Baker-designed lenses with several aspheric surfaces. James Baker personally ground and made the final bench tests on each lens before releasing it to the agency. These lenses resolved sixty lines per millimeter, a 240-percent improvement over existing lenses.

Once Baker and Scott had redesigned the twenty-four-inch lens for the K-38 devices, they continued to pioneer aerial photography for the U-2 with Baker's new camera design, known as the B model. It incorporated an entirely new concept, a high-resolution panoramic-type framing camera with a much longer thirty-six-inch f/10.0 aspheric lens. The complex B camera engineered by Hycon's chief designer, William McFadden, used a single lens to obtain photography from one horizon to the other, thereby reducing weight by having two fewer lenses and shutter assemblies than the standard trimetrogon configuration. Because its lens was longer than those used in the A cameras, the B camera achieved even higher resolution—one hundred lines per millimeter.

The B camera used an 18- by 18-inch format achieved by focusing the image onto two counter-rotating but overlapping 9.5-inch-wide strips of film. Baker designed this camera so that one film supply was located forward, the other aft. Thus, as the film supplies unwound, they counterbalanced each other and did not disturb the aircraft's center of gravity. The B camera's two modes of operation increased the available number of exposures, almost doubled the camera's operating time and provided stereo coverage from three of the seven B-camera frames.

The C model with a 240-inch focal length was James Baker's idea for the ultimate high-altitude camera. In December 1954, he designed a camera with a folding optical path using three mirrors, a prism and a f/20.0 lens system. Before working out the details of this design, however, Baker flew to California in early January 1955 to consult with Kelly Johnson about the weight and space limitations of the U-2's payload compartment. Despite every effort to reduce the physical dimensions of the C camera, he needed an additional 6 inches of payload space to accommodate the bigger lens. When he broached this subject to Johnson, the latter replied, "Six more inches? I'd sell my grandmother for 6 more inches!"

Baker continued his efforts to design a better camera for the CIA. He later decided to make the mirrors for the system out of a new, lightweight foamed silica material developed by Pittsburgh-Coming Glass Company that reduced the weight significantly. Hycon flight-tested the C camera on

January 31, 1957, and discovered that its 180-inch focal length, five times longer than that of the B camera, made the camera very sensitive to aircraft vibration and led to great difficulty in aiming the C camera from altitudes above sixty-eight thousand feet. The engineers, therefore, decided to shelve the camera. More than five years later, a redesigned C camera employed during the Cuban Missile Crisis in October 1962 proved very satisfactory.

The failure of the C camera design was not a serious setback to the high-altitude reconnaissance program because the B camera proved highly successful. Once initial difficulties with the film-transport system were overcome, the B camera became the workhorse of high-altitude photography. An improved version known as the B-2 was still in use. Both earlier A-model cameras were phased out after September 1958.

During the period when he was designing lenses for the CIA's overhead reconnaissance program, James Baker was also working on a classified lens designed by the air force for the Smithsonian Institution. To protect the security of Baker's work for the agency, Herbert Miller of the Development Projects Staff told Baker to work on lenses for the U-2 in the open and did not make any effort to classify the documents connected with the project. Miller believed that by not calling attention to the effort using special security measures, the project could be completed faster without compromising it. This "hiding in the open" strategy proved very successful.

In addition to the camera systems, the U-2 carried one other important item of optical equipment: a periscope designed by James Baker and built by Walter Baird of Baird Associates to enable pilots to recognize the targets beneath the aircraft and to provide a valuable navigational aid.

Selecting Area 51 for the U-2

The work continued in California on the airframe, in Connecticut on the engines and in Boston on the camera system. The construction of the first few U-2 aircraft was nearing completion, and it was ready for flight tests. However, the top officials of the Development Projects Staff had not found a venue offering safety and secrecy to flight test the U-2.

On April 12, 1955, U-2 designer Kelly Johnson sent project pilot Tony LeVier and Lockheed Skunk Works chief foreman Dorsey Kammerer in an unmarked Beechcraft V-35 Bonanza on a two-week survey mission to scout for a new flight test location for the CIA.

A few days later, Bissell, with his air force liaison, Colonel Osmond J. "Ozzie" Ritland, departed on a two-day survey where they reviewed fifty potential sites in a small Beechcraft V-35 Bonanza plane piloted by Lockheed's chief test pilot, Tony LeVier.

They used the cover story of them going on a hunting trip in Mexico. They made it realistic by dressing and packing appropriately to keep their hunting trip cover realistic. During their two-week mission, they photographed and explored desert areas that had potential as a test site in Southern California, Nevada and Arizona.

None of the sites met the stringent security requirements of the program. Bissell rejected Johnson's proposed Site 1 (Mud Lake, Nevada) because of its closeness to the populated area of the Tonopah mining district and the Tonopah U.S. Army Air Force Bombing Range. Ritland, however, recalled a little X-shaped field located at the eastern side of dry Groom Lake that was once the Nellis Auxiliary Field No. 1. It was one hundred miles north of Las Vegas, Nevada, outside the Atomic Energy Commission's (AEC) Nevada Atomic Proving Ground at Yucca Flat.

On a later flight, LeVier, Johnson, Bissell and Ritland flew out to Nevada on a two-day survey of Groom Lake, the most promising of all the lakebeds. They found the abandoned airfield that Ritland remembered as sandy, overgrown and unusable.

They debated landing on the airstrip but feared to attempt landing on the airstrip at the risk of nosing the plane when the wheels sank into the loose soil. They ran the risk of killing or injuring all the key figures in the U-2 project, so instead, LeVier chose to set the plane down on the lakebed. They walked to examine the strip and found it covered ankle-deep with dust after more than a decade of disuse and littered with shell casings from gunnery practice during World War II.

Unmarred by either hummock or furrow, no tree or bush grew on this dry pluvial lakebed, its parched clay and alkaline surface smoothed through the centuries to glass-like flatness from desert winds sweeping water from winter rains across the lakebed in a timeless cycle. Receiving an average annual precipitation of only five inches of rain and snow, only occasionally did water stand on the lake more noted for hosting dusty whirlwinds. Bissell later described the playa as "a perfect natural landing field as smooth as a billiard table without doing anything to it." It was an area of flat, dried-up land, a desert basin from which water evaporated quickly, except on the lakebed. The lakebed was a clay-like, impermeable sediment with particles smaller than silt.

Kelly Johnson initially opposed the choice of Groom Lake because it was farther from Burbank than he liked and because of its proximity to the Nevada Proving Ground (later renamed Nevada Test Site). Conducting a flight test program adjacent to an active nuclear test site and directly in the primary downwind path of radioactive fallout from atomic blasts concerned Johnson.

The ancient dry lakebed's surface provided sufficient hardness for aircraft operations and marked airstrips. However, for all practical purposes, the CIA treated the entire surface as an active runway under the jurisdiction of the Area 51 air traffic control tower.

With the selection made, the key people went to work, with Bissell and his colleagues all agreeing that Groom Lake provided the ideal site for testing the U-2 and training its pilots. Bissell returned to Washington, where he discovered that Groom Lake lay outside the AEC proving ground. He undertook to secure a presidential action adding the Groom Lake area to the AEC proving ground. Bissell and Miller consulted with Dulles before asking the Atomic Energy Commission to add the Groom Lake area to its real estate holding in Nevada. He wrote three memos to the U.S. Air Force, the AEC and the Training Command in charge of administering the gunnery

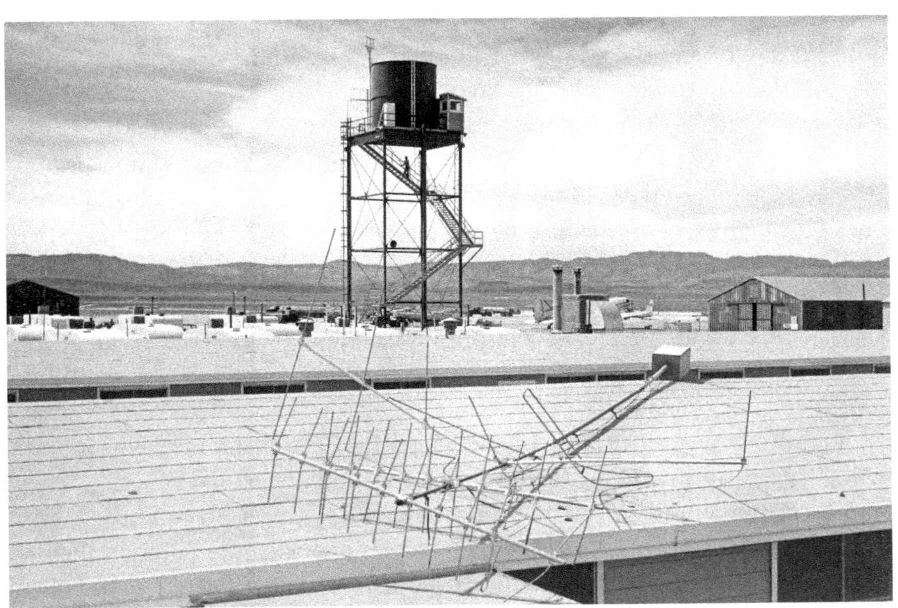

Note the damaged TV antenna from a sandstorm and the guard climbing the water tower to his guard shack. *CIA via TD Barnes Collection.*

range. AEC chairman Admiral Lewis Strauss readily agreed, so Dulles approached President Eisenhower, who approved the addition to the AEC holdings of this strip of wasteland, known by its AEC map designation as Area 51. Signed by Assistant Air Secretary for Research and Development Trevor Gardner, this ensured other range activities not involving the new test site and thus ensured the security needs for Project AQUATONE.

The Groom Lake site in Lincoln County, Nevada, with its excellent flying weather and unparalleled remoteness, was perfect for providing the secrecy and security needed for the CIA's U-2 Project AQUATONE. The entire county had less than two thousand population, with none residing near the dry Groom Lake except for a few miners sporadically working the lead and silver Groom Lake Mine owned by the Sheahan family since 1889. The federal government owned virtually all the land in the region, rendering it dormant, unpopulated and downwind of the radioactive fallout from the atomic tests at the Atomic Proving Grounds.

The mountains around the valley contained large sagebrush and semiarid pinion juniper. In the blistering heat and desolate valley surrounded by mountains, nothing moved during the day—and at night, predators, spiny reptiles, poisonous rattlesnakes and stinging insects came out of hiding from the blazing sun amid sparse cactus or otherwise thorny plant life. The average temperature ranged from 104 degrees Fahrenheit in the summer to minus 21 degrees in the winter. Everything at Groom Lake either chapped, punctured or bit those working there.

In 1955, the AEC's Federal Protection Services operated the check stations on the Nevada Proving Grounds through the Yucca Flat region of Area 51, the location of 739 of the 928 nuclear tests. The road split a few miles past Camp 12 on the atomic test site. The road to the right branched off the AEC property where it passed a CIA security check station into Area 51. The rectangular, six- by ten-mile (9.7- by 16.1-kilometer) facility lay in a silty valley of a sparsely populated desert, vegetated with scrub plants on the desert floor underlying the soon-to-be restricted air space called the "Groom Box."

The following month, in May 1955, Tony LeVier, Dorsey Kammerer and Johnson returned to Groom Lake in Lockheed's Bonanza. They used a compass and surveying equipment to lay out a place for a 5,000-foot, north–south runway on the southwest corner of the lakebed. While there, they staked out the facility's general layout along the salt flat, an ancient dry pluvial lakebed of parched clay and alkaline. Located in the Emigrant Valley at a 4,462-foot elevation, Groom Lake provided a perfect landing strip for any size or type of plane anywhere on the lakebed except when it rained.

LeVier and fellow Lockheed test pilot Bob Matye spent nearly a month at Groom Lake removing surface debris from the gunnery practice during World War II. LeVier drew up a proposal for marking four three-mile-long runways on the hard-pack clay. Johnson, however, refused to approve the $450 expense, citing a lack of funds.

While Groom Lake was Johnson's second choice for the test location, it was the top choice of hundreds of possible sites. At that time, there was no Highway 375 or the town of Rachel. Groom Lake lay on the Nevada Nuclear Test Grounds divided into numbered area grids during atomic bomb testing. It was on the grid number 51. The grid number Area 51 existed long before it became widely known as the infamous Area 51.

Nevada: From Battle-Born to the Battlefield State

The state of Nevada, 85 percent of its land owned by the federal government, and having a population of only 237,000, was perfect for the CIA wanting to test a top-secret reconnaissance plane. Nevada was born into battle during the Civil War and has remained a battle state to this day. Though the Nevada Territory barely even qualified as a territory, three years after it became a territory, Union sympathizers in the Civil War ensured Nevada's entry into statehood as the thirty-sixth state to provide the vote needed to elect Abraham Lincoln as the sixteenth president and first ever Republican president of the United States.

In 1942, Nevada, the "battle-born" state, became the "battlefield" state when the United States established a defensive network in Nevada to repel a feared Japanese invasion of the West Coast. The navy established its West Coast base outside Fallon, Nevada, and the army air corps established several military bases throughout the state to contain the Japanese army should it invade the West Coast of the United States. Nevada became the front line.

During World War II, the Wendover Army Air Field straddling the Nevada-Utah line was the training site for the 509th Composite Group, the B-29 unit that carried out the atomic bombings of Hiroshima and Nagasaki. Beginning with the Korean War, the Marine Corps Mountain Warfare Training Center near Lake Tahoe and the town of Gardnerville, Nevada, provided cold-weather training for replacement personnel bound for Korea.

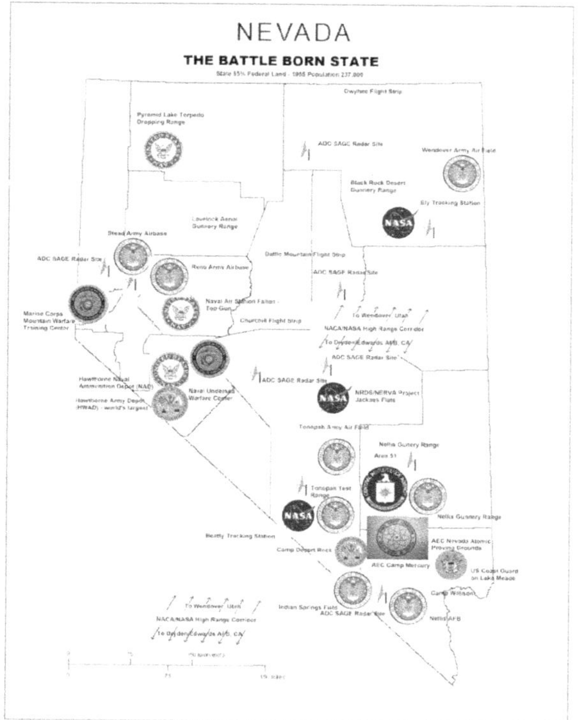

Nevada, the western coast line of defense, beginning during World War II. *TD Barnes.*

When the Central Intelligence Agency chose Area 51 in Nevada for flight testing the U-2, it picked a state long known as a military state, a military test venue where no one would notice yet another war activity. Many of its 237,000 residents depended on the military and the Atomic Energy Commission for jobs.

Next door at Yucca Flats, Yucca Mesa and Frenchman Flats, the Atomic Energy Commission was exploding atomic bombs that created mushroom clouds, entertaining tourists watching from Las Vegas hotels and casinos and forming fallout clouds that traveled directly over Area 51 before dissipating over Utah.

At Jackass Flats, the National Aeronautics and Space Administration (NASA) and the Atomic Energy Commission were developing a nuclear rocket engine for a manned flight to Mars.

Area 51 lay near the center of the four-hundred-mile NASA High Range Flight Corridor, where the United States was preparing to fly the X-15 that carried eight astronauts flying over the NASA High Range Corridor in Nevada. The CIA's Groom Lake in Area 51 soon became an issue between the CIA and NASA when NASA designated it an emergency landing site for the X-15 Project.

The CIA "weather research" project and the AEC activities received scant attention because the U.S. Army, Navy, Marine Corps and even the Coast Guard were all present, with most of the services conducting classified activities within the state. The U.S. Coast Guard patrolled Lake Meade near Las Vegas, and the army ran the largest weapons depot in the world at Hawthorne, Nevada.

The U.S. Navy used the nearby Tonopah Test Range as impact targets for its Regulus II, Model XR33M-N-9A, tactical missile launched at sea. The navy also operated a naval air station at Fallon, Nevada, and operated at the Naval Undersea Warfare Center in Walker Lake near Hawthorne, Nevada. More than 7,000 armed forces and civilians worked at the Hawthorne arsenal during the war, making Hawthorne the busiest Nevada boomtown in a generation. In early 1950, nearly 2,500 people lived in government housing at nearby Babbitt while working for the U.S. Navy and Marine Corps at Walker Lake.

The CIA's creation of its Area 51 facility and combination of its air space with the adjoining U.S. Air Force Nellis gunnery range created the largest contiguous air and ground space available for peacetime military operations in the free world.

One might say the CIA chose Nevada because it was already hosting the unique and highly classified activities of four distinct worlds. These included the military world (army, navy, marine corps, coast guard and air force), the white world (atomic), the space world (NASA) and the black world (Area 51, the nucleus of black projects extending worldwide). A cloak of secrecy already shrouded Nevada's guided missile and leadership in the national security of the United States, making it ideal for hiding the CIA's U-2 spy plane posing as a NASA plane for weather research.

Area 51 No Secret

The CIA did not build the Area 51 facility in secrecy. The "facility that didn't exist" was public knowledge at the beginning in 1955 with the construction of the airstrip at Groom Lake, Nevada. The Atomic Energy Commission announced the construction on behalf of the CIA in the name of NASA, the use being weather research. Despite numerous such announcements over the decades, test site insiders, government officials, military personnel and the public perpetuated the myth that the existence of the facility was a closely guarded secret.

Herb Miller of the CIA Development Projects Staff used the cover of the Atomic Energy Commission to organize a team of construction crews after he issued $800,000 in contracts for construction of the facility. Seth Woodruff Jr., manager of the AEC's Las Vegas field office, participated in the cover by announcing to the news media his instructing the Reynolds Electrical and Engineering Co., Inc. (REECo) to commence the preliminary work on a small, satellite Nevada test site installation. He noted work underway at the location a few miles northeast of Yucca Flat and within the Las Vegas Bombing and Gunnery Range.

Woodruff announced that the installation included "a runway, dormitories, and a few other buildings for housing equipment." He described the facility as "temporary." The press release distribution included eighteen media outlets in Nevada and Utah, including a dozen newspapers, four radio stations and two television stations. At the time and under the existing circumstances, the news release hardly rated as newsworthy.

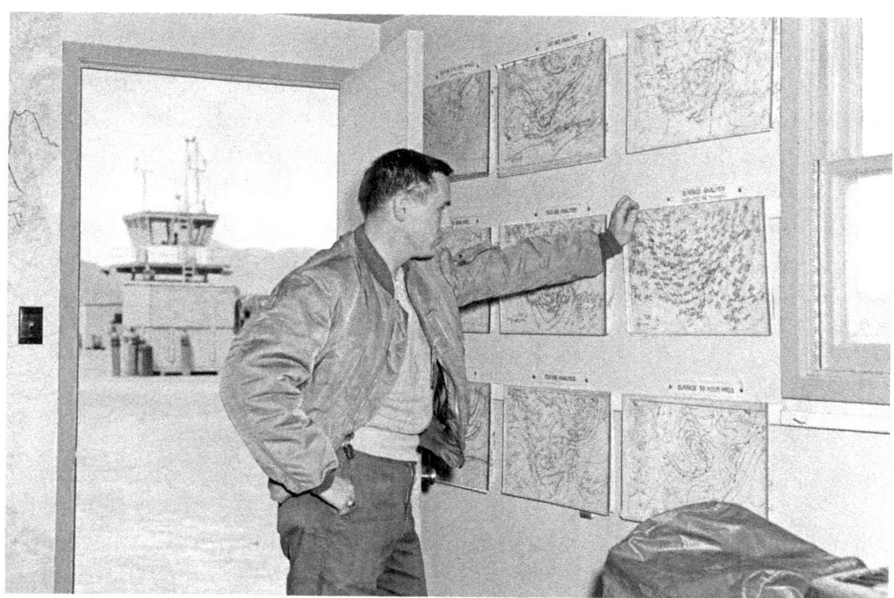

The latest weather maps at Watertown. *CIA via TD Barnes Collection.*

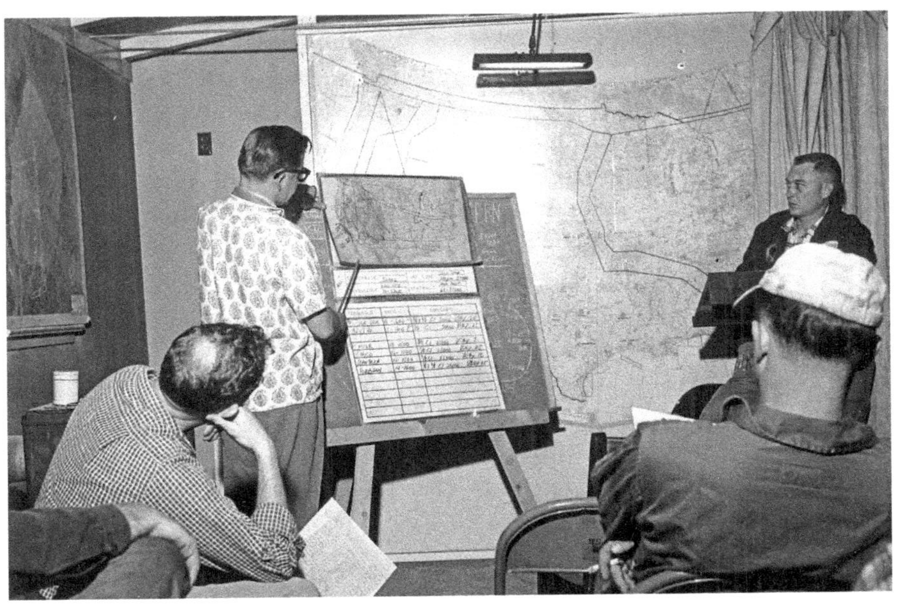

Watertown weather briefing prior to U-2 flight. *CIA via TD Barnes Collection.*

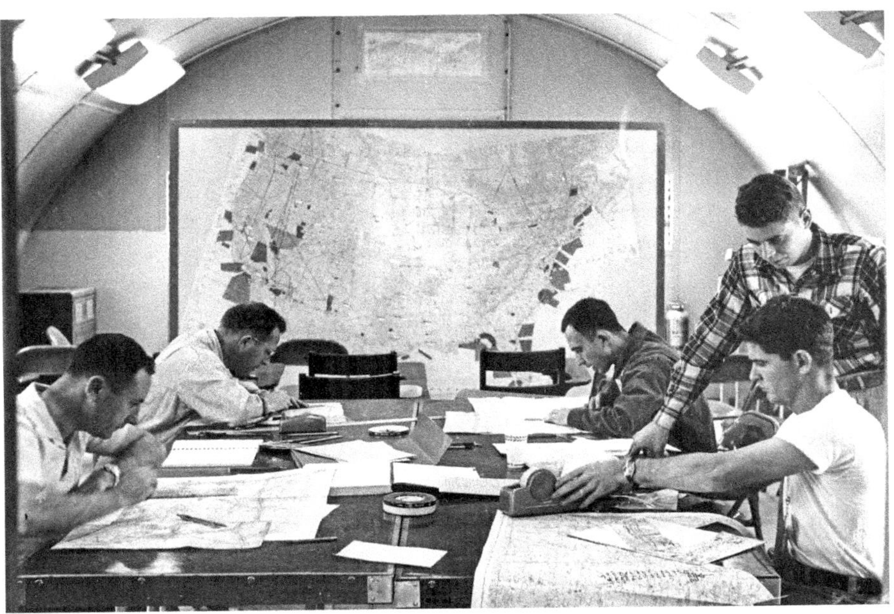

Preparing maps for photo rooms at Watertown. *CIA via TD Barnes Collection.*

By July 1955, the AEC had provided the CIA with a secret facility by expanding its Area 51 boundaries to include Groom Lake. The CIA and AEC invented C.L.J, a fake construction firm, to oversee the construction done by subcontractors. The CIA contractors constructed hangars, a mile-long runway, a concrete ramp, a control tower, a mess hall and other amenities. Official records referred to the facility as Watertown Strip. The pilots and ground crews called it "Area 51."

History had shown the CIA took the right approach at the beginning by announcing through the AEC the construction of the facility. The CIA even identified it as a test site for the U-2, using the cover story of NASA building the facility to conduct weather research, thus providing enough information to satisfy the public's curiosity without revealing agency involvement or classified operational details about the U-2's mission. Only the security surrounding the U-2 belied the innocuous "weather research" cover story. The security for the project created little speculation considering the U.S. Air Force Gunnery, Atomic Proving Grounds and the Tonopah Test Range all having similar closed borders due to the classified nature of their activities.

What's in a Name?

The CIA never officially acknowledged or named the rectangular former World War II bombing and artillery practice airfield, now a CIA test area hidden inside a 38,400-acre Atomic Energy Commission grid identified as Area 51. The CIA chose to use this same name to unofficially identify its new facility only for internal administrative reference purposes.

It wasn't until 1979, when the CIA turned its Area 51 facility over to the air force, that the public even knew the former U-2 test facility was still operating. Many wondered what had occurred at the secret facility between when the U-2 planes left and the air force took over. Consequently, the Area 51 name conjured images of government conspiracy and unexplained mysteries. Since the CIA's arrival in 1955, this nonexistent flight test facility had acquired several identities: Groom Lake, Dreamland, Nevada Test Site, Nellis Test Range, Paradise Ranch, Area 51, Watertown Strip and the Pig Farm, to name a few. People attempting to name an unnamed secret activity caused as much speculation, debate and skepticism as did the classified activities suspected of occurring there.

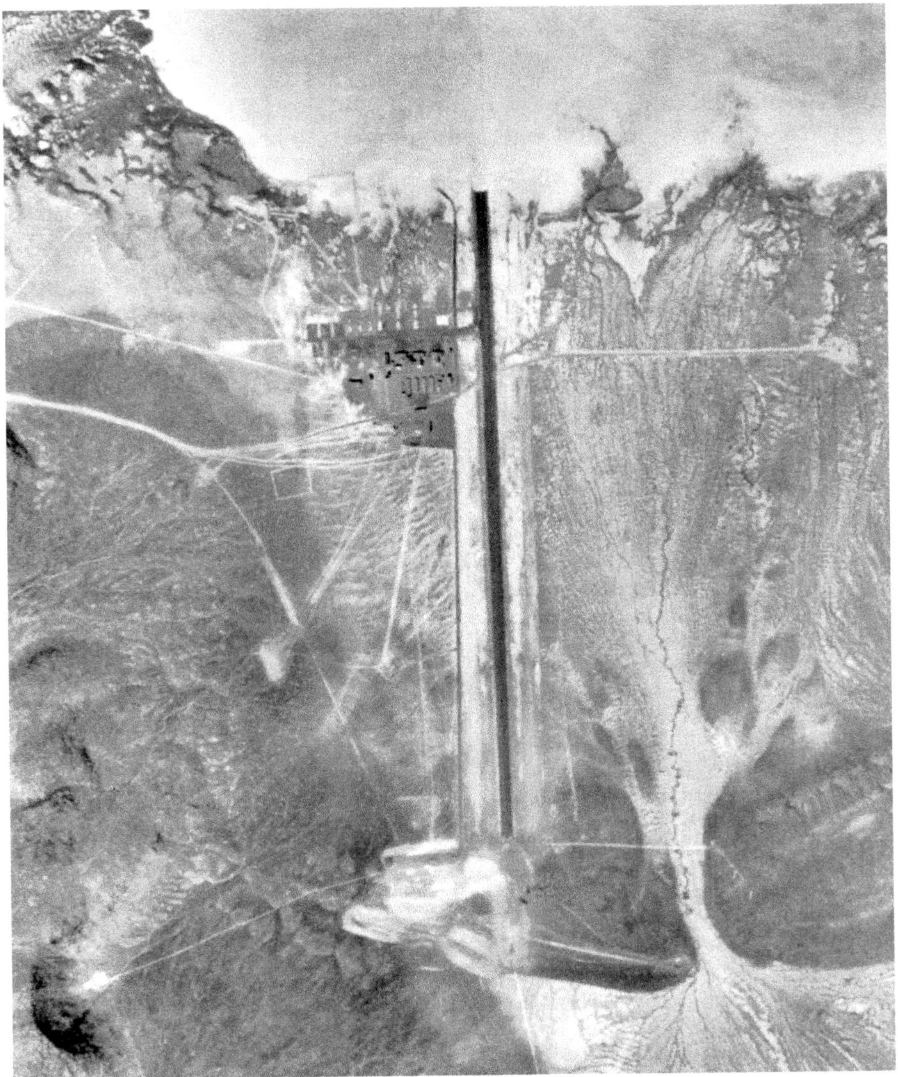

An overhead view of the CIA Watertown facility at Area 51 in 1955 with the new six-thousand-foot runway. *USGS.*

During the CIA era, its existence stayed secret because no one working there talked about it. The workers used the mailing address Pittman Station, a former one-room post office in a rundown area along Boulder Highway in Henderson, Nevada. The U-2 workers identified the facility as Watertown Airstrip, adopting the name of CIA director Allen Dulles's birthplace of

Watertown, New York. Even the Watertown name was debatable, with some thinking the name referred to rainwater flooding the Groom Lake dry lakebed from the runoff from the nearby mountains.

CIA declassification of formerly top-secret documents had confirmed that the CIA adopted the name depicted on the AEC map dividing the Atomic Proving Grounds into areas. Identifying the number 51 adjacent to the much lower area numbers and out of sequence suggested the AEC most likely added Area 51 later in the sequencing.

Some today think of Area 51 being a top-secret place where the United States tested new aviation technology. However, most of the world believed Area 51 was a mythical mecca for black conspiracies and cover-ups. Many believe the CIA constructed massive underground facilities for harvesting colonies of extraterrestrial alien species for their alien technology. For years, the media, movies and authors have competed to generate conspiracy stories concerning the CIA conducting reverse engineering at Area 51. The media feeds an endless number of diverse political and social groups throughout the world that associate with all sorts of trivial, superficial and sensationalist phenomena. It's not because of what the media and some authors believe. Paranormal ufology and alien hypotheses simply sell. After all, 80 percent of the world believes in flying saucers and little green men.

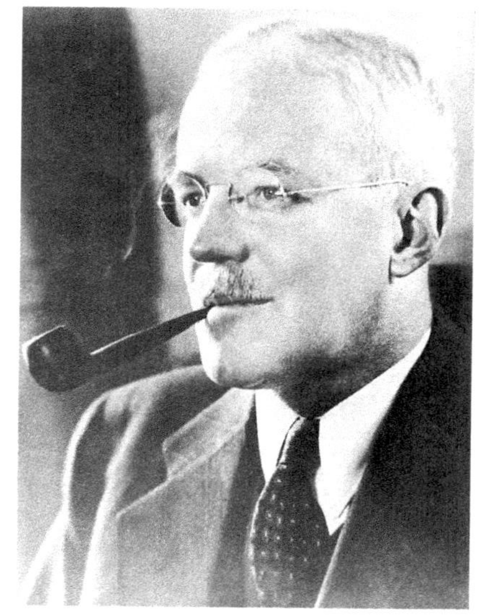

Allen Welsh Dulles, director of Central Intelligence from February 26, 1953, to November 29, 1961, under Presidents Dwight Eisenhower and John F. Kennedy. *Wikipedia.*

According to theories, Area 51 had underground tunnels, subterranean chambers, flying saucers, little green men or wreckages from Roswell. In reality, it was the most unlikely place on the planet for such things when one considered that Area 51 became the most monitored spot on earth when the Russians launched their Sputnik satellite in October 1957, knowing at the time about Area 51. Other than base support, security and the special projects technical services team, Area 51 always served transient occupants, here today and gone as soon as they completed their project. Several low-skilled workers have come and gone at

Area 51. No way could one of them not have said something over the past half century had the stories been true.

Contrary to what the world wants to believe, Area 51 provides an operating technical laboratory for the advancement of aerial military systems, a business serving customers. Yes, a cloak of secrecy covers Area 51, but not necessarily because of military activities. In most cases, the secrecy exists to protect the customers competing with one another through proof-of-concept systems undergoing testing for sale to the military. They knew their trade secrets were safe at Area 51.

CHAPTER 5

ORGANIZING IN SECRECY

The staffing called for a large number of communications engineers and technicians and security investigators, all having top-secret clearances. Security was so sensitive that the CIA performed its security clearance investigations rather than trust the Federal Bureau of Investigation to do it. Everything was on a need-to-know basis regardless of one's rank, position or level of security clearance.

The CIA considered the changing requirements and revised the staffing within the month to delete the support aircraft crews, who became an air force contribution. It increased the administrative support area, targeting clerical. It added a communications reserve cadre to permit retention of personnel while training on project equipment before their assignment to the field. For the four deployment bases, the staff changes replaced civilian contract guards with staff security investigators and added a supply depot.

The director of personnel received a sterile version of the staff so he might produce agency candidates to fill the vacancies and provide support in keeping personnel records. The CIA assigned the highest priority to the project's requirements and made every effort to staff it with the best candidates. However, the CIA found it more difficult getting the actual bodies on board than getting approval to add them.

To handle the task, the Offices of Communications and Security set up their own recruiting and training programs to meet the requirements for personnel without depleting their staffs. The office reached an early decision disallowing accompanying dependents at either the ZI or foreign bases. Thus, the CIA chose single men wherever possible. To this end, the project made excellent use of air force enlisted men in clerical slots. The "no dependents" rule continued in effect until the end of 1957.

Dick Bissell and the deputy director for support, Colonel Lawrence K. White, soon realized the complexities of organizing all the functions required for Project AQUATONE. They had to find qualified personnel having a top-secret security clearance in departments that they had never envisioned. Everything was compartmentalized and on a need-to-know basis, so it wasn't a matter of publishing help wanted ads in the newspaper. The project required staffing experts in building the plane, the engines, the cameras, everything. Thus, the project's operating organization evolved slowly from January to April 1955, with most of the individuals working on AQUATONE remaining on the rolls of their agency components.

Toward the end of April 1955, Bissell's staff finished developing, and the deputy director for support approved the organization staffing for AQUATONE. Now operational, the project totaled 357 personnel divided among project headquarters, a U.S. testing facility and three foreign field bases. The CIA employees represented only one-fourth (92) of the total. The U.S. Air Force personnel commitment totaled 109 positions, not counting many other air force personnel, such as SAC meteorologists, who supported the U-2 project in addition to their other duties.

Contract employees made up the largest Project AQUATONE category, with 156 positions in 1955. This category included 5 maintenance and support personnel per aircraft from Lockheed, the pilots and support personnel from other contractors for items such as photographic equipment. By October 1956, AQUATONE would reach a high-water mark of 600 personnel and face a reduction in force. The training stopped, and the detachments left Area 51.

Security for the U-2 Project

On April 29, 1955, Richard Bissell signed an agreement with the U.S. Air Force and the Navy, which exhibited interest at the time. The services agreed with the CIA assuming primary responsibility for all security concerning the overhead reconnaissance Project AQUATONE. From this time on, the CIA took responsibility for maintaining the security of overhead programs.

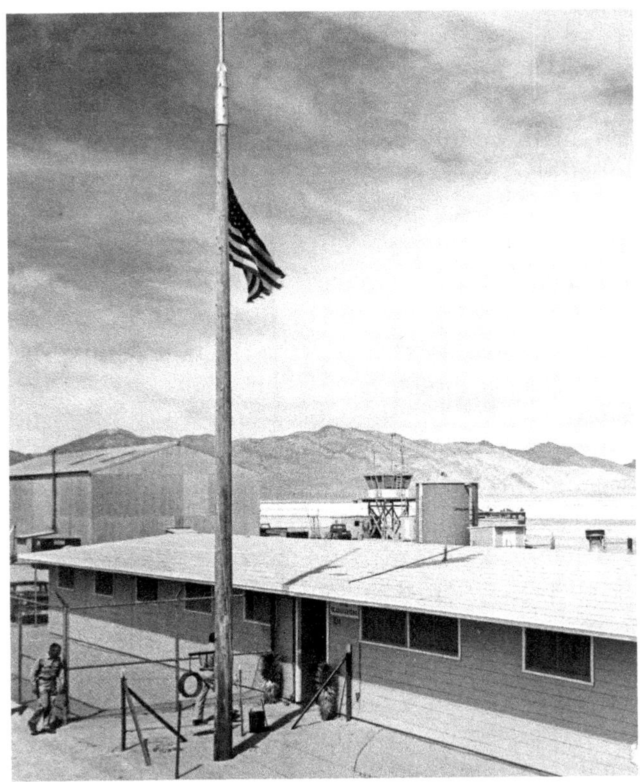

Left: Headquarters building at Watertown. The flag is at half mast following U-2 pilot Sieker's fatal crash. *CIA via TD Barnes Collection.*

Below: Watertown control tower at sunset. *CIA via TD Barnes Collection.*

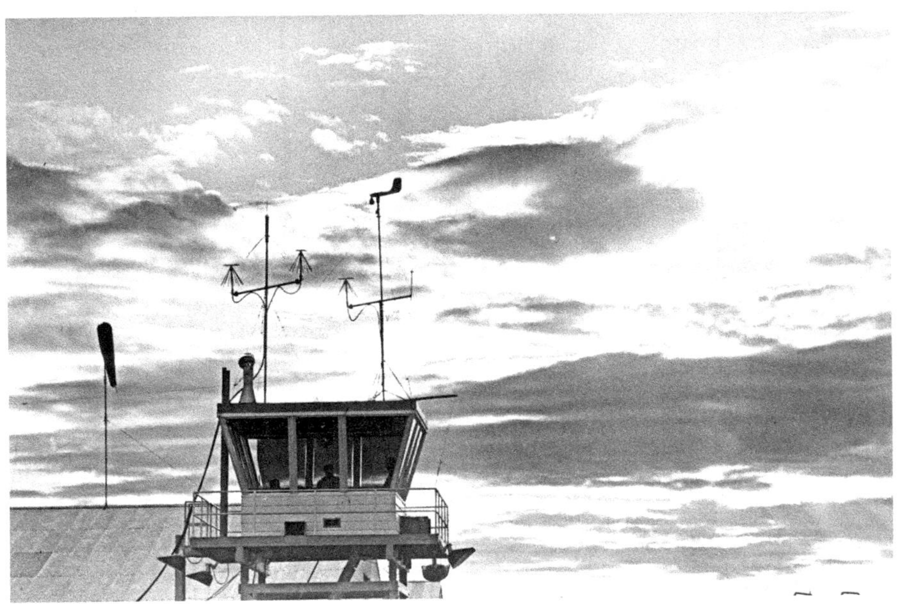

This responsibility placed a heavy burden on the Office of Security. The challenge called for establishing procedures to keep scores of contracts untraceable to the CIA. The responsibility included determining which contractor employees required security clearances and devising physical security measures for the various manufacturing facilities.

The Office of Security found keeping the U-2 and subsequent overhead systems secret a time-consuming and costly undertaking. The most important aspect of the security program for the U-2 project called for the creation of an entirely new compartmented system for the product of U-2 missions. Strict control of access to the photographs taken by the U-2 often limited the ability of the CIA analysts to use the products of U-2 missions.

The terminology used to describe U-2 aircraft and pilots played a part in maintaining the security of the overhead reconnaissance program. The CIA reduced the chances of a security breach by always referring to its high-altitude aircraft as "articles," with each aircraft having its "article number," and the CIA referred to each U-2 with its article number of classified internal documents. Similarly, the CIA referred to the pilots as "drivers," a name that never sat well with the former fighter pilots. (The prototype U-2, Article 341, never received a USAF serial.)

Cable traffic referred to the aircraft as KWEXTRA-00 with the two-digit number identifying the precise aircraft; these numbers were unrelated to the three-digit article numbers assigned by the factory. The CIA identified the pilots by a two-digit number identifying the precise pilot. Thus, even if a message or document concerning overflight activities fell into unfriendly hands, the contents could refer to articles and code numbers without indicating the identity of the program.

Access to Area 51 required top-secret and SCI security clearances. Obtaining such clearances—or, for the Atomic Energy Commission, "Q" clearance—entailed passing a background investigation. The procedure involved the applicant submitting an executed Standard Form 86 (SF86) for the background check process. Standard elements included background checks of employment, education, organizational affiliations and any local agency where the subject lived, worked, traveled or attended school. These checks led to interviews with persons who knew the subject both personally and professionally. The investigation included the subject's spouse or cohabitant for the past ten years or to age eighteen, the lesser of the two. The investigation expanded as necessary to resolve issues and address employment standards unique to individual agencies.

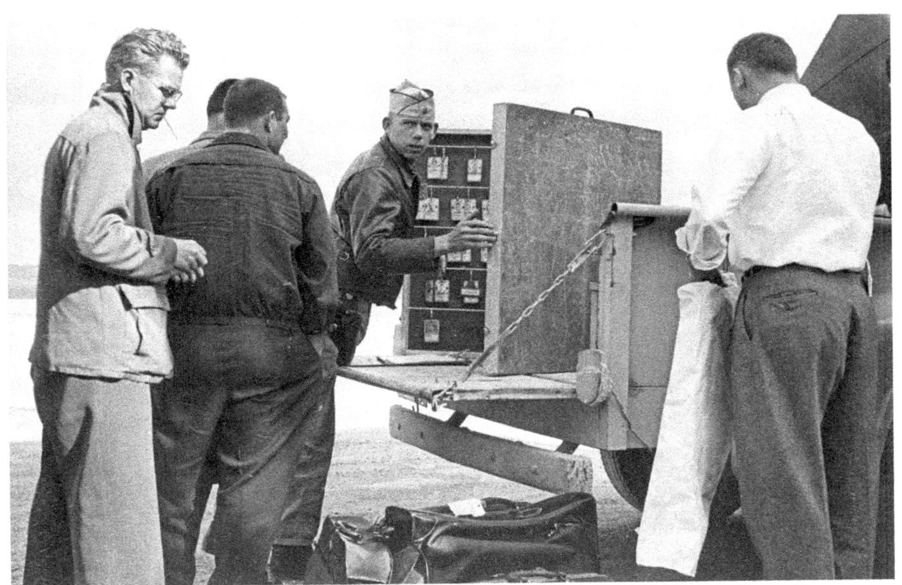

Workers passing through security to a shuttle flight from Watertown to Burbank. *CIA via TD Barnes Collection.*

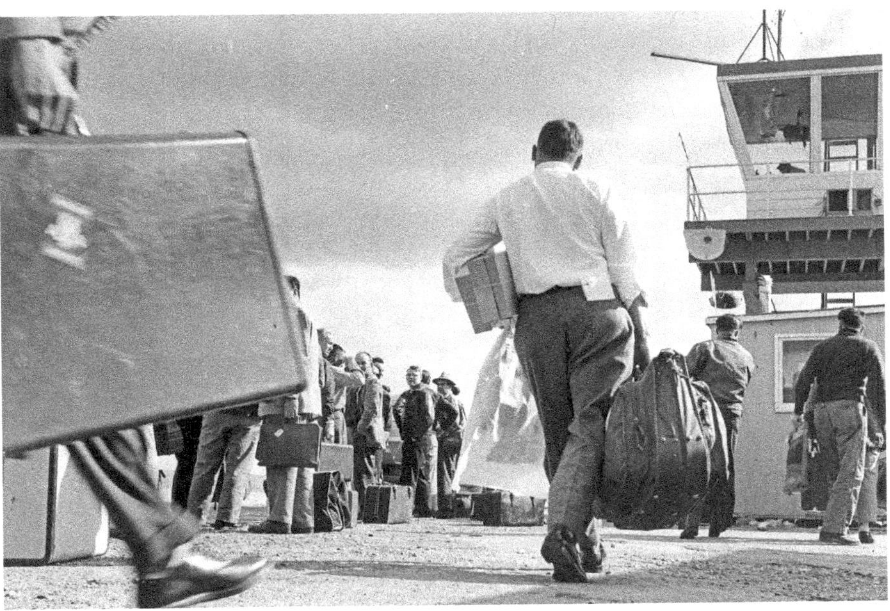

Workers arriving at Watertown for security check following a shuttle flight. *CIA via TD Barnes Collection.*

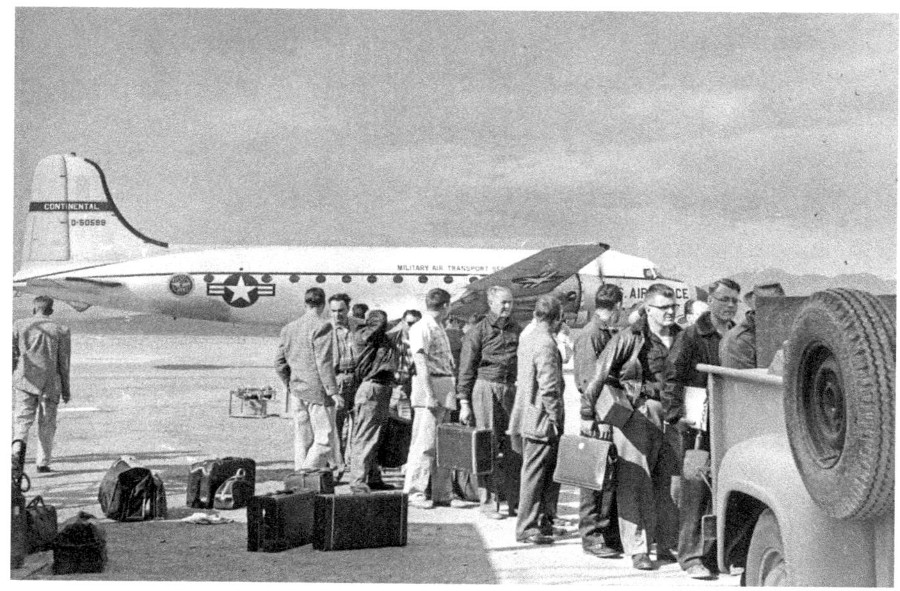

Arriving workers at Watertown lining up to pass through security. *CIA via TD Barnes Collection.*

Early on, the security concern focused on cleared personnel discussing classified matters where those lacking a need-to-know might overhear them. About the only other concern in this area regarded mishandling of classified material. Secret procurement of the aircraft components proved to be more challenging. Even the aircraft's onboard equipment involved the CIA security planners. For example, Johnson ordered altimeters from the Kollman Instrument with instructions for calibrating the devices to eighty thousand feet. Johnson's choice raised eyebrows at Kollman because its instruments only went to forty-five thousand feet. The CIA's security personnel briefed several Kollman officials and produced a cover story saying it planned to use the altimeter for experimental rocket planes.

In May 1955, while the CIA dealt with security concerns and recruiting pilots, Osmund J. Ritland, one of the first air force officers assigned to Project OILSTONE, began coordinating air force activities in the U-2 program with Richard Bissell. A month later, Ritland became Bissell's deputy, although Air Force Chief of Staff Twining did not approve this assignment until the day after.

Air force officer Lieutenant Colonel Leo P. Geary, using the U.S. Air Force Inspector General's Office as a cover, joined the program in June 1955 and remained as a project officer until August 1966, longer than any of the other project managers. As an air force colonel (later brigadier general), he was James Cunningham's air force counterpart in the U-2 program. He was instrumental in diverting engines from other air force projects for use in the U-2 and served as the focal point to provide a high degree of air force continuity for all Defense Department support to the U-2 programs during his eleven years with the overhead reconnaissance projects.

Building the CIA Flight Test Facility at Area 51

The dry lakebed provided a great landing strip except when it rained enough for the lake to collect rainwater runoff from the surrounding mountains. To solve this problem, the project managers provided the project a paved runway to allow testing during these times.

On May 4, 1955, a survey team arrived at Groom Lake and laid out a five-thousand-foot (1,500-meter) north–south runway on the southwest corner of the lakebed and designated a site for a base support facility. Area 51, initially known as Site II, consisted of little more than a few shelters, workshops and trailer homes in which to house its small team.

The CIA's facility requirements soon changed, however, calling for a permanent facility nearly 300 percent larger than Johnson's original design. Before the Groom Lake selection, Johnson had estimated the construction of a larger Site I facility would cost $450,000. His estimate for building the same facility at Site II (Groom Lake) was $832,000.

The CIA maintained its cover during the construction of the Groom Lake flight test facility by using secret funds to pay the C.L.J. Construction Firm—C.L.J. being the initials of Kelly Johnson—by placing in Johnson's mailbox blank envelopes filled with cash for all work (runways, hangars, quarters, water wells, sewers and so on).

By July 1955, the CIA's flight test facility was ready for occupancy, and the agency, air force and Lockheed personnel began moving in under the CIA's commander, Richard A. "Dick" Newton, USMCR (Ret). Newton would serve from 1955 to 1956 and Landon McConnell from 1956 to 1957.

By now, the CIA's fledgling Groom Lake facility had two dirt landing strips, one approximately five thousand feet and one seven thousand feet long, both scraped into the barren desert floor on the east side of the lake. At this same time, Earnest Williams, a REECo employee, drilled a well that

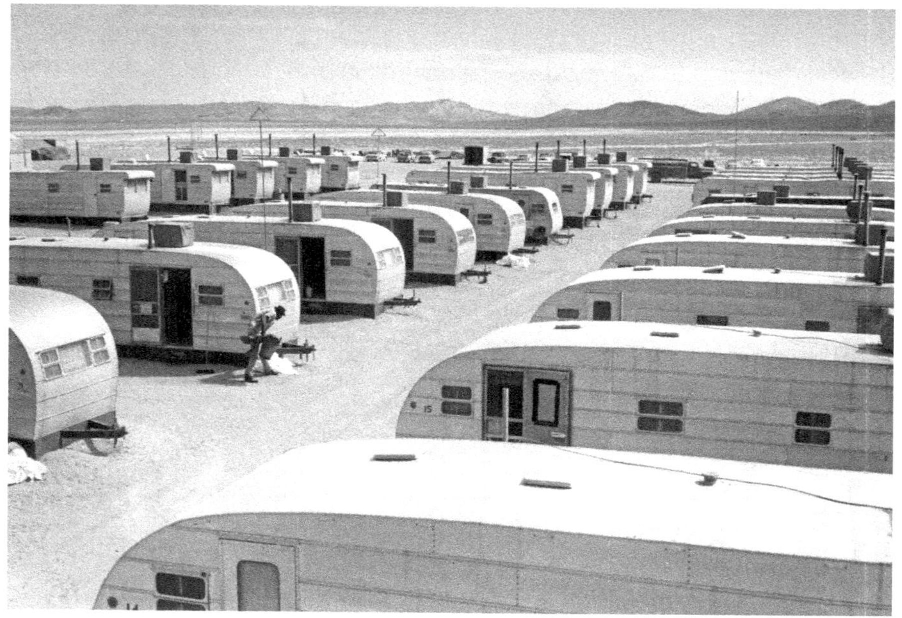

Workers at Area 51 laying out laundry for pickup at Area 51 in 1956. *CIA via TD Barnes Collection.*

provided a limited water supply; however, trouble with the well still required trucking in water.

The facility contained three hangars, a control tower and rudimentary accommodations for test personnel. The facility's few amenities included a movie theater and a volleyball court in addition to a mess hall and fuel storage tanks. Many today tend to refer to the Groom Lake operating facility in Area 51 as a base, as in an air force base. During the CIA stewardship, Groom Lake remained a flight test facility with no official name or designation as an air base.

Bissell's plan for the project was to have the Lockheed test pilots train some air force instructor pilots to fly the U-2 and for these instructor pilots (IPs) to train the pilots selected to fly U-2 missions for the CIA.

Earlier, in February 1955, Colonel Ritland had sought a direct line to General John S. Mills, the air force deputy chief of staff, personnel, to recruit the best candidates available. He tried to expedite the paperwork required to transfer them to the project separately from that of the regular military assignees to other CIA duty. The liaison officer in the Pentagon would furnish him the candidate files for review by senior

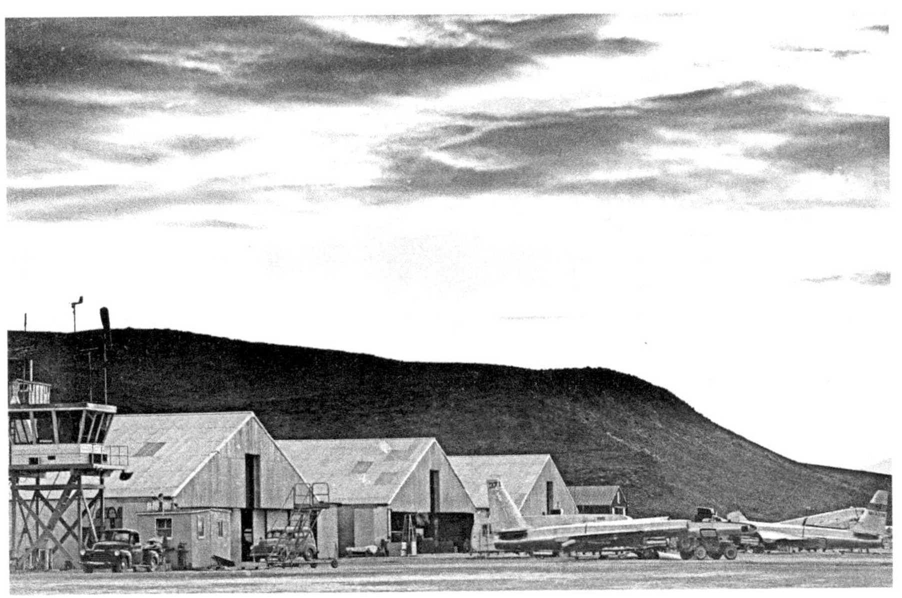

Watertown flight line at sunset. *CIA via TD Barnes Collection.*

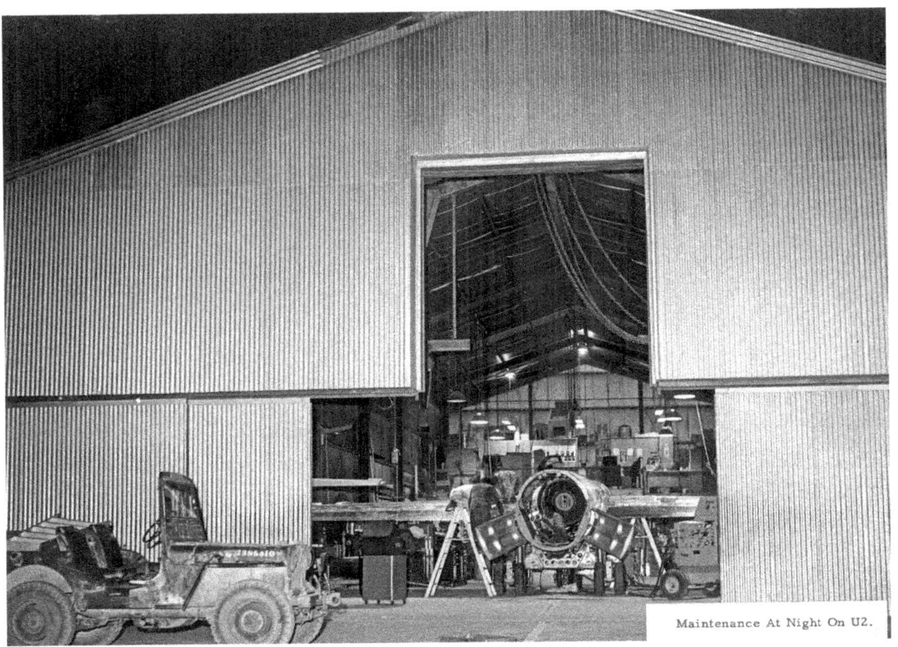

Night view of maintenance on U-2 at Watertown. *CIA via TD Barnes Collection.*

project officers. This worked well until General Mills encountered the U.S. Air Force's reluctance to release so many extraordinary men from critical categories. The signing of a joint agreement in August 1955 solved the problem. However, these delays had a sharp effect on the training, equipping and deployment. The U.S. Air Force's reluctance to meet the aerial reconnaissance needs justified the decision to have the CIA take the lead in training and deploying the U-2 detachments.

Lieutenant General Emmett "Rosy" O'Donnell, the U.S. Air Force's deputy chief of staff for personnel, authorized the use of air force pilots and provided considerable assistance in the search for pilots meeting the high standards established by the CIA and the U.S. Air Force. Most of the air force pilots, the instructor pilots and those sheep dipped into the CIA alike had trained at Turner Air Force Base in Georgia.

The U.S. Air Force attached its assigned project personnel to the 1007th Air Intelligence Service Group Headquarters Command, where a special unit of the Military Personnel Division handling their records approached the selectees through a form letter that described the proposed assignment to the CIA as a sensitive activity overseas without their dependents. The personnel division requested their personal history statement for use in a security office investigation and granted preliminary approval for administrative processing.

While the CIA won the bitter battle with General LeMay and SAC over control of Project AQUATONE, General LeMay won the right to name the staff and the military people who would run the flying part of the program. He chose Colonel Yancey to command the training wing at Area 51 out of March Air Force Base in California.

Even before the recruiting effort was underway, the U.S. Air Force and the CIA developed a pilot training program. Under the terms of the OILSTONE agreement between the CIA and the U.S. Air Force, responsibility for pilot training lay with Colonel William F. Yancey.

The CIA screened and selected the mission pilots from SAC F-84 pilots with long-range navigation training. The CIA organized three squadrons, and General LeMay chose the commanders. Colonel McCoy commanded Detachment A, Colonel Perry commanded Detachment B and Colonel Stan Berrli commanded Detachment C.

Each candidate received orders to Washington and completed the entry-on-duty processing, including physical and psychological examination, security briefing and voluntary participation in a polygraph interview. Once the candidate received a final security clearance, the individual entered duty status and received a briefing on his assignment. Only after reporting in at

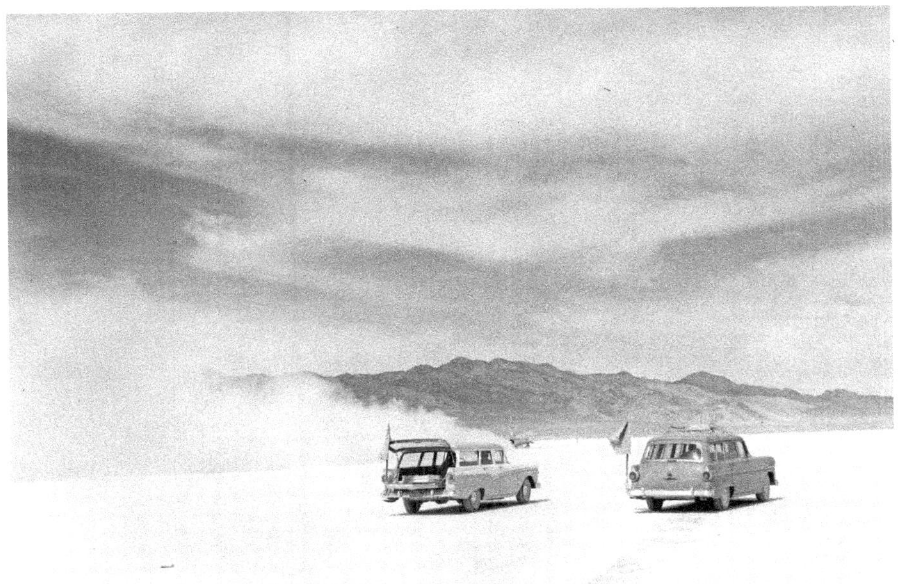

A mobile car following a U-2 across Groom Lake at Watertown. *CIA via TD Barnes Collection.*

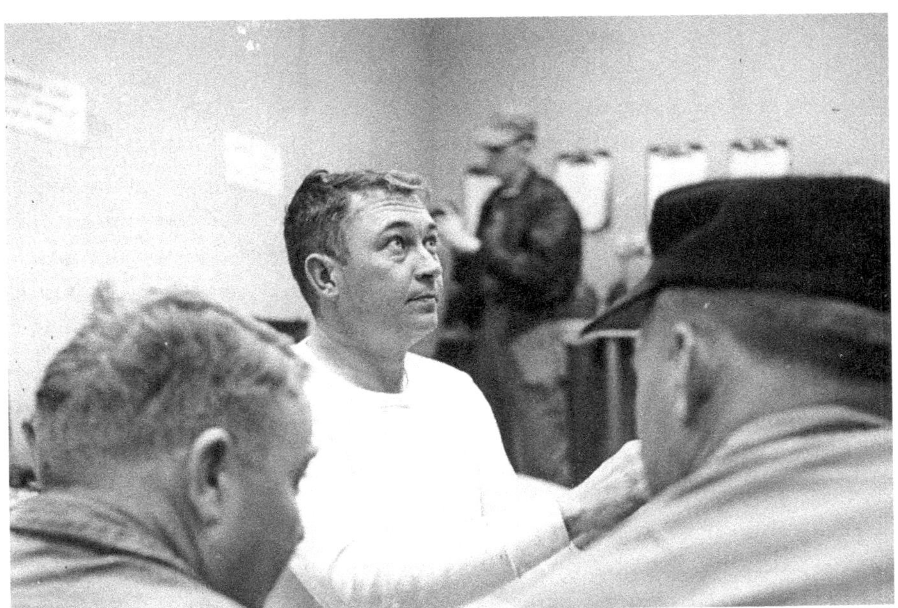

Stress showing on the face of a U-2 pilot following an eight-hour flight. *CIA via TD Barnes Collection.*

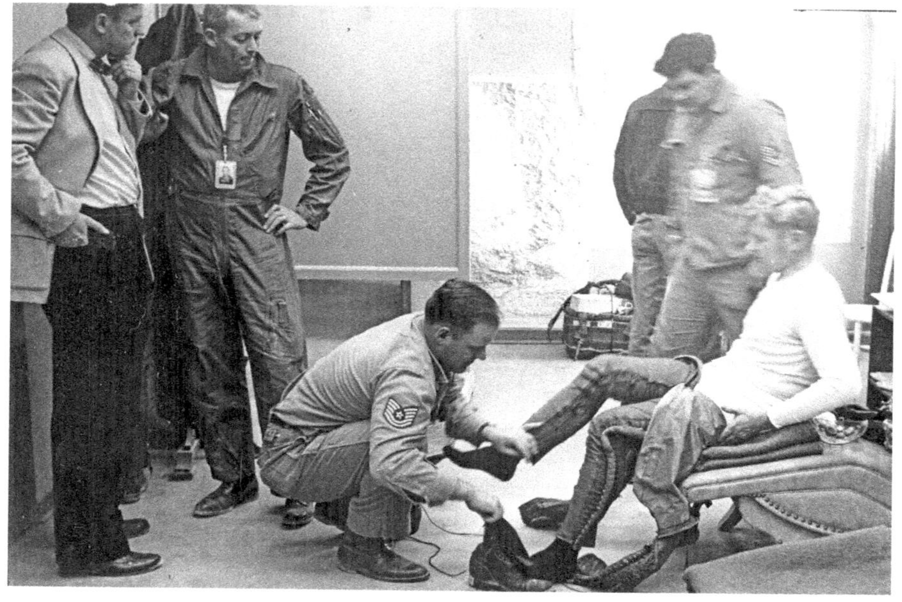

A USAF sergeant suit technician assisting a U-2 pilot out of his partial-pressure suit following a flight. *CIA via TD Barnes Collection.*

March Air Force Base in Riverside, California, did the pilots selected meet the other personnel making up this group.

The first few months of this procedure saw a moderately high rate of washouts of military personnel for various reasons when subjected to agency tests. Despite efforts made to explain the necessity for it and to minimize the reaction to it, the CIA could do little to make this type of examination more palatable to senior air force officers. The career air force officers found it patently difficult to accustom themselves to civilian command with stringent security control over all their activities and movements. Only a moderate number of problem cases came from the screening to give trouble later.

While the recruitment of military personnel was underway, Richard Newton of the CIA took command of Area 51. At the same time, on July 24, less than eight months after the go-ahead call from Trevor Gardner, Kelly Johnson readied the first aircraft, known as Article 341, for delivery to the "Paradise Ranch" site. Lockheed completed the final inspection, flutter and vibration tests and control proof tests and disassembled the aircraft for transport to the Groom Lake remote test facility for taxi and first flight.

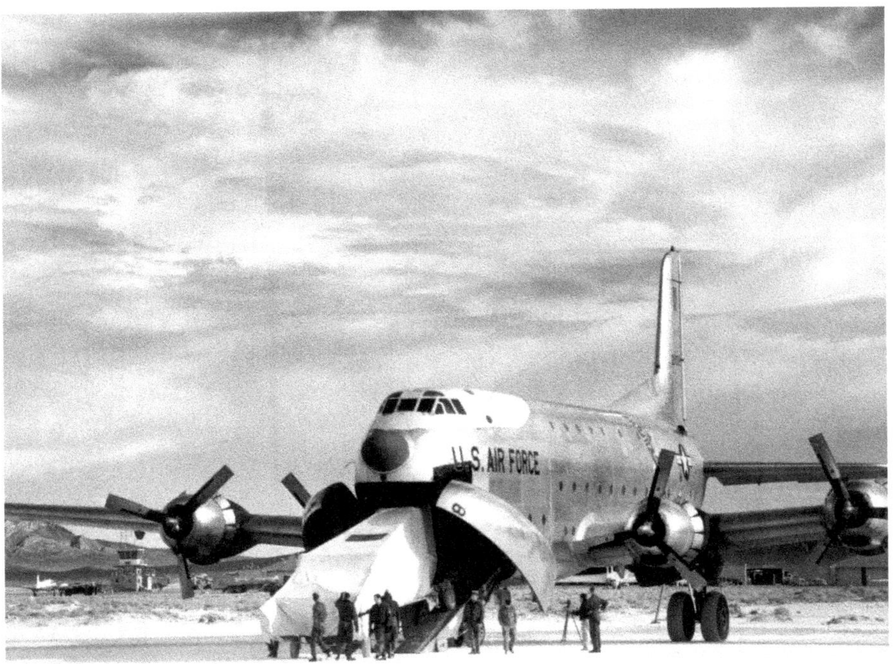

Virtually all of the U-2s were delivered from Burbank to Area 51 by air force Douglas C-124 Globemasters. *CIA via TD Barnes Collection.*

Three days later, Lockheed transported the first U-2 prototype number 101, disassembled and wrapped in cloth, to the Watertown Groom Lake facility from a small Lockheed factory at Oildale, California, on board a C-124 transport plane. The C-124 pilots delivering the plane did not know their destination. Their instructions were to fly (at night) to a certain point on the California-Nevada border and follow radio directions to their unknown landing site. The cargo plane landed on the Groom Lake dry bed rather than the runway after base commander Richard Newton expressed his doubts to Kelly Johnson concerning the new asphalt runway supporting the weight of the loaded C-124. The CIA security personnel required the crew to turn in their regular IDs upon arrival and use aliases while at the Groom Lake facility.

The Lockheed U-2 #001 arrived at Area 51 to commence flight tests under the FAA designation N308X. It was a lightweight, unusual-looking plane with an eighty-foot wingspan resembling a glider. Among other equipment, it came armed with two telescopic-lens cameras with extraordinary capabilities, including a high-resolution lens capable of

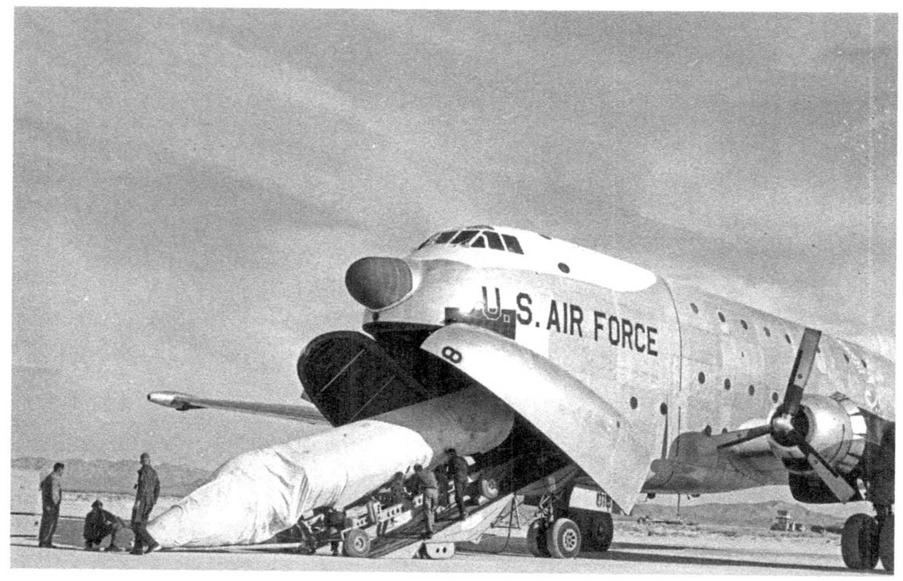

C-124 unloading U-2 at Watertown. *CIA via TD Barnes Collection.*

focusing on a newspaper headline over the shoulder of a person on the ground from an altitude of fifteen miles. Johnson's aircraft provided the unprecedented potential for espionage and was vital for investigating the "bomber" and "missile" gaps threatening the U.S. national security.

At Groom Lake, Lockheed mechanics spent the next six days readying the craft for its maiden flight. Colonel Allman T. Culbertson from the U.S. Air Force's Office of the Director of Research and Development pointed out to Lieutenant Colonel Geary that before "Kelly's Angel" could take to the air, it needed an air force designator.

The two officers looked through the aircraft designator handbook to see their options and decided they could not call the project aircraft a bomber, fighter or transport plane. Not wanting anyone to know the CIA intended to use the new plane for reconnaissance, Geary and Culbertson decided to place it in the utility aircraft category along with the only two utility aircraft on the books, a U-1 and a U-3. Thus, Johnson's CL-282 design, called the "angel" by the Lockheed test pilots, the "article" by the CIA and the "Dragon Lady" by the air force, became simply the U-2. The CIA referred to all the U-2s as articles. The difficulty experienced by the pilots flying the U-2 led to it being called the "Dragon Lady" because the aircraft was extremely unforgiving on pilot ineptitude or incompetence.

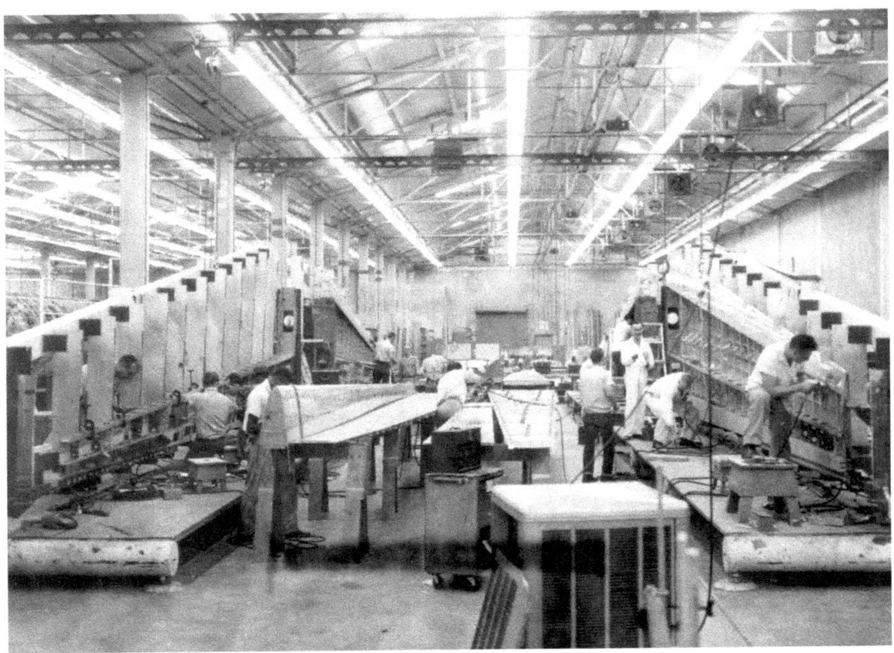

U-2 planes being constructed at Lockheed's low-profile Oildale facility near Bakersfield, California. *CIA via TD Barnes Collection.*

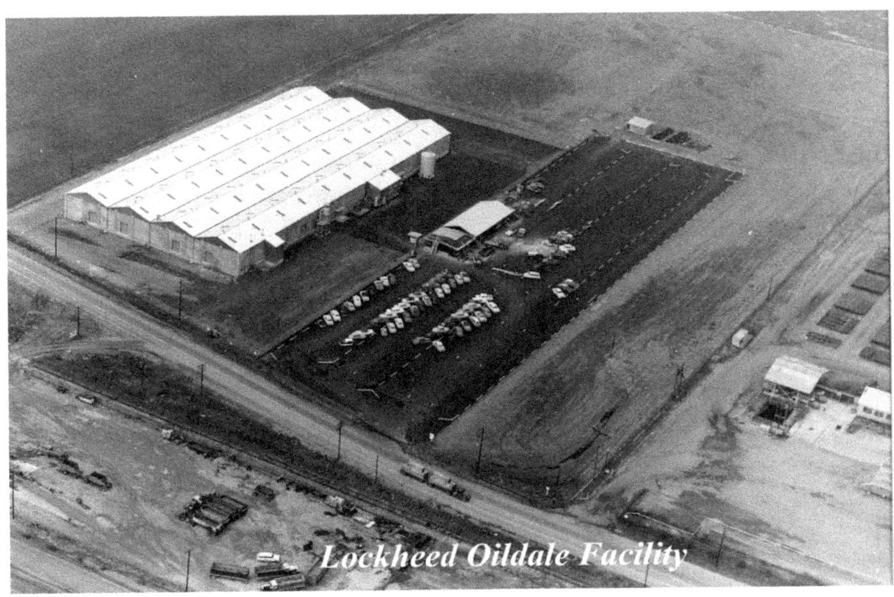

Lockheed's U-2 production facility at Oildale, California. *Lockheed.*

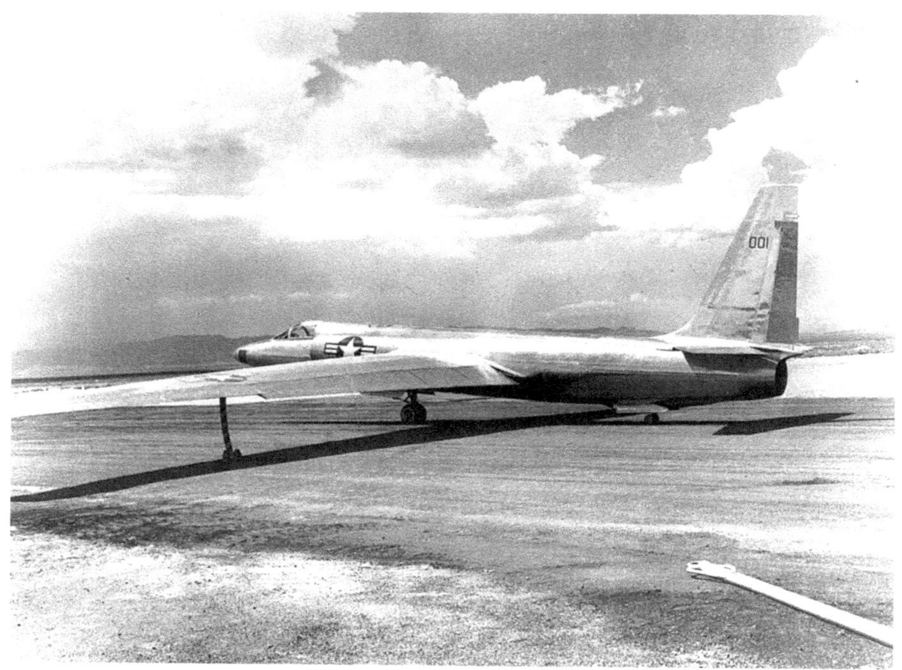

A U-2 on the runway at Area 51 with pogos installed to support the wings during takeoff. *CIA via TD Barnes Collection.*

Six days after the U-2 Article 341 arrived, Lockheed test pilot Tony LeVier piloted the unofficial maiden U-2 flight during a taxi test. The CIA and Lockheed intended LeVier to conduct only a high-speed taxi test. The sailplane-like wings were so efficient that the aircraft jumped into the air at 70 knots (81 miles per hour, 130 kilometers per hour), amazing LeVier, who, as he later said, had no intentions whatsoever of flying. The lake bed had no markings. The lack of markings made it difficult for LeVier to judge the distance to the ground. The brakes proved too weak, causing the U-2 to bounce once before it stopped rolling. He tried the ailerons only to discover the plane airborne. The transition to flight occurred so smoothly he did not notice.

Levier cut the power and contacted the ground in a left bank of ten degrees in a hard landing that blew both tires and caught the brakes on fire, only to bounce back into the air. He brought the plane back down for a second landing. He applied the brakes, with little effect. The aircraft rolled for a long distance before coming to a stop.

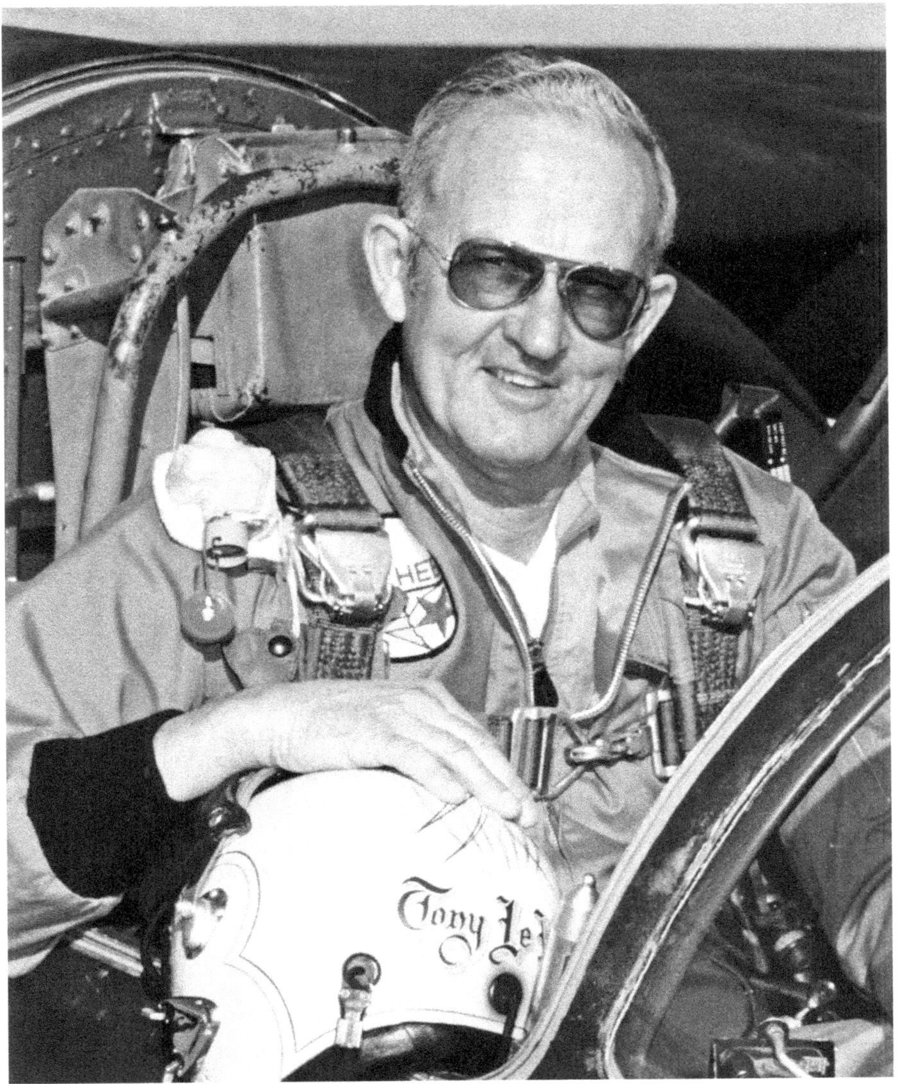

Lockheed test pilot Tony LeVier flew the first test flight of the U-2 at Watertown. *area51specialprojects.com.*

Bissell, Cunningham and Johnson saw the aircraft fall and bounce. Leaping into a jeep, they rushed to the plane and saw the brakes were on fire. The ground crew followed in radio trucks carrying extinguishers. They signaled to LeVier to climb out and then used fire extinguishers to put out the fire before it damaged the airframe.

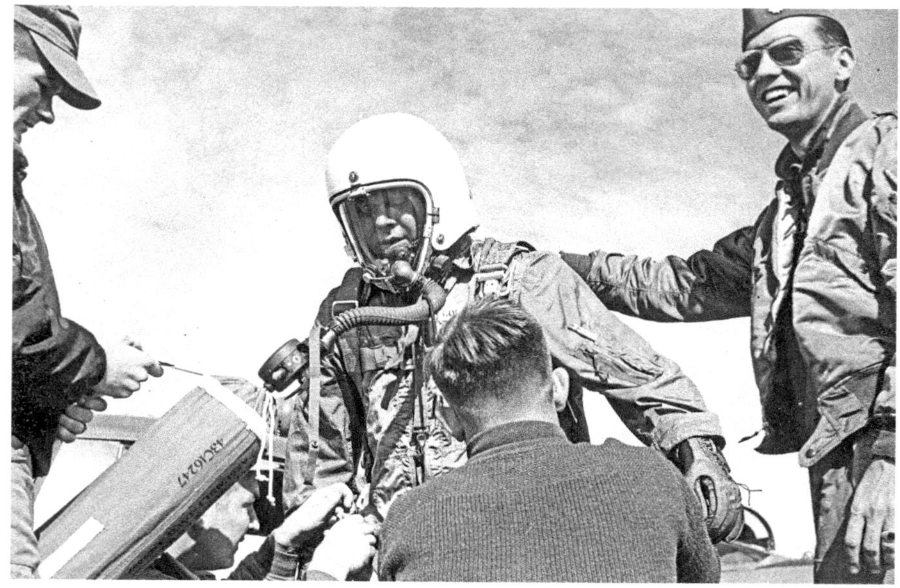

A pilot entering a U-2 for high flight. *CIA via TD Barnes Collection.*

Thus, Lockheed test pilot Tony LeVier was the first to learn the U-2 had a mind of its own when it came to flying. At a debriefing session that followed, LeVier complained about the poor performance of the brakes and the absence of markings on the runway.

The prototype U-2 suffered only minor damage: blown tires, a leaking oleo strut, a pneumatic air–oil hydraulic shock absorber on the landing gear, on the undercarriage and damaged brakes. This unplanned flight foretold the airworthiness of the U-2.

Taxi trials continued for one more day. The CIA knew now that the U-2 loved to fly and refused to land. At low speeds, it remained in ground effect and glided effortlessly above the runway for great distances.

Little did the CIA know that the plane's design, expected to fly two years, would still be flying today, more than half a century later. In eight months and under budget, the CIA produced at Area 51 the most capable and reliable high-altitude intelligence, surveillance and reconnaissance (ISR) platform ever, even compared to any system flying today—manned or unmanned.

Three days following the U-2 taxi trials, on August 4, 1955, LeVier piloted the U-2 at Groom Lake on its first official flight, flying it to eight thousand feet in a rainstorm. It flew beautifully. Having only two landing wheels, it

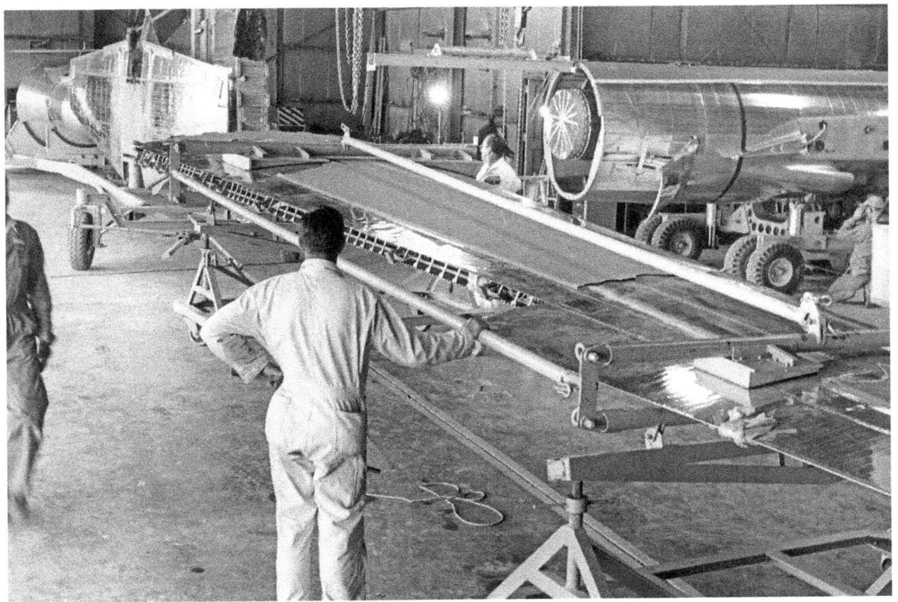

U-2 assembly in a hangar at Watertown. *CIA via TD Barnes Collection.*

landed like a bicycle. LeVier wanted to touch the rear wheel down first. However, Kelly Johnson insisted on him landing the plane by touching the nose wheel down first.

LeVier disagreed with this approach, believing the U-2 would bounce if he attempted to touch down on the forward gear first. LeVier took the aircraft up to eight thousand feet, leveled off and cycled the landing gear up and down. He tested the flaps and the plane's stability and control systems before making his first landing approach. As the U-2 settled down, the forward landing gear touched the runway, and the plane skipped and bounced into the air. LeVier made a second attempt to land front wheels first, and again the plane bounded into the air. Kelly Johnson watched from a chase plane and gave a constant stream of instructions as LeVier made three more unsuccessful landing attempts.

With the light fading and a thunderstorm fast approaching from the mountains to the west, LeVier made one last approach using the method he first advocated: letting the aircraft touch on its rear wheel first. This time the U-2 made a near-perfect landing ten minutes before the thunderstorm dumped a rare two inches of rain, flooding the dry lakebed and making the airstrip unusable.

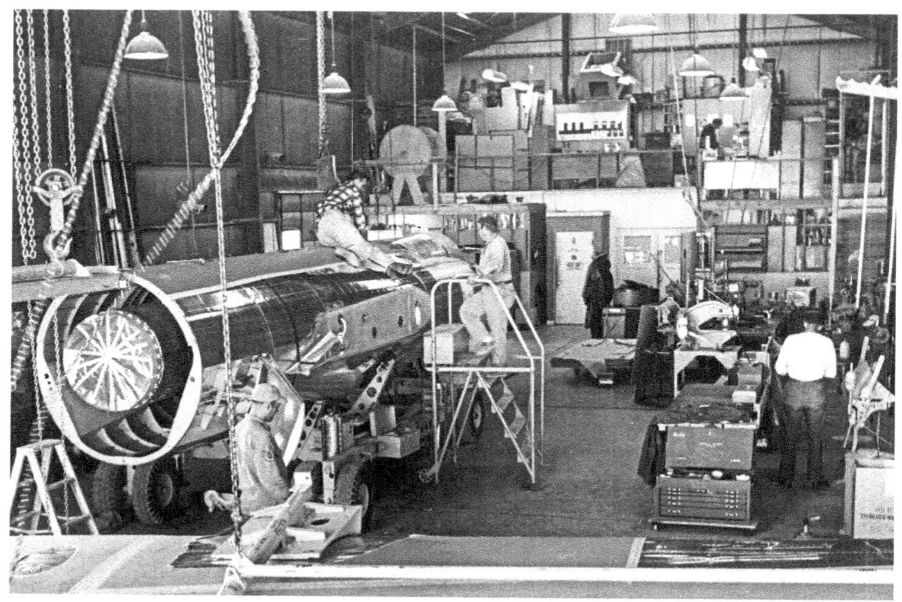

U-2 assembly in a hangar at Watertown. *CIA via TD Barnes Collection.*

Legend had it that LeVier climbed from the cockpit while giving Johnson a "one-fingered" salute for almost getting him killed with his insistence on a nose-first landing. Johnson supposedly returned the "one-fingered" salute and yelled, "You, too." The story spread among the pilots, and the plane itself became known as the "You, too," or U-2. Again, this was another name legend derived at the CIA's mythical facility with many names.

Now with the first problems in flying and landing the U-2 worked out, Kelly Johnson scheduled the "official" first flight for August 8, 1955. This time, outsiders present included Richard Bissell, Colonel Osmond Ritland, Richard Homer and Garrison Norton.

LeVier, using the call sign ANGEL 1, made the first real flight in Article 341 with Bob Matye flying chase in a C-47 and Kelly Johnson on board as an observer.

The U-2 ascended to thirty-two thousand feet and performed well, meeting Kelly Johnson's eight-month deadline. LeVier made an additional nineteen flights in Article 341 before moving on to other Lockheed flight test programs in early September. This first phase of U-2 testing explored the craft's stall envelope, took the aircraft's maximum stress limit (2.5 gs)

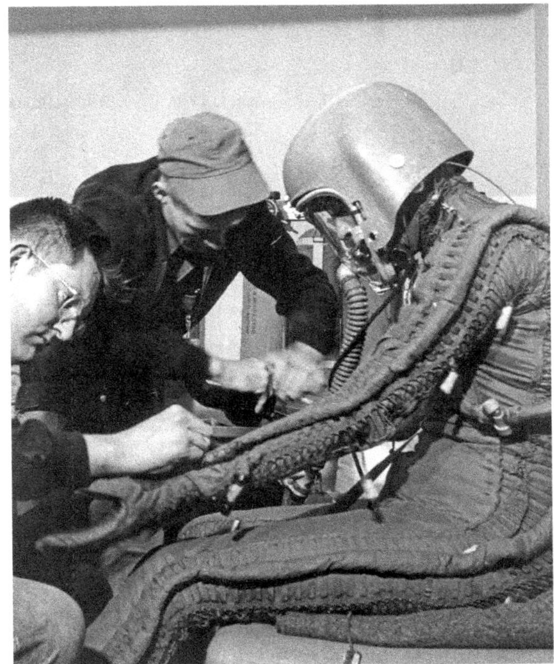

Right: A pilot being suited up in a partial-pressure suit at Watertown. *CIA via TD Barnes Collection.*

Below: U-2 flight at Watertown, 1956. Note the U-2 flying overhead. *CIA via TD Barnes Collection.*

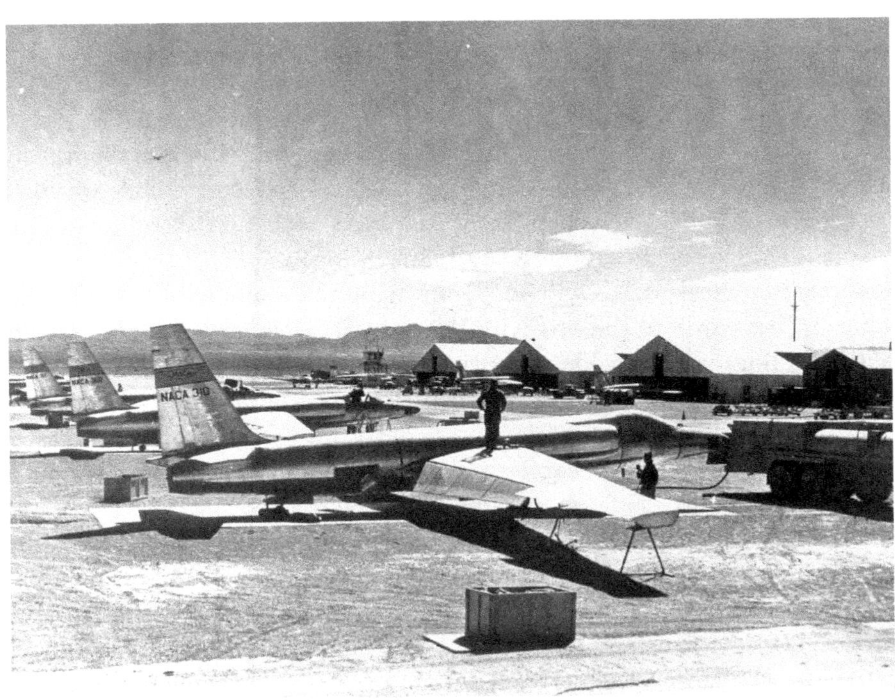

and explored its speed potential. LeVier was soon flying the aircraft at its maximum speed of Mach 0.85.

Flight tests continued, with the U-2 ascending to altitudes never attainable in sustained flight. Almost every day, the U-2 broke the world's altitude record of sixty-four thousand feet, but due to the secrecy, those present could not tell anyone. On August 16, LeVier took the aircraft up to fifty-two thousand feet. During preparation for this flight, the forty-two-year-old test pilot completed the U.S. Air Force partial-pressure suit-training program, becoming the oldest pilot to do so.

LeVier completed Lockheed's Phase 1 testing that included taking the U-2 to 50,000 feet, achieving the maximum design speed of Mach 0.84 and making a successful dead-stick landing. The Lockheed test pilots Bob Matye and Ray Goudey expanded the altitude envelope to 74,500 feet. The two pilots replaced LeVier shortly before the second U-2 (Article 342) arrived at Area 51.

The rest of the Lockheed test pilots arriving at Area 51 to flight test this latest plane entering the world of aviation were Tony LeVier, Robert Matye, Ray Goudey, Robert Sieker and Robert Schumacher.

Anthony W. "Tony" LeVier began his aviation career with air racing in a Keith Rider racer dubbed the Firecracker. Following World War II, he bought a war surplus P-38 Lightning that he modified, painted bright red and used for air racing. He began his career at Lockheed ferrying Hudson bombers to the Royal Air Force. In 1942, he became an engineering test pilot flying the PV-2 Ventura. At Lockheed, he made the first flight of the XP-80A. He flew the first flight of the XF-104 Starfighter and the first flight of the U-2. When Tony LeVier, Lockheed's chief test pilot for the F-104, was chosen by Kelly Johnson to fly the U-2 prototype, he reportedly remarked, "I switched from flying the plane with the shortest wings in the world to the one with the longest." LeVier was an air racer and test pilot for the Lockheed Corporation from the 1940s to the 1970s. During his flight career, LeVier survived eight crashes and one midair collision.

Robert L. Matye was a career experimental test pilot for the Lockheed Aircraft Company. Being an accomplished fighter pilot in World War II, he received an assignment to the first jet-powered fighter group. After the war, Lockheed hired Matye as a test pilot, and he enjoyed an outstanding career there lasting twenty-six years. He was only the second pilot to fly the famous U-2 spy plane and the first person to take it to its maximum altitude capability. He flew every Lockheed aircraft produced during that time.

Ray Goudey first soloed on September 25, 1937, and had enjoyed a career where he flew 258 different types of aircraft and accumulated 23,708 flight hours. He flew single-engine jets, multi-engine jets, multi-engine turboprop planes, single-engine reciprocating, multi-engine reciprocating, single-engine helicopters, single-engine seaplanes, multi-engine seaplanes and even one hundred hours in gliders. Goudey trained civilian pilots for the army air corps and was the U.S. Navy acceptance pilot at Grumman, Chance Vought, Curtis and the U.S. Naval Factory. He flew in air shows for the flying circus and was the chief pilot for the Hank Coffin Flying Service. From 1952 to 1990, he flew as a test pilot for Lockheed, where he set several speed and altitude records and flew several first flights.

Robert "Bob" Schumacher was a navy dive bomber assigned to the USS *Bennington* in World War II. He received the navy's Distinguished Flying Cross for his part in sinking the Japanese battleship the *Yamamoto*. He joined Lockheed in 1953 as a test pilot. In 1956, he began testing the U-2 spy plane. In 1965, he would become the first pilot to land the U-2 on an aircraft carrier.

CHAPTER 6

WE CAN'T TELL YOU THE ASSIGNMENT, GENTLEMEN

EXPERIENCED PILOTS WANTED

The Atomic Energy Commission covered for the CIA adding additional infrastructure to the Area 51 facility by releasing a statement to the *Las Vegas Review-Journal* that discussed the progress on the Watertown Project. The news release stated that Reynolds Electrical and Engineering Company, Incorporated would complete the additional work sometime in 1956 under the direction of the Atomic Energy Commission's Las Vegas branch office.

The increase in logistics involving equipment, supplies and personnel made it necessary to fly the essential personnel to the site on Monday morning and return them to Burbank on Friday evening. The AEC provided trailers for the workers to live in during the week and a mess hall for their meals.

Personnel already on the site to train the arriving air force pilots included the Lockheed pilots, Bob Matye, Ray Goudy, Bob Schoemacher and Bob Sieker. The Lockheed pilots briefed the USAF pilots and Colonel Phillip O. Robertson (ops officer) on the expected idiosyncrasies not yet learned.

Richard Newton was the CIA station chief at Watertown. The 4070th SAS was composed of Colonel William F. Yancey, commander; Major R.E. Mullin, pilot navigator and classroom instructor; Navigation Officer Jack Delap; Lieutenant Colonel Art Lien, chief of supply; Colonel Herbert Shingler, deputy commander and material chief; Louis A. Garvin, development and test flight officer; Phillip O. Robertson; and Captains Hank Meierdierck and Louis Setter, U-2 pilots and test flight officers. This air force transition team, in turn, trained the first CIA pilots. The unit had a few enlisted personnel for administrative and maintenance duties.

The U.S. Air Force cadre instructor pilots received only a few flights before the agency (Central Intelligence) pilots, all F-84 qualified, arrived from Turner and Bergstrom Air Force Bases as recruits. Major Delap, a USAF navigator, devised a system of flight planning and navigation while the cadre officers learned the systems with help from the Lockheed and other contractor people. Using this "learn-as-they-go" process, the staff officers used their flight experience to brief the student CIA pilots in ground school and subsequent flights. Robertson, Garvin, Meierdierck and Setter all flew their first low-level flight on the same day.

The air force 4070 Special Activities Squadron participants in the U-2 Project AQUATONE worked for the CIA, including Colonel Yancey. In a memorandum to Colonel Yancey, Dick Bissell instructed Yancey in his assumption of duties at Area 51. He told Yancey to assume the duties as chief of base, representing the Central Intelligence Agency at Area 51, Nevada. He informed Yancey that his status was that of commanding officer, 4070 Special Activities Squadron, and that his status as chief of base would be made known to those U.S officials and industry personnel from whom he solicited cooperation in furtherance of his mission.

When the first air force U-2 squadron trained at Area 51, the U.S. Air Force intended to activate an air force U-2 squadron at Turner Air Force Base in Georgia. Colonel Yancey sent Captain Meierdierck to Turner to advise them on the placement of the ground approach control (GAC) vans on the base. At Turner, the division commander refused to take suggestions from a lowly captain until Colonel Gerald Johnson, who knew Captain Meierdierck, intervened.

Training and flight testing were beginning at Area 51 with the Watertown support aircraft consisting of one C-47, four T-33s, one B-25, a Twin Bonanza and two Navions. Meierdierck went to the Sacramento Air Depot to pick up one of the Navions only to learn it belonged to General LeMay. In those days, the wing and base commander signed all flight clearances, except the pilots in the unit. Meierdierck lacked authority for his taking General LeMay's plane. Nonetheless, he signed for it and headed to Watertown with no known repercussions.

Hiring Foreign U-2 Pilots

In authorizing the U-2 project, President Eisenhower told DCI Dulles he wanted non-U.S. citizens to pilot these planes. He believed this made it easier for the United States to deny any responsibility for a U-2 coming down in hostile territory.

In mid-1955, the CIA had assigned the directorate of plans Air/Maritime Division (AMD) the task of hiring the pilots, with Lieutenant Colonel Geary in charge of training the recruits.

Using foreign pilots soon ran into trouble at Luke Air Force Base, where all except four of the Greek pilots selected to fly the U-2 flunked from the training program. None of them qualified to advance to Watertown for flight training. In May 1956, Luke Air Force Base sent the four Greek and one Polish pilot to Watertown for pilot familiarization in the U-2 at the same time that the CIA's Detachment B, the second class, arrived.

SAC instructor pilot Louis Setter found they lacked the proficiency to fly operations. While the later famous Francis Gary "Frank" Powers's class was in training, the Greek pilots all washed out, and the U.S. Air Force instructor pilot never allowed the Polish pilot to fly the U-2.

One Greek student pilot did complete the standard transition training in the T-33 that consisted of dozens of "drag in" approaches to simulate the U-2 approach. He flew the U-2 only once, and it was without a pressure suit. He experienced trouble communicating in English, making radio calls to him quite difficult. On his first U-2 landing on the lakebed, he leveled off at thirty feet in the air at near stall speed. With the tail down, the airplane stalled, hitting hard and kicking up a cloud of dust. Lou Setter, his instructor pilot, was a short distance behind him in the chase car, talking to him on the radio, and saw it all. Kelly Johnson saw it as well and decided, "No more U-2 flying for this pilot."

Even before eliminating the Greek students, Bissell realized the CIA lacked enough trained foreign pilots available in time for deployment. He resumed the search for U-2 pilots by going with SAC F-84–trained pilots.

The CIA U-2 Pilots

The search for the agency pilots to fly the U-2 was limited to only SAC F-84 fighter pilots holding reserve commissions. The CIA and the U.S. Air Force refused to consider using regular air force pilots because of the complexities involved in them resigning from the U.S. Air Force to become hired civilians for the AQUATONE project. The CIA selection required SAC pilots with an interest in the U-2 project to resign from the U.S. Air Force and assume civilian status—a process known as sheep dipping. Although air force pilots felt an attraction to the challenge of flying over hostile territory, they remained reluctant to leave the service and give up their seniority. To overcome the pilots' reluctance, the CIA offered handsome salaries, and the U.S. Air Force promised each pilot that he could return to his unit upon satisfactory conclusion of his employment with the CIA. In the meantime, the pilot retained consideration for promotion along with his contemporaries who declined the job to continue their air force careers.

Initially, the recruiters used the criteria of the former OSS, seeking single men with little or no family ties. They found the single men less responsible and lacking the stability of married men. Consequently, with the U-2 program, the U.S. Air Force and CIA found it more practical to recruit married candidates with families. The strong bonding and support within the family proved essential to the performance of their candidate. The screening process, in most instances, included the candidate's family.

In all cases, the individual only learned of someone considering him after the Federal Bureau of Investigation and the various agencies wishing to recruit him completed a meticulous scrutiny of his background. If the candidate failed to pass this scrutiny, the individual never knew about the agency even considering him.

The CIA U-2 pilots endured a rigorous selection process. Because the strain involved flying at extreme altitudes for extended periods of time, the selection process took painstaking efforts to exclude all pilots who were nervous or unstable in any way. The exclusions included those having excessive debt, alcoholism or drug dependency or being homosexual. The Lovelace Foundation for Medical Education and Research in Albuquerque, New Mexico, under a contract signed with the CIA on November 28, 1955, conducted the physical and psychological screening of potential U-2 pilots.

The CIA recruited a tough breed of pilots from the best. The CIA required that pilots already have 1,500 hours of flying time, with 900 being first pilot/instructor time. It also required they have experience in one, two and sometimes three aircraft, plus outstanding records and a wing commander's recommendation. With all this, they might undergo an interview lasting two weeks.

The CIA's insistence on more stringent physical and mental examinations than those used by the U.S. Air Force to select pilots for its U-2 fleet resulted in a higher rejection rate of candidates. The CIA's selection criteria remained high throughout its manned overflight program and resulted in a much lower accident rate for agency U-2 pilots than for their counterparts in the U.S. Air Force program.

Of the prospective pilots, 50 percent or less made it past interviews conducted by the wing commander, his squadron commanders and ops officers. Once they passed the interview stage, they received a physical and three in-flight evaluations in the U-2.

Each of the detachment commanders chose his military staffs consisting of Operations, Flight Planners, Physiological Trainers and Engineering officers. Each of those chosen received orders to report to the 1007th Air Intelligence Service Group in Washington, D.C. Upon arrival, the individual pilot signed in at Bolling Air Force Base for billeting in the BOQ (bachelor officers' quarters). He next reported to the 1007th Air Intelligence Service Group located in an old World War II building near Fort McNair.

Despite the list, if those recruited possessed Q or top-secret security clearances, the CIA required they attend orientation classes, physiological tests, interviews and the infamous lie detector examination. The CIA dismissed those not passing this phase of the recruitment after a strict debriefing to the effect that none of this ever happened.

When the agency requested the unsuspecting individual appear for a personal interview, it invariably went something like: "Mr., Sergeant, Captain" (or whatever), the no-name person would say. "You've been recommended for a job of the utmost importance to your country. I have reviewed your records, and I have asked you and your spouse here today to request that you volunteer for this assignment. I will tell you both upfront: this is something dangerous that you cannot discuss with your wife or anyone else. At times, it may become a remote assignment unaccompanied by family. If you choose to decline, no one is to know what we discuss here today. I need you and your spouse to please sign this security agreement."

For military recruits, the recruiter advised them that they had to leave the military and became civilians. The recruit signed the security agreement, thinking this something to do with an earlier application to become an astronaut, navy seal, test pilot or whatever. At this point, the questions and answers went like:

"Where is this assignment?"

The recruiter answers, "Sorry, that's classified. I can't tell you."

"What will I be doing?"

"Sorry, I can't tell you that either."

"Whom will I be working with?"

"Sorry, I can't tell you."

The man turns to his spouse and asks, "What do you think, Hon?"

"Just whatever you think. You know the kids and I will stand by whatever you decide."

Recruiter: "Do you need some time to think it over?"

The recruit says to the recruiter, "Negative, Sir. I'll take the assignment."

The recruiter smiles and tells the recruit to return to his old job—he will hear from someone later.

Those the CIA recruited as pilots arrived at March Air Force Base with no idea at this point of why the CIA picked them or for what reason. All of them reaching this recruitment stage volunteered, which meant resigning their air force commissions and signing a contract with the CIA. Only then did they report as civilians to Project AQUATONE Headquarters in a super secure area of the Matomic Building at 1717 Street in downtown Washington. There, they met the CIA members of the team, including the project director, Richard Bissell, executive officer James Cunningham and the others recruited for their detachment.

This same procedure applied to the support team members, except they retained their rank in the U.S. Air Force. Where the CIA project pilots received four times their air force pay, with some withholds based on performance, the U.S. Air Force support members of the team received seven dollars per day per diem when deployed.

Most of the new recruits rented apartments at 1600 Fifteenth Street, near the Russian Embassy, next door to the Cairo Hotel and within walking distance of the Matomic Building.

At the time, no Dash-1 operating manuals existed for the U-2 plane. The recruit pilots reviewed notes and documents filed in loose-leaf binders. They studied the flying manual for the T-33 aircraft, which played a major part in the U-2 training.

The high operating altitude and the partial cockpit pressure were equivalent to twenty-eight thousand feet pressure altitude. The pilot wore a partial-pressure space suit to deliver his oxygen supply and provide emergency protection in case of cabin pressure loss. While pilots could drink water and eat various liquid foods in squeezable containers through a self-sealing hole in the face mask, they lost up to six pounds of weight on an eight-hour mission. While in Washington, the pilots, in CIA fashion, met with

Dave Clark of the Clark Clothing Company of Worcester, Massachusetts, in a nondescript hotel in Washington for measurement for their individual partial-pressure suits.

After passing the extensive physical and psychological tests, the first group of pilots for Detachment A sheep dipped into an existence of name changes, separation from the service and anonymity. The CIA Detachment A pilots trained at Area 51 were Hervey Stockman, Marty Knutson, Carmine Vito, Glendon Dunaway, Carl Overstreet, Howard Carey and Jake Kratt.

Following a general security briefing, the pilots flew to Area 51 for an introduction to the secret, high-flying reconnaissance aircraft. There, they met the Lockheed engineers, led by Ernie Joiner and his staff of experts on the U-2. Arriving at Area 51, they met Lockheed test pilots Ray Goudy, Bob Sieker and Bob Schumacher, who did all the phase testing, testing the aircraft coming off the assembly line while training the Strategic Air Command pilots.

The United States did not have pilots qualified to fly a plane at the high altitude or the long-lasting flights intended for the U-2. Nor were they qualified to fly a plane whose unique landing gear resembled a bicycle, with its wheels aligned under the center of the plane. No one was qualified to fly a plane as lightweight as a glider, a plane that wanted to fly and refused to land.

The U-2, being a mixture of glider and jet, made training pilots more difficult even for the qualified fighter pilots chosen for the overflight program. The purpose of the training program was to teach the fighter pilots to fly the delicate U-2, a revolutionary new plane design concept with large wings and tremendous lift but too fragile to survive the stresses of loops and barrel rolls to which the pilots were accustomed. Moreover, the original placard U-2s found that flying in the smooth air at sea level limited their speed to a mere 190 knots or even lower to 50 knots in rough air.

Arrival at Area 51

The selected pilots flew out of Burbank, California, in an air force C-54 transport plane, thinking they were preparing all this time for space flight. At Watertown, the plane pulled up to an aircraft with long, glider-type wings: the U-2. Four of the six pilots got off the plane; Marty Knutson and another pilot did not, saying thanks, but no thanks. After some persuasion, the two joined the other four.

All six of the pilots came from a fighter background, flying planes with control sticks or, if a bomber pilot, wheels or yoke-type controls. The fighter pilots in those days considered bomber pilots below them. They looked into the cockpit of the U-2 and saw the wheel/yoke control, and all six returned to the transport plane saying, "No way." Again, after much persuasion by the CIA, they all decided to give it a try.

Checking Out in the U-2

All the selected pilots arrived at Area 51 as experienced fighter pilots, so it was a matter of becoming familiar with the plane and high-altitude flight. Aside from its extraordinary gliding ability, the U-2 proved to be a tough aircraft to fly. Its light weight that enabled it to achieve extreme altitudes also made it fragile. The aircraft was very sleek, and it sliced through the air with minimal drag. The U-2 design could not withstand high-speed G-forces, which made it very dangerous. Flying at high operational altitudes required the pilots to be extremely careful to keep the aircraft in a slightly nose-up attitude. If the pilot dropped the nose only a degree nose-down, it caused the plane to gain speed at a dramatic rate. In less than a minute, the speed could exceed the placard structural limit and come apart. Pilots, therefore, paid close attention to the aircraft's speed indicator because at sixty-five thousand feet, they had no objects nearby to use as a reference to give them a physical sensation of speed.

The P-37 model engine demonstrated poorer combustion characteristics than the preferred but unavailable P-31 version. The P-37 tended to flame out at high altitudes. The combustion problems became apparent as the U-2 began the final part of its climb from fifty-seven thousand to sixty-five thousand feet. The pilots referred to this area as the "badlands" or the "chimney."

The U-2 encountered some developmental and technical problems, as did all new aircraft designs. One such issue involved an oil film often appearing on the windscreen, which clouded the forward visibility and increased the landing problem. During the interval, until Kelly Johnson solved the problem, the pilots used a sanitary napkin on the end of a stick to clean enough of the windscreen for them to see to land.

Flameouts at altitude proved a significant problem because it depressurized the cockpit and inflated the suit, thus preventing the pilot talking on the radio. It forced oxygen into the faceplate and mouth at a great rate while the aircraft slowly descended. Also, the neckpiece of the helmet often popped out, requiring the pilot to hold it in as far as possible with one hand and fly the plane with the other. The procedure created a dangerous predicament, to say the least. It did not take Johnson and the Pratt & Whitney engineers long to solve the flameout problem using a bleed valve—making the U-2 much less hazardous to fly at altitude.

The flameouts bedeviled the U-2 project until sufficient numbers of the more powerful P-31 engines became available in the spring of 1956. Meanwhile, with the airworthiness of the U-2 airframe proven, Lockheed set up a production line in the Skunk Works. Nonetheless, delivery of even the second-choice J57/P-37 became a major problem. The CIA learned of Pratt & Whitney contracting with the U.S. Air Force its full production capacity to provide these engines for the next year. The U.S. Air Force needed the engines for its F-100 fighters and KC-135 tankers.

Colonel Geary, with the help of a colleague in the U.S. Air Force Material Command, managed to arrange the diversion of several of these engines from a shipment destined for Boeing's KC-135 production line, making it possible to continue building the U-2s.

Thus, the CIA and the United States Air Force initiated the development of high-flying aircraft capable of penetrating the airspace of the Cold War enemies of the United States. They screened personnel to engineer, test and fly this new type of aircraft. Loyalty to the United States, physical and mental condition and skills set the criteria in the selection of personnel to participate in these black, secret projects.

CHAPTER 7

FLYING THE ANGEL

America's First Spy Plane

The U.S. Air Force instructor pilots and the CIA pilots arriving at Area 51 were experienced military pilots. Nonetheless, before allowing them to fly the U-2, the U.S. Air Force instructor pilots began their training with the ground school on the aircraft systems, emergency procedures, flight planning, navigation and so on.

Before starting the ground school, the instructor pilots devised procedures to use in the air and in preparation for a flight. The preparation included the route, fuel consumption, checkpoints, pre-breathing for two hours and the myriad details necessary for an overflight of denied territory in a new type of aircraft flying in an environment never flown before. To ready these pilots to fly the U-2, the instructor pilots first verified the Central Intelligence pilots' flying experience and qualifications before allowing them to fly the U-2, the first million-dollar airplane. To do this, the instructor pilots first placed the trainee pilots in the back seat of a two-place T-33 jet for flight evaluations.

The instructor pilot took control of the airplane at the end of each T-33 flight. He climbed to ten thousand feet; put the gear, flaps and speed brakes out; and shut off the engine. The lakebed contained a paint cross mark, the pilot's target to land as close as possible. After a few practice flights, most pilots touched down within one hundred feet of the mark.

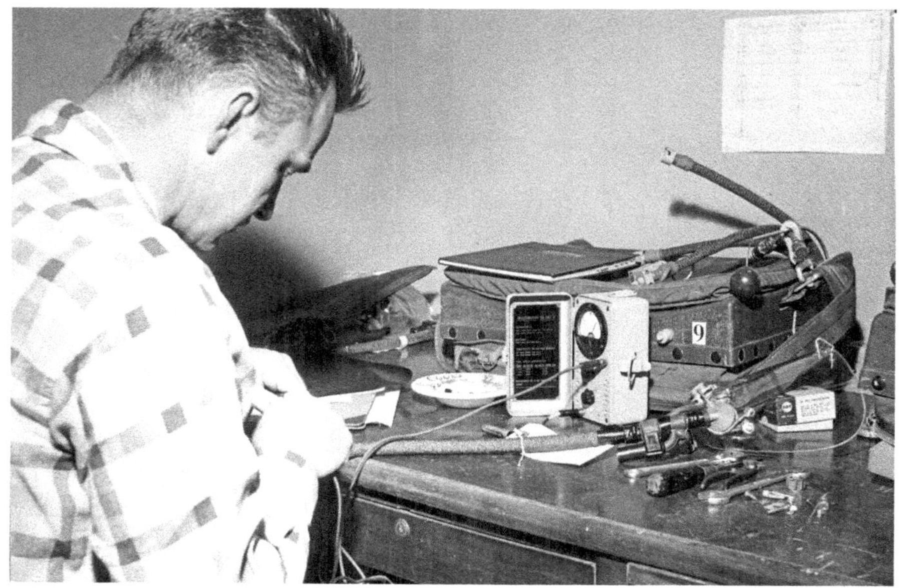

Maintenance on C-packs. *CIA via TD Barnes Collection.*

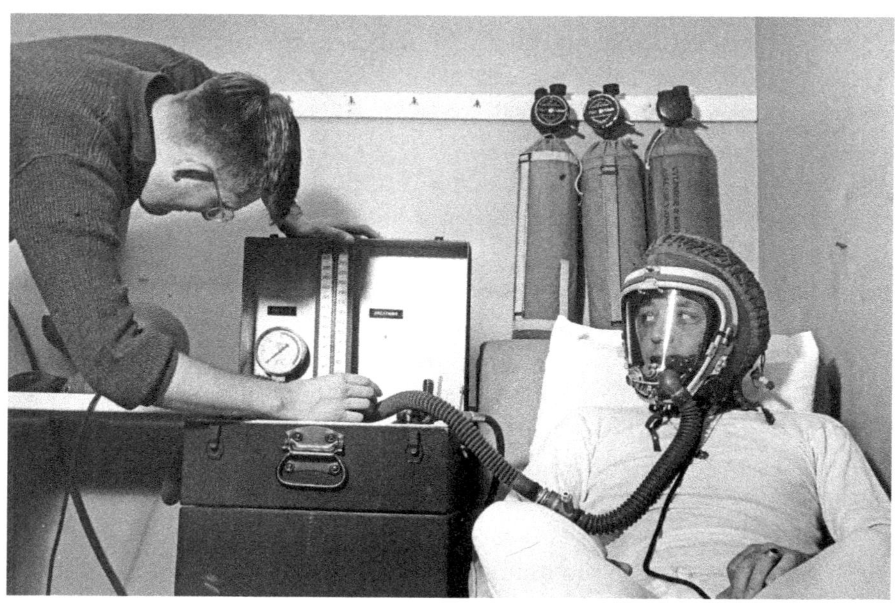

Lockheed test pilot Robert Schumacher watching a life support technician while undergoing oxygen pre-breathing before a U-2 flight. *CIA via TD Barnes Collection.*

Even with the T-33 trainer, the U.S. Air Force used a souped-up Mercury station wagon for mobile control and to chase the plane on takeoff and landing. On landing, a driver and an instructor pilot raced alongside and to the rear of the plane while calling out his altitude above the ground: "Two feet, two feet, one foot, one foot, OK, ease her on down."

Even for experienced pilots, landing the U-2 proved difficult and required flying inside a two-mile-per-hour range to make a safe landing. When flying the CIA's U-2A and U-2C models close to its operational ceiling, the maximum speed (critical Mach) and the minimum speed (stall speed) approached the same number, presenting a narrow window of safe airspeed. Knowing the exact stalling speed of the T-33, the instructor pilots instructed the pilots to fly at two knots above the stall speed, two feet above the surface of the dry lake. The instructor pilots induced contact with the lake to let them develop the correct recovery procedures. When satisfied with the pilots' capability of transitioning to this new airplane, the instructor pilots checked them out in the U-2.

On their second flight, the pilots flew to seventy thousand feet to learn the idiosyncrasies of the coffin corner. The range of indicated airspeed in the U-2 was around 100 to 105 knots. Too slow and the plane goes into a low-speed buffet; too high and it goes into a speed buffer.

Testing at even higher altitudes continued, and on September 8, 1955, the U-2 reached its initial design altitude of 65,600 feet.

The flameouts were not the only problem developed by high flight. On a flight, Captain Meierdierck had departed from Watertown and over the Pacific Ocean to check the wind patterns when he developed engine problems and the engine quit. The pressure suit blew up, forcing him to descend to thirty thousand feet to attempt an air start. It worked, and he climbed back to altitude, only to have it blow out again. Once again, he descended to air start the engine. The suit malfunction occurred fifteen times during his return to Area 51.

Meierdierck returned to the David Clark Co in Worcester, Massachusetts, to solve the communication problem that occurred when the engine flamed out and the suit blew up. David Clark Co. built a new suit for him containing a chest bladder that placed pressure on the pilot's chest to enable the pilot to talk with his suit pressure. To verify this, the CIA sent Meierdierck to the altitude chamber at Wright-Patterson Air Force Base, where they lowered the pressure to a simulated altitude of 120,000 feet and broke the seal. The suit inflated, and he shouted to see if they could hear him. They heard him, solving the inability to communicate during a flameout.

A U-2 pilot always took care not to hit the front gear first, as it caused the plane to bounce and porpoise near the stall speed. The problems occurred once when a pilot who was coming in for a landing hyperventilated. Lou Garvin, the mobile control officer, drove to the end of the runway to assist the landing by calling out the plane's altitude above the runway as he raced alongside in a souped-up Ford Thunderbird. In his hyperventilated condition, the pilot heard Garvin call "two feet, two feet, one foot." The pilot said, "Screw you," and jammed the front gear onto the lakebed with the nose a foot off the ground and the tail high in the air. He conducted this impossible maneuver by leaving the power on and continuing two or three miles before he pulled the power off and let the plane settle to the runway. When the flight surgeons met him, they grounded him until they could evaluate his condition. The grounding set him off again. He gave them all hell for a little while until the effects of too much oxygen wore off and he returned to normal.

The U-2 program developed a unique device for the U-2: a small sextant for making celestial fixes during the long overflights. With cloud cover often preventing U-2 pilots from locating navigational points on the earth through the periscope, the sextant became the pilot's principal navigational instrument during the first three years of deployment. Otherwise, the periscope proved accurate for navigation. During the final tests before the aircraft became operational, U-2 pilots found they could navigate by dead reckoning with an error of less than one nautical mile over a one-thousand-nautical-mile course.

As early as August 1955, the CIA realized that even with air force support, establishing a secret flight test facility in the Mojave Desert did not come easily. A shortage of supply personnel remained a recurring problem for setting up the depot and the assembling of supplies for training the CIA's Detachment A, scheduled to commence early in 1956. The shortage continued through the training and deployment of Detachment B.

Despite the difficulties involved in training U-2 pilots, Colonel Yancey's cadre of six qualified air force U-2 pilots began training agency pilots by September 1955.

In the face of this shortage, the SAC support group, headed by Colonel Herbert Shingler, carried the burden of getting Detachment A logistically ready at the time of deployment. From July 1955 until June 1957, he, while stationed at March Air Force Base in California, was the director of material for the 4070th Support Wing and later the wing commander. Now, he was at March AFB and commuting to Area 51 to train the pilots selected by the

Central Intelligence Agency to fly the U-2. The shortage of aeromedical staff and personnel at March AFB and Watertown forced Shingler to borrow personnel to staff Detachment A at the time of deployment. Colonel Ritland reported the problem to the project director on March 30, 1956, saying:

> *Because the overall expansions and the lack of sufficient personnel, they had drawn on the U.S. Air Force commands to assume definite project responsibilities. It was apparent that although work was proceeding rapidly, personnel outside of the project and not under the control of the project director were accomplishing the buildup. The lack of control was not a satisfactory situation and should be watched as the scope of the project expanded.*

As the flight tests developed, flameouts became a frequent occurrence. Lockheed test pilot Bob Matye experienced the first flameout on his third high-altitude flight. The experience proved the pressure suit, regulator and emergency oxygen system worked.

During the final test in the spring of 1956, the U-2 once again demonstrated its unique airworthiness. On April 14, 1956, James Cunningham received a call from Watertown while in his office in Washington. The caller informed him of a westward-bound U-2 experiencing a flameout over the Mississippi River along the western border of Tennessee. After restarting his engine, the pilot reported a second flameout and engine vibration so violent it prevented him from getting the power plant to start again.

Early in the program, Bissell and Ritland had foreseen such an emergency and, with the cooperation of the U.S. Air Force, arranged for delivery of a sealed order to every airbase in the continental United States giving instruction concerning what to do if a U-2 needed to make an emergency landing.

Cunningham instructed the project officer to ask the pilot how far he could glide so they could determine which air force base to alert. The pilot, now over Arkansas, radioed back giving the prevailing wind and the U-2's 21:1 glide ratio; he thought he could reach Albuquerque, New Mexico.

Within minutes, Cunningham phoned Colonel Geary in the Pentagon. Geary, the U.S. Air Force's assistant director of operations, and Brigadier General Ralph E. Koon called the commander of Kirtland Air Force Base near Albuquerque. General Koon warned the base commander to expect an unusual aircraft to make a dead stick landing at Kirtland within the next half

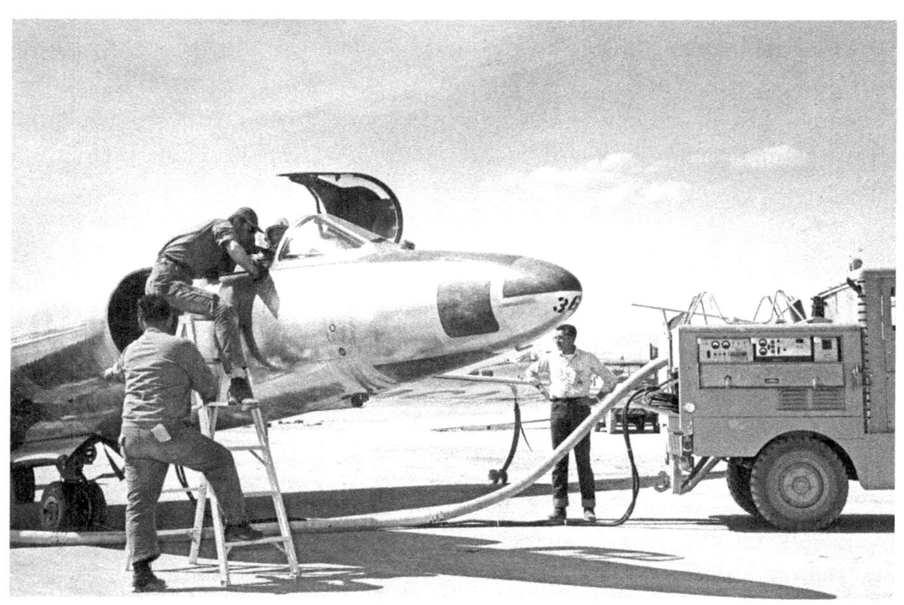

Ground crew and U-2 pilot performing preflight and engine start for a flight at Watertown. *CIA via TD Barnes Collection.*

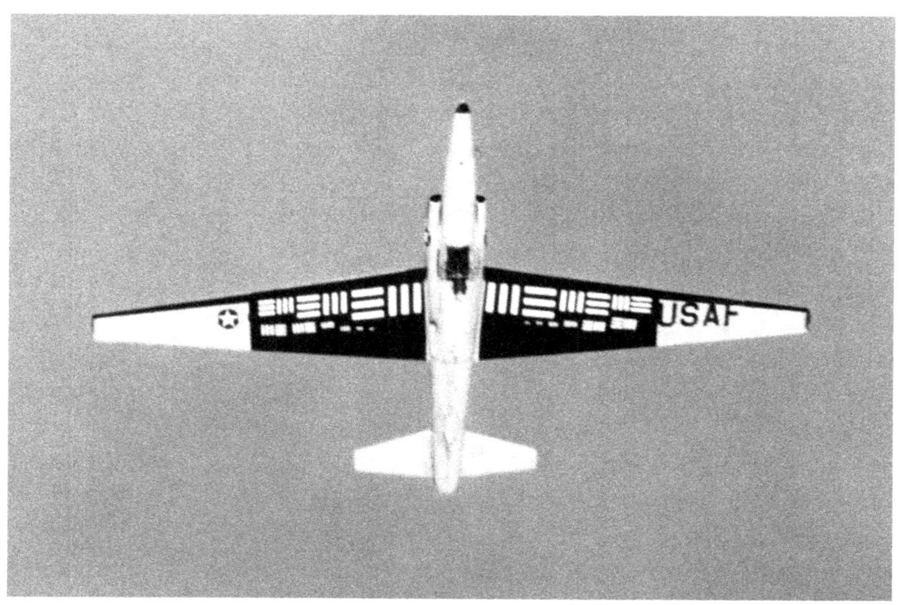

U-2 flying over Watertown by USAF 4080th Strategic Reconnaissance Wing pilots training at Watertown in early 1957 before transferring to Laughlin AFB, Texas. *CIA via TD Barnes Collection.*

hour and told him to make use of the sealed orders. The general instructed the base commander to have air police keep everyone away from the craft and quickly secure it out of sight inside a hangar.

After a half hour passed, the base commander called the Pentagon to ask where the crippled aircraft was. As he spoke, the officer saw the U-2 touch down on the runway and remarked, "It's not a plane, it's a glider." It surprised the air police surrounding the craft even more when it came to a halt and the pilot climbed from the cockpit in his "space" suit. One air police officer remarked that the pilot looked like a man from Mars.

The pilot, Jacob Kratt, later reported to Cunningham how from the first flameout to the landing at Albuquerque, the U-2 covered over nine hundred miles, including more than three hundred by gliding.

Adjusting to High-Altitude Flight

Putting a man into high flight required a change that spawned several experiments with both the pilot and the plane throughout the aviation industry. The U.S. Air Force undertook high-altitude bailout experiments from balloons in the autumn of 1955 to determine if the suit designed for the U-2 pilot protected him during his parachute descent once he separated from the life-support mechanisms inside the aircraft.

The CIA's instructor pilots and its agency pilots flying the U-2 at Area 51 pioneered the prevention of pilots suffering the effects of decompression sickness that could cause permanent brain damage, with initial symptoms such as disorientation and inability to read.

The U-2 pilots used a procedure known as pre-breathing to avoid getting the "bends" during such descents or long flights. They donned their pressure suits and breathed 100 percent oxygen an hour before taking off to remove nitrogen from the body. They used a portable oxygen supply while entering the aircraft, where they then connected to the aircraft's oxygen supply.

The pilots found eating, drinking and urinating major problems while wearing their suits. The first model of the pressure suit used by Lockheed test pilots made no provision for urination. At first, they had to catheterize the pilot to permit urination during flight. The catheter proved uncomfortable, so by the autumn of 1955, an external bladder arrangement made the catheter unnecessary.

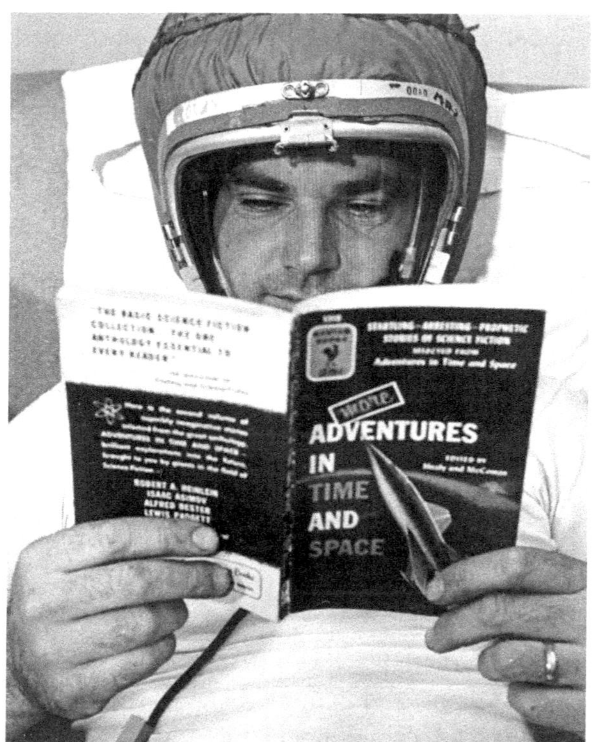

Left: Lockheed test pilot Ray Goudey pre-breathing for a flight while reading the 1955 sci-fi edition of *Adventures in Time and Space*. *CIA via TD Barnes Collection.*

Below: The back room of the flight planning Quonset containing classified material storage and work area for classified planning and target review. *CIA via TD Barnes Collection.*

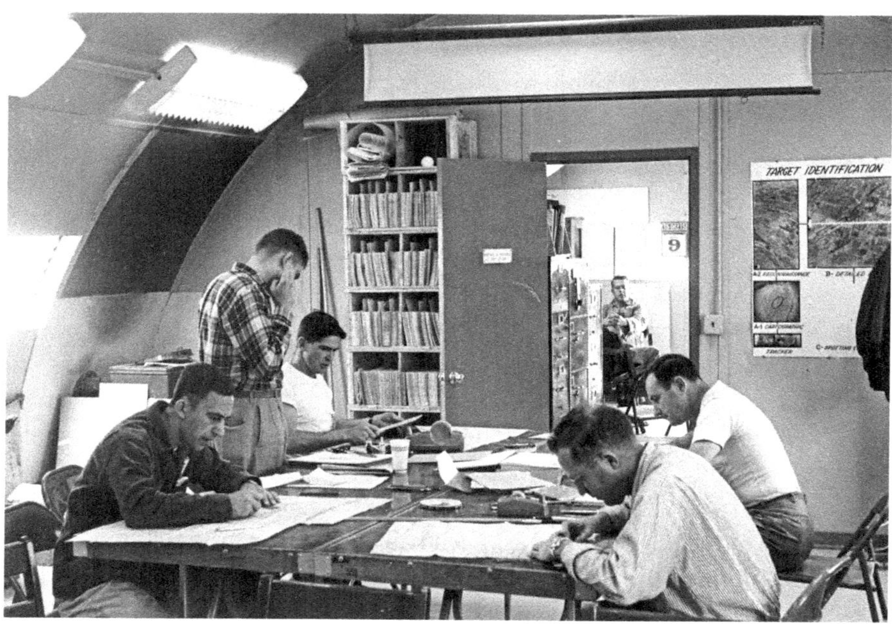

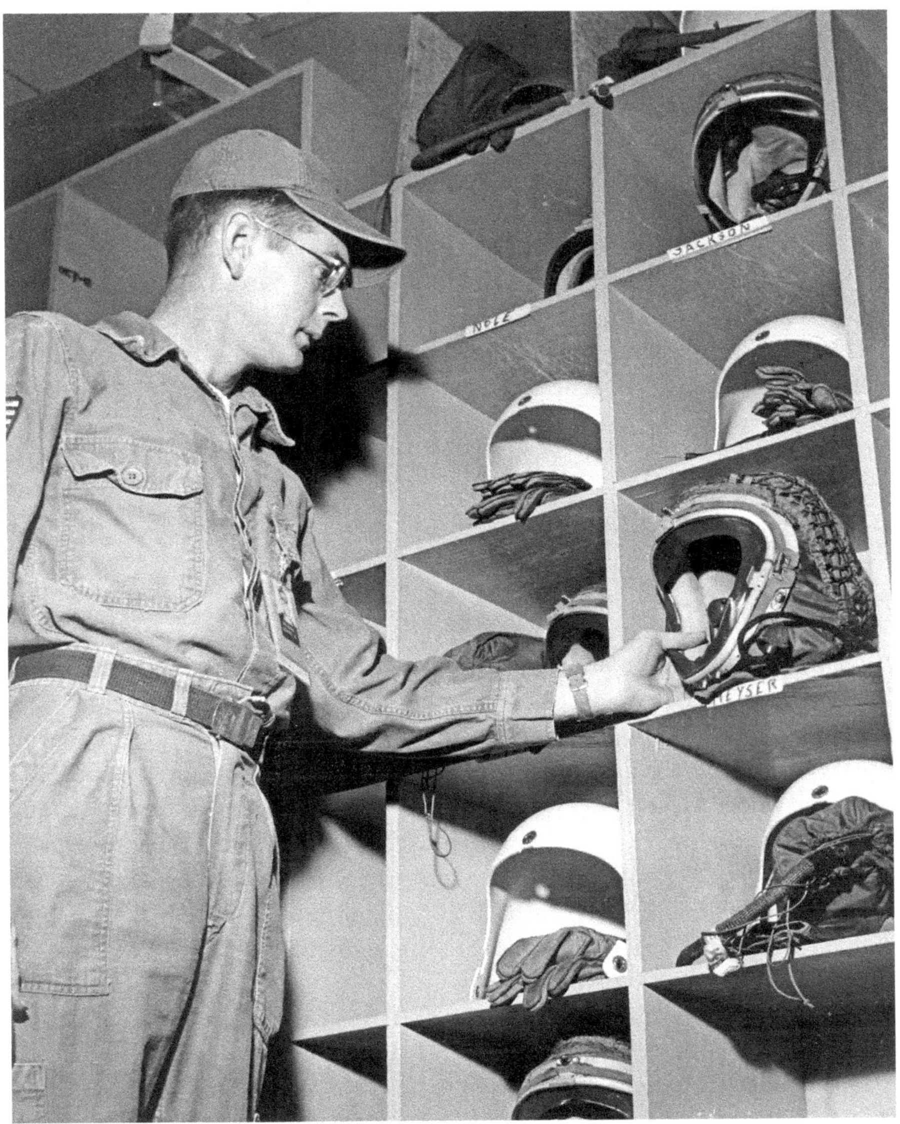

Sergeant Weldon C. Lewis checking Major Richard Heyser's inner flight helmet assembly. The model MA-2 helmet, made by International Latex Corporation of Dover, Delaware, provided constant pressure and oxygen to the pilot's head with a tight-fitting liner and seal covered by a hard shell. *CIA via TD Barnes Collection.*

The pilots reduced their stimulation by eating a low-bulk, high-protein diet on the day before and the morning of each mission. They drank sweetened water to prevent desiccation during the long missions, a condition exasperated by their breathing pure oxygen. They accomplished this by providing a small self-sealing hole in the face mask to allow the pilot to push in a straw-like tube attached to the water supply.

The CIA project personnel pioneered the development of the ready-to-eat foods in squeezable containers used today. They chose bacon- or cheese-flavored mixtures that the pilot squeezed into his mouth using the self-sealing hole in the face mask. Despite all these precautions, the U-2 pilots lost three to six pounds of body weight during an eight-hour mission.

Greatest Loss of Life at Area 51

Each day during the week, USAF C-54 transport planes flown by the Military Air Transport Service (MATS) secretly transported the CIA officials, USAF personnel and contract support, along with supplies, from Norton AFB and Burbank, California, to Area 51 and back. Everyone working at Area 51 commuted from out of state, with most staying at Area 51 the entire week. James Cunningham dubbed this activity "Bissell's Narrow-Gauge Airline" in November, less than seven weeks after it began.

On November 17, 1955, a Douglas MC-54M Skymaster transport plane attached to the 1700th Air Transport Group of the Military Air Transport Service at Kelly AFB, Texas, departed Norton AFB with five military personnel on board. Following the daily routine, the plane landed at Burbank, a few miles away, to pick up nine civilians from the Lockheed Skunk Works. The civilians included five from the Central Intelligence Agency, two from Hycon and two from Lockheed.

Due to the secrecy of the U-2 program, the commuter planes always maintained radio silence. At the early hour of departure, the passengers usually slept while en route to Watertown.

A few miles west of Las Vegas, Nevada, the plane hit a severe blizzard as it approached Mount Charleston and the Spring Mountain range. The plane became lost in the clouds, and the blinding blizzard blew it off course. An error in plotting the plane's position caused the plane to crash only 50 feet below the crest of an 11,300-foot ridge leading to the peak of Mount Charleston.

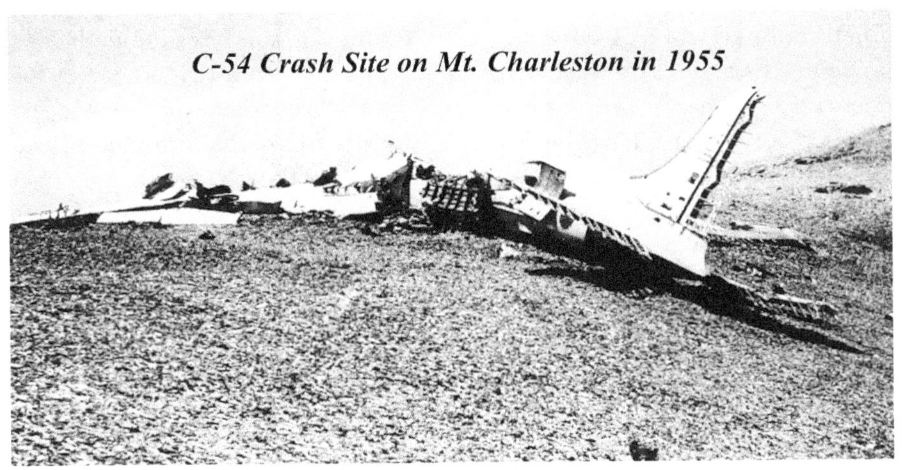

The C-54 employee transport crash site on Mount Charleston, Nevada, in 1955, where fourteen were killed en route to Area 51. *coldwarmonument.org/the-accident/accident-photos.*

When the plane failed to land at Area 51, the CIA and air force frantically initiated a search for the wreckage. Searching for a secret plane carrying secret documents and personnel to a secret facility proved delicate to the organizers. To maintain the secrecy of the U-2 project, no one could identify the type of plane, who was flying it, who and how many were on board, where the flight originated or its destination. Such flights never communicated with air traffic control or anyone else.

During the afternoon of Thursday, November 17, 1955, Captain Meierdierck was flying search out of Watertown when he located the wreckage on Mount Charleston. The mountain was experiencing the worst weather conditions seen in years, bad enough for the Forest Service to predict the crash site remaining inaccessible until the middle of June. The CIA found this, a seven-month delay, unacceptable for the top-secret U-2 project.

Two air force parachute rescue teams arrived from March Air Force Base in California with the intention of offering first aid to any surviving the impact, only to have to abort the paratrooper drop because of the intense wind conditions at the top of the mountain. The U.S. Air Force then deployed the Forty-Second Air Rescue Squadron, a trained mountaineer team from March Air Force Base under the command of Colonel Frank Schwikert.

Las Vegas sheriff Butch Leypoldt also deployed the Sheriff's Mounted Posse to assist in military rescue efforts, along with two paratroopers from the original March team. No one expected to find any survivors. Nonetheless, providing first aid to any survivors remained their priority. Recovery of classified documents and body recovery was a secondary priority for the U.S. Air Force and CIA. The Sheriff's Mounted Posse had no idea of the top-secret documents scattered at the crash site or the identity of the crash victims, for that matter. It would stay that way for nearly half a century.

The first rescue party, the paramedic group from March Field, California, left on Friday morning on foot wearing snowshoes. One of the posse members became severely ill during the climb and returned down the mountain, aided by the other three members of the posse. The two parachute rescuers continued their climb. They reached the crash site and radio base camp, confirming there were no survivors and their intent to remain near the site to wait for the arrival of a horse party headed up the mountain.

A forest ranger, a deputy sheriff and two members of the Second Air Rescue Unit headed out on foot early Saturday morning as a second rescue party. At 6:00 a.m., the sheriff headed out with another group of Sheriff's Mounted Posse members, along with two air force colonels. After several days of struggling through the deep snow and subzero weather while using skis and snowshoes, the team aborted their attempts to climb the north side of the mountain in time to save any survivors. The team became bogged down in the deep snow as it returned to base camp.

The top-secrecy of this accident posed many problems for the CIA and air force. The CIA was extremely concerned about the top-secret documents and equipment needing recovery before the civilian rescue party approached the wreckage. Securing the area now became the mission.

To this end, Colonel Schwikert from March Air Force Base and Colonel Pittman from Norton Air Force Base met up with the sheriff, fifteen members of the Sheriff's Mounted Posse and seventeen horses at the base camp set up at the bottom of the mountain. They briefed the sheriff on the situation to ensure the posse and he stood down while the U.S. Air Force attended to classified matters.

The group departed the base camp, taking a horse-friendly but longer route to the south of the mountain. They traveled up a switchback trail toward the ridge with the snow drifts so deep the horses' feet never touched the ground. The riders at times dragged their feet in the snow behind their saddles or dismounts to slide on their stomachs while hanging on to the horses' tails. Conditions became much worse, with the rescue team realizing they had no water to drink and had only a few cans of SPAM for food.

Sheriff Leypoldt led the rescue party up the mountain along an old hiking trail, where snow varied up to six feet deep. In temperatures below zero and drifts twenty feet deep, the rescue party worked its way up the mountain in increasing wind velocities that covered them with powdered snow. The horses often slipped off the narrow trail, at times pinning their riders beneath them in the snow.

The rescue party, traveling on skis and snowshoes, overtook and joined the first army rescue team six miles from the plane. Finding them so cold and miserable, the leader of the party ordered them to return to the lodge. The rescuers traveled along the ridge near the summit to the crash site in the freezing wind, the shallow snow turning to ice that the horses' hooves broke through.

The rescue party arrived at 1:00 p.m. at the wreckage, where they stood down, shivering in the blizzard wind and snow, to allow the sheriff and Colonel Schwikert time to inspect the crash site before allowing them to proceed.

The pilot appeared to have seen the mountain at the last moment and tried to climb over it. It was too late. The plane pancaked against the mountain and disintegrated, causing cargo and ten passengers to erupt through the top of the cabin and scatter forty or fifty feet in all directions. The plane's motors lay twenty or thirty feet from the plane, and the plane's nose and wings were downslope in front of the fuselage tail.

The sheriff and his posse grouped a few yards away while the U.S. Air Force collected the classified documents and material. When finished with collecting the classified material, Colonel Schwikert turned the recovery of bodies over to the sheriff.

The sheriff's posse had to break the frozen bodies to bend them before tying them onto the saddles of spooked horses for the trek back down the mountain. Otherwise, the frozen bodies would have extended to the sides of the narrow trail and caught in the brush. The first group of five rescuers departed on foot, leading the horses through a cold blizzard down slippery slopes. It became necessary for the rescuers to clear the trail with a shovel. Several times, the horses carrying the recovered bodies and lunging through the snow slipped and rolled down the slopes. In one incident, one of the horses slipped, falling and rolling down the mountainside, leaving the body on the trail. The rescuer managed to return his horse to its feet but was too exhausted and weak to put the body back on the horse.

The sun set with the blizzard howling around the rescue party with no flashlights. They groped in the darkness, hanging on to the saddles to prevent their staggering and falling off the steep mountainside. They finally met up with the half-frozen snowshoe troops from March Field now in their third day of the encampment in small pup tents on the side of the frozen mountain.

The rescue and recovery effort ended with the Sheriff's Mounted Posse volunteers taking an oath of secrecy concerning everything they had seen. Following this, the greatest single loss of life in the entire U-2 program, Lockheed assumed the responsibility of transporting personnel to Watertown using a Lockheed-owned C-47. Lost were the lives of key CIA, Lockheed and Hycon personnel so essential that their deaths almost ended the U-2 project entirely.

CHAPTER 8

WATERTOWN GOES OPERATIONAL

"WEATHER RESEARCH"

While the CIA made its final preparations for U-2 overflights, the U.S. Air Force began a reconnaissance project causing considerable protest around the world and threatened the existence of the U-2 spying program before it even began.

Project GENETRIX, a project originating from the 1951 RAND Corporation study, involved the use of camera-carrying balloons to obtain high-altitude photography of Eastern Europe, the Soviet Union and the People's Republic of China while claiming to be weather research connected with the International Geophysical Year.

President Eisenhower gave his approval on December 27, 1955, two weeks before the CIA's U-2 began flights from bases in Western Europe. Meanwhile, the U.S. Air Force had launched 516 balloons by the end of February 1956. Once launched, the balloons flew at the mercy of the prevailing winds, missing the prime target areas, which lay in the higher latitudes, and instead, many drifted toward southern Europe, across the Black Sea and the desert areas of China.

Large numbers of balloons failed to cross the Soviet Union and China because of hostile aircraft shooting them down or because they prematurely expended their ballast supplies and descended too soon. Of the 516 balloons launched, the U.S. Air Force recovered only 46 payloads. Only 34 balloons

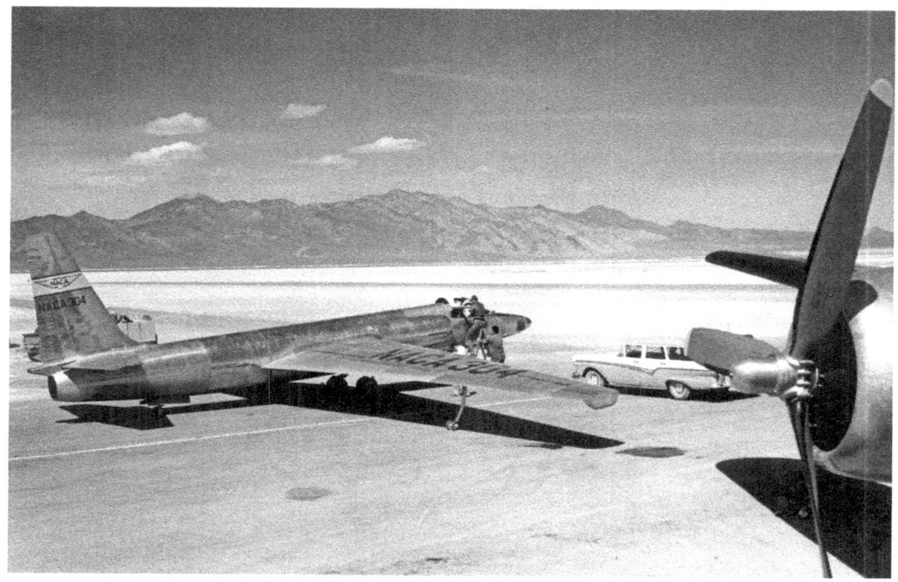

Photo taken from the shuttle plane of a U-2 preparing for flight. Note the NACA markings. The CIA attempted to reduce visual sightings of the U-2 by painting it. The weight of the paint cost the plane 1,500 feet of altitude. *CIA via TD Barnes Collection.*

succeeded in obtaining useful photographs while causing the United States problems from the balloon overflights provoking a storm of protest and unfavorable publicity.

All this publicity and protest led President Eisenhower to conclude the balloons giving more legitimate grounds for irritation than matching the benefit obtained from them. He ordered the project halted.

Although Project GENETRIX gained limited quality photo intelligence, it still rated as some of the best and most complete photography obtained of the Soviet Union since World War II. The U.S. Air Force and the CIA considered it as "pioneering" photography because it provided a baseline for all future overhead photography, including the U-2. Even innocuous photos of forests and streams proved valuable in later years when U-2 and satellite photography revealed construction activity.

The data obtained by NATO and U.S. radars tracking the paths of the balloons at an average altitude of 45,800 feet over the Soviet Bloc proved of still greater importance to the U-2 program for the most accurate record to date of high-altitude wind currents. Knowledgeable meteorologists later used these for determining optimum flight paths for U-2 flights.

One fortuitous development from Project GENETRIX involved a steel bar that secured the top rigging of the huge polyethylene gasbag with the camera payload and automatic-ballasting equipment. By sheer chance, the length of the bar corresponded to the wavelength of the radio frequency used by Soviet TOKEN S-band radar that the Soviet forces used for early warning and ground-control intercept.

The bar on the GENETRIX balloons resonated when struck by TOKEN radar pulses, making it possible for radar operators at the U.S. and NATO installations on the periphery of the Soviet Union to locate several unknown TOKEN radars. These radar findings, coupled with other intercepts made during the balloon flights, provided extensive data on Warsaw Pact radar networks, radar sets and ground control interception techniques.

Nonetheless, the ill will generated by the balloon overflights concerned the CIA officials and soured the Eisenhower administration on all overflights, including those flights by the U-2, near ready for deployment. The CIA feared President Eisenhower might curtail a balloon program of the Free Europe Committee, a covert agency operation base in West Germany used to release propaganda pamphlets over Eastern Europe.

By January 1956, everyone working on Project AQUATONE saw the U-2 nearing operational deployment. During tests, the aircraft met all the criteria established in late 1954. Its range of 2,950 miles was sufficient to overfly continents, its altitude of seventy-two thousand feet was beyond the reach of all known antiaircraft weapons and interceptor aircraft and it carried the finest camera lenses available.

The main targets for the U-2 lay behind the Iron Curtain. Bissell and his staff considered this and looked for operational bases in Europe. The CIA felt America's closest ally, the United Kingdom, was the logical choice for U-2 bases.

On January 10, 1956, Bissell flew to London to discuss the matter with the Royal Air Force (RAF) and MI-6 officials. Initially, they responded favorably. Nonetheless, they referred Bissell to a higher level for approval of the proposal. Bissell reported his findings to Director Dulles, who arranged to meet with Foreign Secretary Selwyn Lloyd in London to explore the possibility of winning the British government's approval for the project. Dulles presented his case to Lloyd on February 2, and by early March, Lloyd had approved the basing of U-2s in the United Kingdom, suggesting the U-2s use Lakenheath Air Force Base, which was already in use by the USAF Strategic Air Command.

In March 1956, Colonel Ritland returned to the U.S. Air Force as the deputy project director, followed by Colonel Jack A. Gibbs. In March 1956,

Colonel Landon McConnell took command of Watertown at Area 51, and CIA director Allen Dulles visited Area 51 to meet the first training class.

Colonel Gibbs, who retired a brigadier general, received an assignment to the CIA as the deputy project director of the U-2 under Richard Bissell. In this role until July 1958, he became responsible for operational control of the three overseas detachments and the one at Area 51. Also, he was the CIA's engineering manager for research and development efforts under Project RAINBOW to reduce the radar detectability of the U-2 and assess the feasibility of developing a new aircraft with lower RCS (radar cross-section) characteristics under Project GUSTO. He received the Legion of Merit in 1958 for his performance in this assignment.

Congress Briefed on AQUATONE

Although a guarded secret within both the CIA and the Eisenhower administration, DCI Dulles decided to tell a few key members of Congress about the U-2 project. On February 24, 1956, Dulles met with Senators Leverett Saltonstall and Richard B. Russell, the ranking members of the Senate Armed Services Committee and its subcommittee on the CIA. He shared with them the details of Project AQUATONE and asked their opinion on informing some members of the House of Representatives.

Because of the senators' recommendation to brief the senior members of the House Appropriations Committee, Dulles met later with the ranking members, Representatives John Taber and Clarence Cannon. Official congressional acknowledgment of the U-2 project remained confined to this small group for the next four years. The House Armed Services Committee and its CIA subcommittees did not receive a CIA briefing on the U-2 Project until after the loss of Francis Gary Powers's U-2 over the Soviet Union in May 1960.

Coordinating Intelligence Collection

From the U-2 program, the CIA saw the apparent need for an interagency task force or office to develop and coordinate collection requirement for the covert overhead reconnaissance effort.

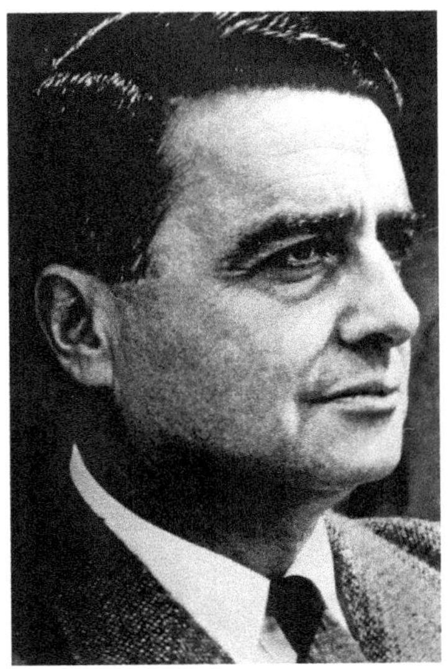

Scientist Edwin Land, who developed the Polaroid Company and was a member of the Beacon Hill Group. *Wikipedia.*

Early on, on November 3, 1954, Edwin Land had written to DCI Dulles setting forth the idea of a permanent task force to consolidate requirements and for planning missions given priority and feasibility. Land's recommendation went into effect when the U-2's development and testing approach completion. On December 1, 1955, following a meeting with Deputy Secretary of Defense Donald Quarles and Trevor Gardner, Richard Bissell established an Ad Hoc Requirements Committee (ARC). He named James Q. Reber as the intelligence requirements officer for the U-2 project and chair of the ARC.

Reber, already experienced in coordination with other intelligence agencies, headed the Directorate of Intelligence DI Office of Intelligence Coordination for four years. The first full-scale ARC meeting took place on February 1, 1956, with representatives from the army, navy and air force present. The CIA membership later expanded to include the Office of Current Intelligence (OCI). The Office of Scientific Intelligence (OSI) and a representative of the Directorate of Plans attended for the CIA.

In 1957, the National Security Agency (NSA) began sending a representative, and the State Department followed suit in 1960. After that, the committee issued its list of targets for the entire intelligence community using all available means of collection and not for the CIA with the U-2. ARC gave the top priority target list to the project director and the project staff's operations section using the list to plan the flight paths for U-2 missions.

Although not responsible for developing flight plans, the requirements committee assisted the planners with detailed target information as required. When ready to submit a flight plan to the president for approval, the committee drew up a detailed justification for the selection of the targets. This paper accompanied the flight plan.

In developing and prioritizing lists of targets, the committee members took into account the varying needs and interests of their parent organizations. Thus, the CIA representatives emphasized strategic intelligence: aircraft and munitions factories, power-generating complexes, nuclear establishments, roads, bridges and inland waterways. In contrast, the military services placed a heavier emphasis on order-of-battle data. The air force had a strong interest in gathering intelligence on the location of Soviet and East European airfields and radars. Although the committee members kept the interests of their services or agencies in mind, their awareness of the vital mission kept the level of cooperation high. Although occasionally impossible, the group always attempted to reach a consensus before issuing its recommendations. One or more agencies added a dissent to the recommendation of the committee.

U-2 Mission Film Handling

Developing the U-2 plane at Lockheed and flight testing it at the CIA's Watertown Flight Test Facility in Area 51 were merely parts and stages of what Project AQUATONE entailed and required. While going through these stages, the CIA was preparing to deploy the U-2 and the three detachments to commence operational flights over the Soviet Union.

On December 13, 1954, DCI Allen Dulles and his assistant, Richard Bissell, briefed Arthur C. Lundahl, the chief of the CIA's Photo-Intelligence Division (PID), on Project AQUATONE. At DCI Dulles's direction, Lundahl set in motion within his division a compartmentalized effort known as Project EQUINE to plan for the exploitation of overhead photography obtained from the U-2 project.

In May 1955, the thirteen-member PID staff found the number of personnel too small to handle the expected flood of photographs expected from the U-2. The Directorate of Support (OS) authorized expanding the PID staff to forty-four persons.

The Photo-Intelligence Division continued expanding in anticipation of large quantities of U-2 photography. It authorized the doubling of the number of staff in January 1956 when a new project known as HTAUTOMAT came into existence to exploit U-2 photography. The changes meant placing all the products from this project in the new control system.

During the summer of 1956, the PID moved to larger quarters in the Stewart Building at Fifth Street and New York Avenue, NW, in Washington, D.C. By now, the PID photo interpreters were already working with U-2 photography following a series of missions in April 1956. The CIA's U-2s photographed several U.S. installations considered analogous to high-priority Soviet installations. These preparations readied the PID for the mass of photography that they knew was coming when U-2 operations commenced in the summer of 1956.

The U-2 Cover Story

The rage and controversy over balloon flights continued into February 1956. Feeling the heat from Project GENETRIX and with the U-2 completing its final airworthiness tests, Richard Bissell and his staff realized the need for a cover story for overseas operations. While the CIA had used weather research for its cover at Area 51, now the CIA needed a plausible reason for deploying such an unusual-looking plane whose glider wings and odd landing gear were bound to attract curiosity.

The CIA's Photo-Intelligence Division grew to prepare for the expected flood of U-2 photographs. At the same time, Bissell decided the best cover for the deployment of the U-2 was that it was flying an ostensible mission of high-altitude weather research by the National Advisory Committee on Aeronautics. Such a cover story, however, needed the approval of all concerned: air force intelligence, the Air Weather Service, the Third Air Force, the Seventh Air Division, the SAC U-2 project officer, the U.S. Air Force Headquarters project officer and NACA's top official, Dr. Hugh Dryden. Before proceeding, Bissell consulted with the CIA Scientific Advisory Committee concerning the coverage plan.

A committee of U.S. Army, Navy, Air Force, CIA, NSA and State Department representatives created lists of priority targets for U-2 and other intelligence-gathering methods. The U-2 project used this list to draw up flight plans that enabled the committee to provide a detailed rationale for each plan for the president to consider as he decided whether to approve it.

With approval from the NACA's director, Hugh Dryden, Bissell's team settled on the NACA high-altitude weather research cover story and arranged for the U-2s to take several weather photographs that later appeared in the press. By the end of March 1956, the project staff had worked out contingency plans for the loss of a U-2 over hostile territory. All press releases would use the weather research cover story that included the suspension of operations and at least an indication of the diplomatic action.

Bissell approved these plans and ensured one final high-level look at the cover story on June 21, 1956.

The cover story of the U-2 conducting weather research turned out to be not entirely bogus when the CIA sent a U-2 flown by Captain Meierdierck to Alaska to check out the high-altitude, high-latitude wind patterns. Meierdierck kept the aircraft on course despite high crosswinds by using the drift sight, a device allowing the pilot to look under the plane to check his course and determine any drift. A C-54 transport plane flew along under the U-2 in case he encountered any difficulty.

The approval occurred the day after the first U-2 mission over Eastern Europe when Bissell met with General Goodpaster, James Killian and Edwin Land to discuss the pending overflights of the Soviet Union.

Killian, as the president of the Massachusetts Institute of Technology, headed a high-level and very secret study of the nation's ability to withstand a surprise attack. While this project was still underway, he and Edwin Land persuaded President Eisenhower to support the development of a high-altitude reconnaissance aircraft, the U-2. Later, Killian headed Eisenhower's

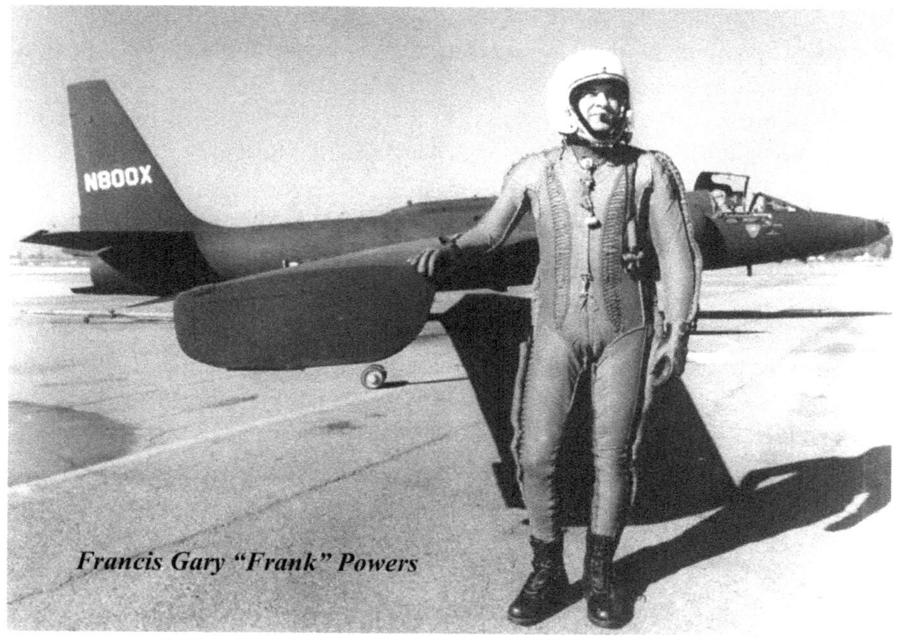

U-2 pilot Francis Gary "Frank" Powers wearing his MC-3 partial-pressure suit, required above fifty thousand feet to prevent hypoxia. *Central Intelligence Agency.*

Board of Consultants for Foreign Intelligence Activities, served as his cabinet-level science adviser and chaired the President's Science Advisory Board. Killian would later serve as the chairman of the President's Foreign Intelligence Advisory Board under John F. Kennedy.

Killian and Land disagreed with Bissell's concept, including the proposed emergency procedures, and made a much bolder and more forthright proposal in the event of the loss of a U-2 over hostile territory. Rather than deny responsibility, the United States should state that it was conducting the overflights to guard against surprise attack.

They all put the proposal aside for further thought, which it never received. Bissell's weather research cover remained the basis for statements made after a loss. The CIA did not follow their advice, and the weather cover story led to the disaster following a May 1960 U-2 loss involving agency pilot Francis Gary "Frank" Powers.

Preparing for U-2 Detachment A's Deployment to England

The CIA was keen to deploy the spy planes in allied countries, and the United Kingdom was a willing partner. The agency was also keen on using British crews to "fool the Soviets" if a spy plane was captured or shot down.

When the first group of U-2 drivers completed their training at Area 51, the CIA immediately deployed them to Royal Air Force Lakenheath to see how much of what the Russians had displayed the previous month was real.

Each year during Russia's May Day celebrations, the United States armed forces went on a worldwide alert while the Soviet Union paraded its latest armament and military might. Knowing the existence of Russia's armament advances meant the United States needed detail data assessing strength. Were the Soviets displaying a demonstrator, or did they have several of whatever it was that they were displaying as an intimidating show of strength? Lockheed felt confident in the ability of the U-2 to fly, obtain information and avoid interception, and the CIA was equally eager to receive it.

NACA announced that the USAF Air Weather Service would use a Lockheed-developed aircraft to study the weather and cosmic rays at altitudes up to fifty-five thousand feet. The CIA U-2 Detachment A was known publicly as the First Weather Reconnaissance Squadron, Provisional (WRSP). The detachment operated at Royal Air Force Lakenheath as a power projection extension of the CIA's Watertown facility that was still training additional detachments at Area 51 for deployment elsewhere. The CIA was already preparing to deploy its second class, Detachment B, to Turkey and its third class, Detachment C, to Japan.

Setting up the deployment venues required considerable planning, negotiations and logistics known to only a few. This top-secret activity allowed only those having a need-to-know in the loop. Advance parties deploying to the United Kingdom, Turkey and Japan included communications personnel at not only the host base but also other countries where the U-2 might fly. The same applied to fuels personnel, Lockheed maintenance personnel and security. Each received a top-secret classification.

On April 30, 1956, the CIA airlifted two U-2A planes to Royal Air Force Lakenheath to await the arrival of the Detachment A personnel from Watertown.

The CIA's First Stealth Attempt: Project RAINBOW, the Dirty Bird

Even before the U-2 became operational in June 1956, the CIA project officials were turning their thoughts to developing a stealth plane. The CIA estimated a short life expectancy for flying over the Soviet Union of between eighteen months and two years. This estimate proved optimistic once the Soviets demonstrated the capability of tracking and attempted to intercept the U-2 overflights. By August 1956, the U-2's vulnerability concerned Richard Bissell to the point that he despaired of its ability to avoid destruction for six months, let alone two years.

To extend the U-2's useful operational life, project officials first attempted to reduce the aircraft's vulnerability to detection by Soviet radars. In December 1956, Lockheed modified Article 341 using radar-absorbent materials for a series of radar cross-section tests called Project RAINBOW.

Antiradar techniques relied on RCS of an object. Radar measured how much electromagnetic (EM) energy an object reflected, expressed as an area defined in square meters. The RCS of an object became a function of the object's size, shape and materials that vary depending on the frequency of the EM energy. Long-distance search/acquisition radars use different frequencies than short-range fire control radars. Thus, it required a variety of techniques to protect the U-2.

All parts of the aircraft created reflections—the fuselage, tail, wings, engine inlets and exhaust. The antiradar technique investigation fell into two categories. It either absorbed the radar energy or created reflections interfering with the reflections from the aircraft.

Purcell's first concept placed on the U-2's fuselage an absorbent material that the Lincoln Lab team and Lockheed developers called "wallpaper." This second approach, tested in early 1958, involved the use of plastic material containing a printed circuit design that absorbed radar pulses in the 65 to 85 MHz range. This material glued to parts of the U-2's fuselage, nose and tail.

Another firm, Edgerton, Germeshausen & Grier (EG&G), which was composed of MIT faculty members, tested the results under an air force contract to evaluate radars. EG&G operated a small testing facility at Area 51 for this purpose.

Although Kelly Johnson had closely involved Purcell with the radar deception project since the early days, he did so reluctantly. Johnson disliked adding attachments that made his aircraft less airworthy. Johnson reflected his dislike of the antiradar attachments in the unofficial nickname "dirty birds" for the modified aircraft.

After the Lockheed mechanics had mounted the various RAINBOW devices on the prototype U-2, a Lockheed test pilot flew the plane over EG&G's installation, little more than a series of tractor trailers containing instrumentation. EG&G technicians could thus record and evaluate the U-2's radar return as it traversed a specific course over their facility. This method of testing radar-deceptive modifications proved both time consuming and dangerous.

Lockheed strung another U-2, Article 344, with piano wire of varying dipole lengths between the nose and wings of the aircraft to reduce the radar signature. This method created extra drag, with a resultant penalty in range and altitude. The U-2 aircraft modified under Project RAINBOW earned the name "dirty bird" from the plane not being aerodynamically "clean." This scheme called "trapeze" attempted to protect the engine inlets by running another wire diagonally from the nose to the slipper tank on each wing. To reduce low-frequency (70 MHz) reflections from the leading and trailing edges of the wings, they placed a wire parallel to and ahead of each wing's leading edge and another parallel to and behind each wing's trailing edge. They placed Ferrite beads on the wires to tune them to the expected frequencies. They called this technique "wires."

A fiberglass pole attached to each wingtip to anchor the outboard end of each wire. The poles provided anchor points ahead of and behind the wings. Each wire ran from the front end of each pole to the slipper tank (which projected in front of the wing) and from the slipper tank to the fuselage. Behind each wing, a wire ran from the back end of the fiberglass pole to the fuselage. The horizontal stabilizer was installed in a similar manner.

Although the "trapeze" and "wallpaper" systems provided protection against some Soviet radars, the systems proved ineffective against radars operating below 65 MHz or above 85 MHz. Furthermore, both additions degraded the U-2's performance. The weight and drag of "trapeze" reduced the aircraft's operating ceiling 1,500 feet, and "wallpaper" acted as a thermal insulator and trapped heat inside the fuselage. Initially, the engineers applied the wallpaper to the upper and lower surfaces. However, after recognizing the heating problem, they applied it only to the lower half of the fuselage. The wires and trapeze installations caused increased drag that cost the U-2 almost a mile, 5,000 feet in altitude and 20 percent in range. The pilots lacked enthusiasm for flying the plane with its reduced performance. One of them likened it to being "wired like a guitar."

The fleet at this point consisted of nine aircraft and the six CIA pilots undergoing flight training at the site. The CIA and its air force support, the 4070th Support Wing (SAC) at Area 51, were at this point preparing for overseas deployment for three CIA detachments. This effort included everything needed for the restricted deployment of a tactical unit, including personnel, finance, base preparation, supply, transportation, fuel, camera film, aircraft maintenance, flight planning and clearance, security and countless other administrative details.

CHAPTER 9

THE OVERFLIGHT MISSIONS

Spy Flights

In October 1955, the Central Intelligence Agency had placed an order for an additional thirty-nine U-2 aircraft at the same time as the Strategic Air Command officers and enlisted men arrived at Area 51 to assist Lockheed in determining the operational capabilities of the U-2 and train the three pilot detachments. By January 1956, the U-2 had impressed the USAF enough that it decided to purchase thirty-one U-2s through the CIA for security in a transaction code named Project DRAGON LADY, using the aircraft's nickname in the air force.

On April 29, 1956, Detachment A, the first CIA crew, deployed to England as the First Weather Reconnaissance Squadron, Provisional (WRSP-1). The "provisional" designation gave the U-2 detachments greater security because provisional air force units did not have to report to higher headquarters. They first located to Mildenhall, England, but moved to Lakenheath shortly after that as Mildenhall's hangar space proved inadequate.

On May 7, 1956, Dr. Hugh Dryden, NACA director, announced the use of the U-2 as a research tool for the study of meteorological conditions. The announcement provided a cover for CIA operatives deploying from Watertown to the United Kingdom via air force. Their travel orders identified them as Department of the U.S. Air Force civilians of the Watertown WRSP. The CIA Detachment A pilots trained at Area 51 and deploying to the

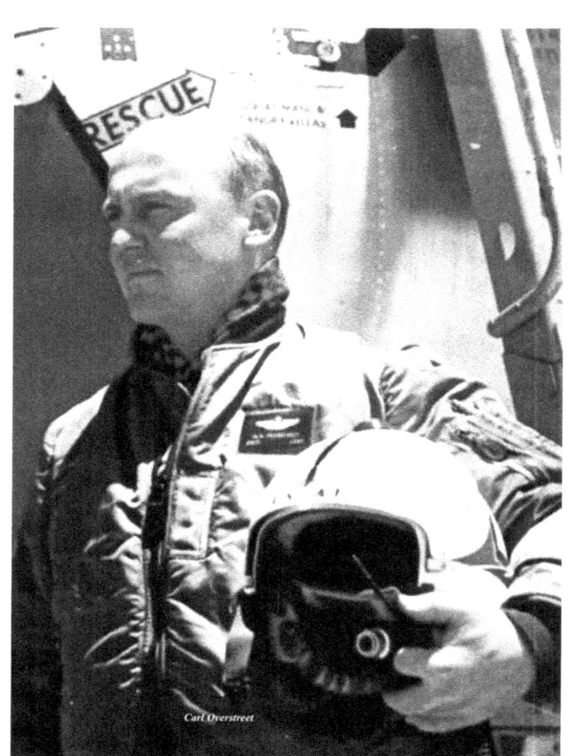

Right: CIA pilot Carl Overstreet, Detachment A at Watertown, flew the first flight over denied territory in Eastern Europe. *Carl Overstreet.*

Below: Watertown Control Tower. *CIA via TD Barnes Collection.*

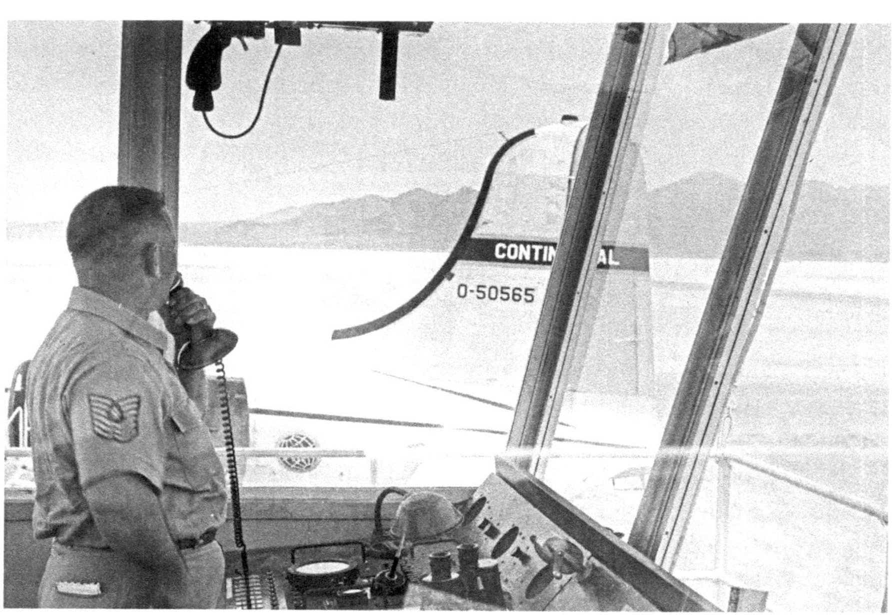

United Kingdom were Hervey Stockman, Marty Knutson, Carmine Vito, Glendon Dunaway, Carl Overstreet, Howard Carey and Jake Kratt.

Six days later, Watertown suffered its first fatality since the C-54 transport plane crash on Mount Charleston. The first fatality while flying the U-2 occurred on May 13, 1956, when test pilot Wilburn Rose, flying Article 345A, experienced trouble dropping his pogo (the outrigger wheel keeping the wings parallel to the ground) during takeoff. Once airborne, Rose made a low-level pass over the airstrip and shook loose the left pogo. He attempted a right turn to come back over the runway to shake loose the remaining pogo. The U-2 stalled and plunged to earth, disintegrating over a wide area.

Four U-2s arrived in secrecy at Lakenheath on April 29, 1956, with the USAF releasing a cover story that the Lockheed-developed aircraft were planes flown by the USAF Air Weather Service to study the jet stream and cosmic rays. Unfortunately, the aircraft could not fly the recon missions over hostile territory for which it was developed and deployed until the fuel control problem was solved. Once the detachment made the fuel control fix, it began testing in the friendly skies of England. This soon ended with an incident between the CIA and the English government in which the United Kingdom ordered all CIA assets off English soil.

Before flights could begin, the agreement with Prime Minister Anthony Eden began to falter as the Suez crisis loomed on the horizon. The CIA informed the British that they would deploy only one plane but sent four to the American base at Lakenheath. The CIA experienced two specific incidents that led it to transfer the U-2s to Wiesbaden in West Germany later in June.

The first incident was the notorious "frogman" incident, when MI6 sent a retired naval commander, Lionel "Buster" Crabb, on a hazardous mission to examine the hulls of ships from a Soviet fleet that were visiting Portsmouth. Crabb's headless body later washed up on the beach, causing huge embarrassment for Eden's government, which was entertaining Soviet leader Nikita Khrushchev.

Adding to the diplomatic faux-pas stacking up in Whitehall, two days later (in May 1956), a U-2 on a training flight from Lakenheath inadvertently penetrated the British radar network, causing Royal Air Force fighters to scramble. The British government, embarrassed at the Russians catching the British spy in the act, asked the United States to postpone the Lakenheath flights. By May 4, all the detachment's personnel and equipment, including four aircraft, were taking the long flight in an old, shaky C-124 to Lakenheath.

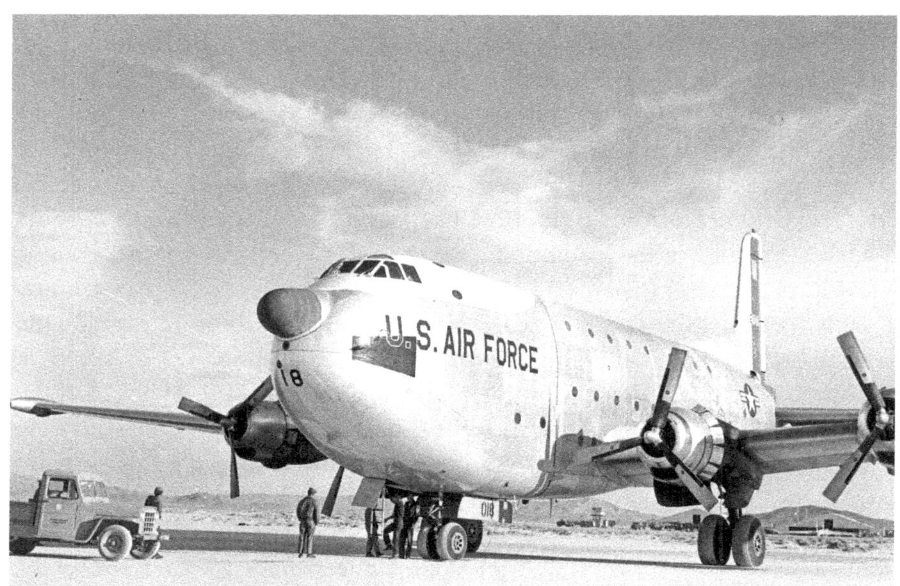

Douglas C-124 Globemaster preparing to take off at Watertown, Area 51. *CIA via TD Barnes Collection.*

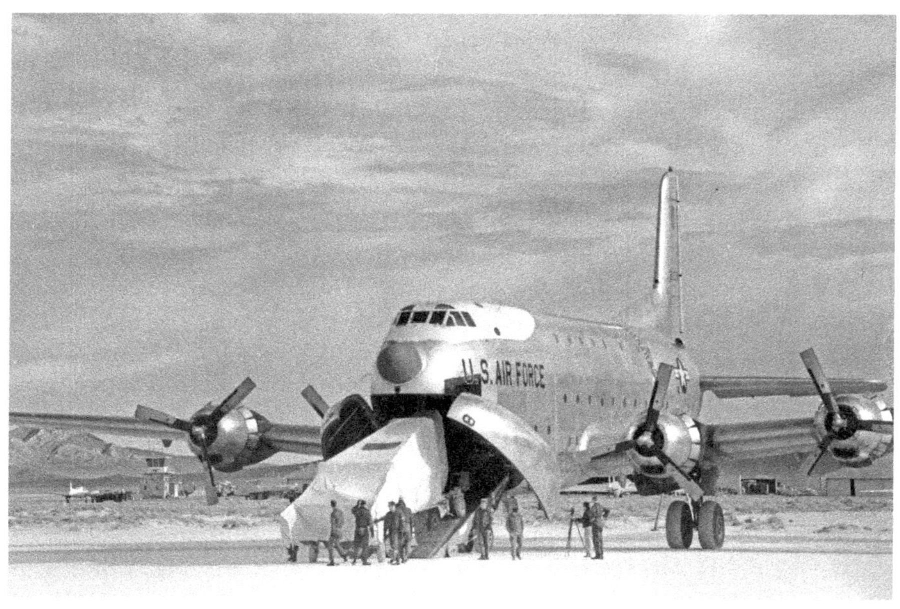

U-2 loading onto a C-124 for overseas deployment. *CIA via TD Barnes Collection.*

After deployment, on May 7, the National Advisory Committee for Aeronautics released an unclassified U-2 cover story. The cover story stated that a Lockheed aircraft flown by the USAF Air Weather Service was intended to study high-altitude phenomena. It identified studies such as the jet stream, convective clouds, temperature and wind structures at jet-stream levels and cosmic-ray effects up to fifty-five thousand feet. The announcement was the first public acknowledgment of the existence of the U-2. In reality, all this research happened much later. The U-2 was a spy plane; the research projects were its cover.

U-2 Detachment A Leaves England for Germany

To avoid delays, on June 11, 1956, following the refusal of the British government to allow mounting U-2 operations from Britain, Detachment A moved to Wiesbaden, Germany, without approval from the German government, while Giebelstadt Army Airfield prepared to become a more permanent base.

It concerned Eisenhower that despite their great intelligence value, overflights of the Soviet Union might cause a war. His fear reached back to the 1955 Geneva Summit, while the U-2 was under development. Eisenhower proposed to Nikita Khrushchev that the Soviet Union and the United States each grant the other country airfields for use in photographing military installations. Khrushchev rejected the "Open Skies" proposal. At the time, the CIA was telling the president that the Soviets lacked the ability to track high-altitude U-2 flights. The CIA based this belief on the Soviet Union still using American radar systems given them during World War II.

Although the Russians could track the overflights, they could not identify the aircraft. Often the U-2s overflying Soviet-denied territory would have an entire squadron of MiGs flying at much lower altitudes beneath the U-2s, which for the pilots was a real pain in the neck because the MiGs blocked the U-2's view of its recon target. In the three weeks from June 20 through July 10, 1956, the CIA U-2s made eight overflights beyond the Iron Curtain, including five over the Soviet Union.

Now, a year after the Geneva Summit, the Office of Scientific Intelligence appeared more cautious, stating that detection was possible but believing the Soviets were unable to track the aircraft. Dulles further told Eisenhower (per Presidential Aide General Goodpaster) that in any aircraft loss, the pilot would not survive. Having such assurances and with the growing demand for accurate intelligence regarding the alleged "bomber gap" between the United States and the Soviet Union, Eisenhower approved ten days of overflights for June 1956.

On July 4, 1956, a month after it was declared operational, a U-2 piloted by Carl Overstreet conducted the first "Operation Overflight" out of Wiesbaden, West Germany. This mission was the first overflight over denied territory of the Soviet Union. It was under the cover designation of the WRSP-1. Meanwhile, the Second Weather Reconnaissance Squadron, Provisional (WRSP-2), in Incirlik, Turkey, and the Third Weather Reconnaissance Squadron, Provisional (WRSP-3), in Atsugi, Japan, were preparing to follow.

Carl Overstreet, the First CIA U-2 Pilot to Fly Over Denied Territory

Carl Overstreet entered the reconnaissance business in the winter of 1954 when Gerry Johnson, his 508 SFW wing CO at Turner AFB, stopped him out on the ramp and suggested he meet some people downtown who had something to offer. Overstreet's thoughts turned to F-86s and the Flying Tigers. Off he went to meet the recruiters for the CIA, who revealed to him a photo of the article, and he agreed to fly it. After physical exams, fitting for a pressure suit and a scary ride in the hypobaric chamber to test the effects of altitude on his body, he arrived at Area 51 in January 1956.

Now, in the summer of 1956, the trained Weather Reconnaissance Squadron A sat ready and waited at Wiesbaden Air Base, West Germany. With events moving rather slowly from his point of view, he took a short weekend trip to Vaduz, Lichtenstein, accompanied by Max Conn, a tech rep for Westinghouse. He returned to Wiesbaden, where he learned of the CIA scheduling him for the first operational flight of the U-2 over Eastern Europe.

U-2 missions from Wiesbaden always departed westward to gain altitude over friendly territory before turning eastward at operational altitudes. The NATO Air Defense mission in that area included No. 1 Air Division RCAF (Europe), which operated the Canadair Sabre Mark 6 from bases in northeastern France. The service ceiling of this aircraft was fifty-four thousand feet. Nonetheless, the U-2 and RCAF "ZULU" recorded numerous encounters between alert flights for posterity.

On Wednesday, June 20, 1956, Carl Overstreet flew Mission 2003 over Eastern Europe, flying north and west from Wiesbaden to gain altitude before looping back to the base and turning east. He entered hostile territory where the borders of West Germany, East Germany and Czechoslovakia met. He flew across northern Czechoslovakia and turned north, passing east of Dresden and into Poland, flying over every major Polish city before turning back to Wiesbaden the way he came via Prague.

The overflights of Eastern Europe continued. In another mission for the CIA, Overstreet photographed the Suez from the Red Sea to the Mediterranean after President Gamal Abdel Nasser shut down the canal in 1957.

On July 2, 1956, Jake Kratt flew Mission 2009 over Eastern Europe, heading south from Wiesbaden across Austria into Hungary. Kratt flew past Budapest and turned south, flying along the Yugoslav border. The route extended all the way across Bulgaria to the Black Sea and back to Wiesbaden, making it a seven-hour sortie.

On the same day, July 2, 1956, Glendon Keith Dunaway flew Mission 2010 over Eastern Europe. He headed north from Wiesbaden over East Germany, southern Poland, eastern Czechoslovakia, Hungary and Romania before turning around at the Black Sea and returning to Wiesbaden after a seven-hour sortie.

The first U-2 overflight had already occurred, using the existing authorization of air force overflights over Eastern Europe. On this flight, the CIA tested the Soviet radar to see if it could track the angel. Eisenhower shared this worry. He nonetheless approved the first overflight over the Soviet Union, Mission 2013, scheduled for July 4, 1956.

The Suicide Pill

During the early 1950s, tales of Soviet secret police torture of captured foreign agents led Bissell and Cunningham to approach Dr. Alex Batlin of the Technical Services Division in the Directorate of Plans for ideas to help "captured" U-2 pilots avoid such suffering. Batlin suggested the method used by Nazi war criminal Hermann Goering: a thin glass ampule containing liquid potassium cyanide. A pilot had only to put it in his mouth and bite down on the glass. Death followed in ten to fifteen seconds. Project AQUATONE ordered six of the poison ampules, called L-pills, and offered one to each pilot before a mission. The CIA left it up to each pilot to decide if he wanted to take an L-pill with him. Some did; most did not. No pilot ever used the pill.

Most pilots chose not to take with them the suicide pill offered before a mission. After a pilot almost ingested an L-pill instead of candy during a December 1956 flight, the CIA placed the suicide pills into boxes to avoid confusion.

When, in 1960, the CIA realized a pill breaking inside the cockpit would kill the pilot, it destroyed the L-pills, and as a replacement, its Technical Services Division developed a needle poison with a powerful shellfish toxin hidden in a silver dollar. The CIA made only one after the agency decided any pilot who needed to use it would cancel the program.

The First Overflight over the Soviet Union

Carl Overstreet's first flight over Eastern Europe was significant. However, Hervey Stockman was suiting up to fly directly over the communist homeland itself. The CIA was preparing to poke the bear itself.

On July 4, 1956, Stockman flew Article 347, marked as NACA 187, on Mission 2013, the first flight over the Soviet Union to target the Soviet submarine construction program in Leningrad, as well as count the number of new Hisasishchev M-4 "Bison" bombers. From Wiesbaden, he flew over East Germany and Poland before crossing the Soviet border near Grodno in Belarus. He flew over various bomber bases around Minsk, north to the naval shipyards and bomber bases at Leningrad, west over more bomber bases in the Baltic states and back to Wiesbaden in an eight-hour-and-forty-five-minute flight. Soviet radar tracked this mission, and several MiG fighters attempted to intercept the U-2.

On July 5, 1956, Carmine Vito in Article 347 flew the second Soviet overflight during Mission 2014, flying a similar route to Mission 2013 except farther south, continuing the search for Russian Bison bombers. He continued to the royal capital city of Krakow in Poland and into the Ukraine over Brest and Baranovici. He headed toward Moscow, following the railway from Minsk to the Soviet capital. He flew over the Fili airframe plant in Moscow and northwest to Kaliningrad and the main Soviet flight test and research center at Ramenskoye, returning to Wiesbaden via the Baltic states, where Soviet radars and MiG-17s again tracked the overflight.

Vito remained the only U-2 pilot to fly over Moscow. His flight was the third operational flight over potentially hostile territory, or what the pilots called "hot" flights.

Eisenhower realized how unrealistic his hope of no Soviet detection from the earlier overflights had been and ordered the overflights to stop if the Russians managed to track the aircraft. The CIA confirmed the Soviets were unable to track the U-2s. Therefore, the Russians did not know of the U-2 overflying Moscow and Leningrad. The aircraft's photographs depicted tiny images of MiG-15s and MiG-17s attempting and failing to intercept the aircraft, proving the Soviets could not shoot down an operational U-2.

The National Air and Space Museum in Washington, D.C., has the U-2 flown by Vito suspended from the ceiling. It still contains a payload from one of its earliest flights: a small lump of Tutti Frutti chewing gum under the left rail. Vito stuck it there on July 5, 1956, before taking off from Wiesbaden, Germany, on his first operational mission.

On July 9, 1956, Marty Knutson flew the third Soviet overflight, Mission 2020, from Wiesbaden north to overfly Berlin, East Germany and the Baltic states to Riga. He headed east and south, covering targets around Kaunas, Vilnius and Minsk before returning via Warsaw to Wiesbaden.

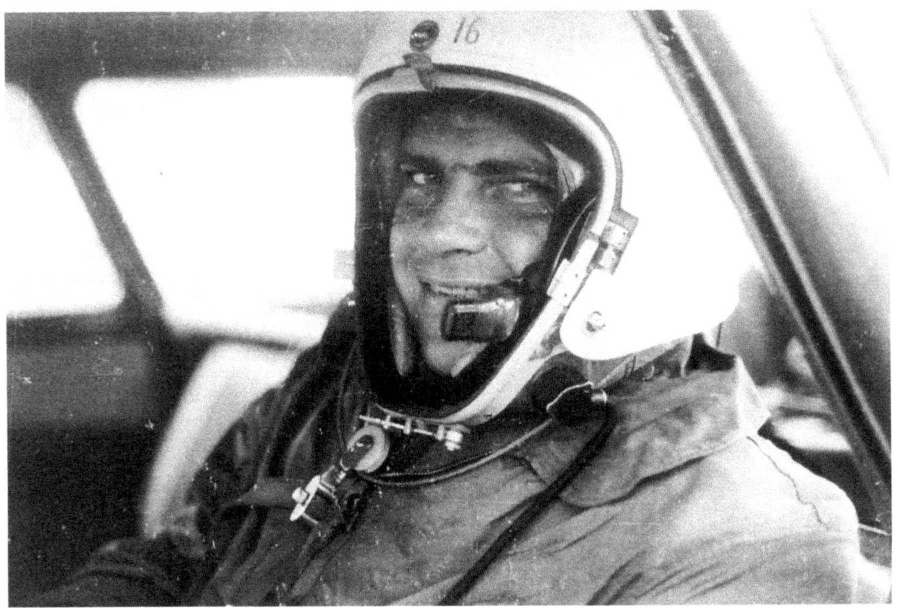

U-2 pilot Marty Knutson, Detachment A at Area 51, flew the third Soviet overflight. *Marty Knutson.*

His mission was to learn how much of a numerical gap existed between the bombers of the United States and Russia. He captured photos of an airfield where all of Russia's Tupolev Bison bombers were based. This informed the United States that the Russians did not have as many bombers as thought by the United States. Knutson's mission lasted nine hours and twenty minutes. He landed with only twenty gallons of fuel remaining. Allen Dulles, the head of the CIA, called the intelligence photos from Mission 2020 "million-dollar photos."

On July 9, 1956, Carl Overstreet flew the fourth Soviet overflight, Mission 2021, from Wiesbaden to head south into Czechoslovakia and Hungary. He flew northeast into the Ukraine as far as Kiev and over various bomber bases before returning to Wiesbaden via Poland.

This same day, the NACA made another announcement about the great research work conducted with the U-2. It informed the public of the need to conduct these types of research flights overseas. The announcement was merely another cover story to explain the presence of U-2s in Germany and other locations.

On July 10, 1956, Glendon Dunaway flew the fifth Soviet overflight, Mission 2024, from Wiesbaden over East Germany, Poland and Ukraine to Kerch on the eastern tip of the Crimean Peninsula. He headed back via Sevastopol, Simferopol, Odessa, Romania, Czechoslovakia and Hungary to Wiesbaden with fighter aircraft radar tracking his flight near Odessa.

Bomber Gap Disproven

On July 10, 1956, the Soviets protested what they described as overflights by a USAF twin-engine medium bomber, believing it a Canberra. The United States knew by July 19, 1956, of no American "military planes" having overflown the Soviet Union. Nonetheless, the fact that the Soviets' report revealed they could track the U-2s for extended periods caused Eisenhower to halt overflights over Eastern Europe. In truth, the president was more concerned about the Soviet protests than he was about the public's reaction to news of the United States violating international law. To avoid project cancellation, the CIA began Project RAINBOW to make the U-2 less detectable.

The eight overflights over communist territory, however, had already proven the bomber gap did not exist. The U-2s did not find any Myasishchev

M-4 Bison bombers at the nine air bases they visited; however, the Eisenhower administration could not disclose the source of its intelligence because of the secrecy of the CIA operation.

The presidential order did not restrict U-2 flights outside Eastern Europe. In May 1956, Turkey approved the deployment of Detachment B at Incirlik Air Base, near Adana, Turkey. Before the new detachment was ready, however, Detachment A in late August used Adana as a refueling base to photograph the Mediterranean. The aircraft found evidence of many British troops on Malta and Cyprus as the United Kingdom prepared for its forthcoming intervention in Suez. The United States released some of the photographs to the British government. As the crisis grew in seriousness, the project converted from a source of strategic reconnaissance, where the priority was high quality over speed (its maker processed the film and then analyzed in Washington), to a tactical reconnaissance unit that provided immediate analysis.

The Photo-Intelligence Division set up a lab in Wiesbaden as Detachment B took over for Detachment A to fly over targets that remain classified today. The Wiesbaden lab's rapid reporting helped the U.S. government predict the Israeli-British-French attack on Egypt three days before it began on October 29.

On August 29, 1956, Missions 1104 and 1105, two U-2s, flew from Wiesbaden to the Suez area during the Suez Crisis, where they photographed preparations for the Suez landings. The missions landed at Incirlik in Turkey. The following day, the two U-2s at Incirlik retraced the previous day's sortie, flying over the Suez area and landing back at Wiesbaden. Meanwhile, the CIA pilots of Detachment B had completed their training and received transfer orders to Incirlik Air Base, Turkey, as Detachment 10-10, Detachment B, Weather Research Squadron (WRSP-2). The CIA pilots were Tom Birkhead, Bill McMurry, E.K. Jones, Buster Edens, John MacArthur, Francis Gary "Frank" Powers, J. Robbie Robinson, Bill Hall, David Dowling and Sammy Snyder.

In August 1956, the third U-2 training class, Detachment C, arrived at Area 51. The Detachment C U-2 pilots were Al Smiley, Lyle Rudd, Jim Barnes, Jim Cherbonneaux, Barry Baker, John Shinn, Al Rand, Bob Ericson and Tom Cull.

Three months following the loss of Wilburn Rose, on August 31, 1956, a second fatal crash occurred at Area 51 during a night-flying exercise. To avoid a stall, experienced U-2 pilots always cut back abruptly on the throttle as soon as the pogo stick falls away. Frank G. Grace, lacking experience,

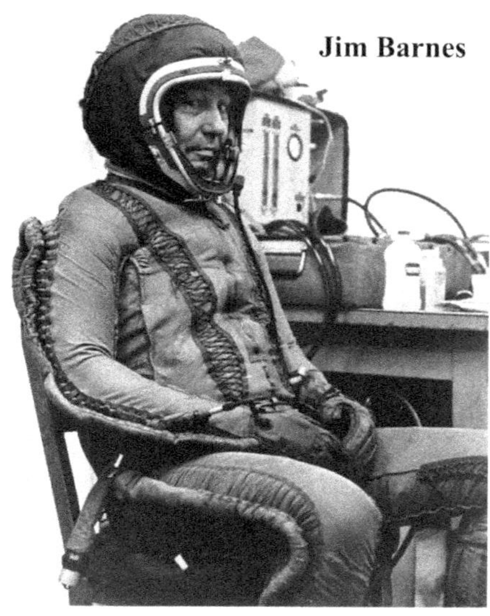

U-2 pilot Jim Barnes, CIA Detachment C at Area 51, flew the U-2 for thirty-two years, a record-setting 5,862 flying hours. *Jim Barnes.*

stalled Article 354 at an altitude of fifty feet when he tried to climb too steeply at takeoff. The falling craft cartwheeled on its left wing and struck a power pole near the runway.

Before the year's end, there were two more U-2 crashes, one of them fatal. On September 17, 1956, Article 346 lost part of its right wing while on its takeoff ascent from Lindsey Air Force Base in Wiesbaden, Germany. The aircraft flew into the jet wash from a Canadian F-86 and disintegrated in midair near Kaiserslautern, West Germany, killing pilot Howard Carey.

Detachment A moved to Giebelstadt in October 1956, placing it within seventeen miles of the Iron Curtain. The CIA flew nine sorties over various Middle Eastern countries involved in the Suez Crisis in the Sinai Peninsula during the build-up to the ten-day Suez conflict on October 19, 1956. Detachment B flew several sorties over the Suez area during the build-up to the conflict after troops landed at the Suez on November 6, 1956. The CIA flew fourteen sorties over Syria between November 7 and December 18, 1956.

Eisenhower refused the CIA pleas in September 1956 to reauthorize overflights of Eastern Europe. It took the Hungarian revolution in November and his reelection that month to persuade the president to renew Eastern Bloc overflights over border areas.

On November 20, 1956, Gary "Frank" Powers flew the sixth Soviet overflight, Mission 4016, from Incirlik, north over Syria and Iraq. He flew over Baghdad into Iran before turning north toward the Caspian Sea. He crossed the Soviet border and flew over Baku before turning west to overfly Yerevan. The flight aborted heading for Tbilisi when electrical problems forced an early return to Incirlik. The flight was the first using the B-Camera. Both radar and fighters tracked the mission.

When its interceptors failed to reach the U-2s, the Soviets protested a December overflight of Vladivostok by RB-57Ds. Eisenhower again forbade communist overflights. However, flights close to the border continued with the first ELINT-equipped U-2s.

On December 10, 1956, the CIA flew Mission 4018 over Eastern Europe from Incirlik over Albania, Bulgaria and Yugoslavia and back to Incirlik.

The same day, December 10, Carmine Vito flew Mission 2019 over Eastern Europe from Wiesbaden over Albania, Bulgaria and Yugoslavia and back to Wiesbaden. On this sortie, Vito, known as the Lemon Drop Kid, almost bit on the suicide L-pill, mistaking it for one of his favorite sweets. A poison needle replaced the L-pill in January 1960.

Nine days later, Watertown suffered the loss of Article 357 on December 19, 1956, resulting from pilot hypoxia. A small leak prematurely depleted the oxygen supply and impaired Robert J. Ericson's judgment as he flew over Arizona. Because of his inability to act and keep track of his aircraft's speed, the U-2 exceeded the placarded speed of 190 knots and disintegrated when it reached 270 knots. Ericson managed to jettison the canopy before the wind sucked him from the aircraft at twenty-eight thousand feet. His chute opened at fifteen thousand feet, and he landed without injury with the aircraft a total loss.

USAF 4028 Squadron U-2 Pilots Arrive at Area 51 for Training

In June 1957, the U.S. Air Force's SAC, which wanted nothing to do with the U-2 at first, now needed more secrecy for its spy plane operations. SAC was concerned about its U-2 pilots assigned to what was originally the 508th Strategic Fighter Wing at Turner AFB, Georgia, flying the F-84 G. Deactivated in 1956, the 508th became the 4028th Strategic Reconnaissance Squadron (SRS), a component of the 4080th Strategic Reconnaissance Wing, Strategic Air Command. The air force activated the wing to fly the Lockheed U-2 spy planes out of Laughlin AFB, Texas.

USAF pilots and support personnel of the 4028th Squadron arrived at Area 51, where the USAF pilots checked out and transferred to the USAF 4070th. The air force pilots trained at Area 51 were Jack Nole (squadron commander), Joe Jackson, Dick Nevett, Howard Cody, Dick "Gordo" Atkins, Ed Emerling, Mike Styer, Joe King, Ray Haupt, Warren "Goog" Boyd, Richard McGraw, John Campbell, Ken Alderman, Leo Smith, Richard

"Steve" Heyser, Dick Leavitt, Bennie LaCombe, Bill "Skip" Allson, Tony Bevacqua and Jack "Curly" Graves.

A second U-2 squadron, the 4029th SRS, received assignments in expectation of the CIA Project AQUATONE ending with the aircraft turned over to SAC. The transfer of U-2s from the CI never happened, and the 4029th SRS never acquired the U-2.

The SAC relocated the 4080th from Turner AFB to Laughlin Air Force Base, near Del Rio, Texas, in early 1957. While the 4080th moved to the new location, the SAC instructor pilots at Area 51 were training a select cadre of pilots to fly the U.S. Air Force's RB-57D replacement, the U-2 Dragon Lady.

On March 20, 1956, U-2 #6696 crashed at Area 51. USAF pilot Tony Bevacqua survived. However, he wiped out the plane's landing gear.

In February 1957, Detachment A (WRSP) moved from Wiesbaden to Giebelstadt Air Base near Wurzburg, West Germany.

On May 6, 1957, Bissell reported to the president concerning the progress of Project RAINBOW, saying that in operational missions, most incidents went undetected. President Eisenhower again authorized overflights of the Soviet Union, with the CIA promising Soviet detection or tracking of the

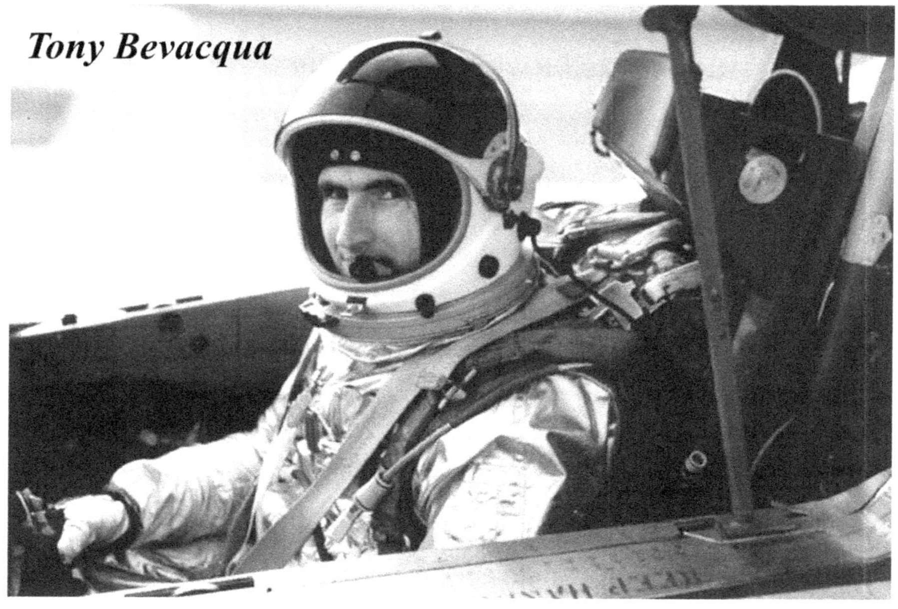

USAF lieutenant colonel Tony Bevacqua trained in the U-2 at Area 51 and later flew the SR-71. He was the youngest of the early U-2 pilots. *Tony Bevacqua.*

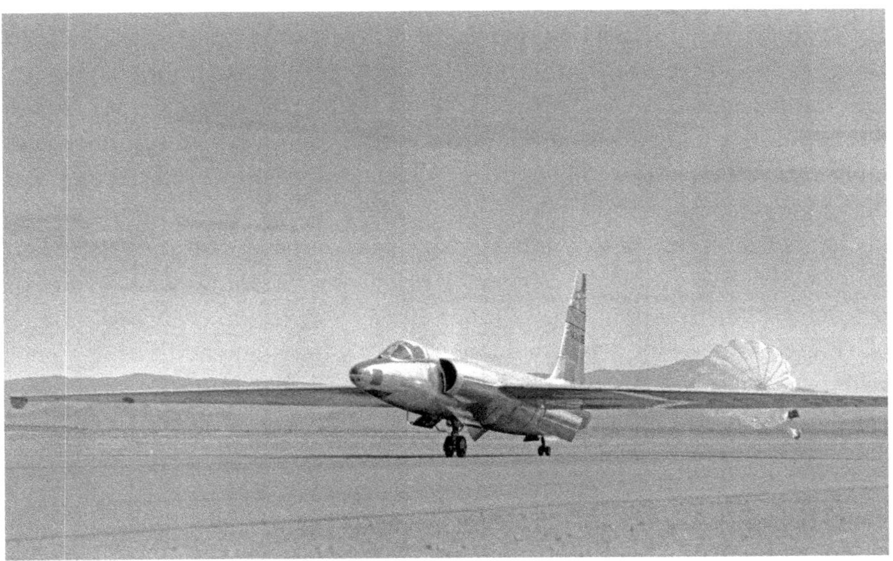

A U-2 plane landing on the Groom Lake bed with drag chute at the Area 51 NASA Beatty, Nevada radar site where the author worked sixty-five miles from Watertown using the same radar as used by the Soviet Union to track the U-2. *CIA via TD Barnes Collection.*

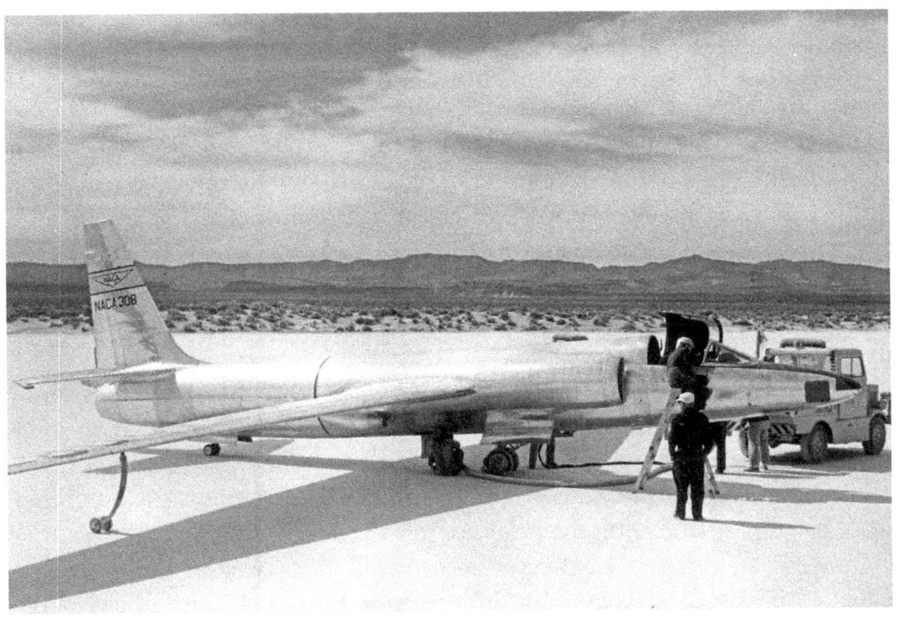

A pilot entering U-2 at Area 51 for takeoff. Note the National Advisory Committee for Aeronautics markings supporting the CIA's cover story. *CIA via TD Barnes Collection.*

U-2 as unlikely. At a meeting on May 6, 1957, with the president, Richard Bissell reported on the progress made in developing radar camouflage.

A month later, during a Project RAINBOW test flight at Area 51, Article 341 suffered a flameout at seventy-two thousand feet due to airframe heat build-up caused by the "wallpaper" modification acting as insulation around the engine. Lockheed test pilot Robert Sieker's pressure suit inflated, but his helmet faceplate failed, and he lost consciousness. The aircraft stalled at sixty-five thousand feet and entered a flat spin. At a low altitude, Sieker recovered enough to bail out. Without an ejection seat, Sieker died for lack of enough altitude for a safe manual egress. By the plane not having a pilot ejection system, the U-2's tailplane struck and killed him in midair. The aircraft crashed in an area so remote that search teams needed four days to locate the wreckage. The extensive search attracted the attention of the press. In April 1957, a headline in the *Chicago Daily Tribune* read, "Secrecy Veils High-Altitude Research Jet; Lockheed U-2 Called Super Snooper." The rescue responders found Sieker's body near the wreck with his parachute partially deployed.

The conclusion was that Project RAINBOW's efforts to mask the radar image of the U-2 were ineffective and made the aircraft more vulnerable by adding extra weight that reduced its maximum altitude. Thus, the CIA canceled Project RAINBOW following Sieker's death, mostly, however, because Soviet radar operators continued to find and track U-2s equipped with antiradar systems.

Because of its large wingspan, an out-of-control U-2 tended to enter a classical flat spin before ground contact. This slow descent lessened the impact. Having no fire to occur after impact often made the remains of crashed U-2s salvageable, as was the case with the wreckage of Article 341. Kelly Johnson's crew at the Skunk Works used the wreckage, along with spares and salvage parts of other crash U-2s, to produce another flyable airframe.

Development Projects Staff noted the U-2's ability to survive a crash in fair condition. The survivability after a crash became a consideration in its contingency plans for a loss over hostile territory. The thought of a plane surviving a crash meant an easy compromise of the weather research cover story because of the equipment on board the aircraft.

The loss of one of Lockheed's best test pilots, as well as the prototype "dirty bird" U-2, led Kelly Johnson to suggest that Lockheed should install a large boom at the radar test facility. Using the boom, which could lift entire airframes fifty feet in the air, technicians could change the airframe's attitude and run radar tests almost continuously without having to fuel and fly the plane.

By the summer of 1957, testing of the radar-deception system was complete, and in July the first "dirty bird" (DB) arrived at Detachment B, an operational detachment, and flew the first mission of a U-2 known as a "Covered Wagon" on July 21, 1957. The CIA flew nine flights of the test aircraft before deeming the system ineffective and ending its use in May 1958.

On June 11, 1957, the 4028th Strategic Reconnaissance Squadron commander, Colonel Nole, led the first of two three-ship U-2 formations from Area 51 to their new home at Laughlin, Texas, for operational duty. Both RB-57s and U-2s graced the West Texas skies until the RB-57s' retirement in April 1960. The U.S. Air Force's U-2 eventually became the United States' sole manned-airborne reconnaissance platform, and most of them were stationed at Laughlin Air Force Base.

U-2 Detachment C Moves to Eielson AFB, Alaska

Detachment C moved to Eielson Air Force Base in Alaska during the summer of 1957. On June 8, 1957, a U-2 took off from Eielson AFB to conduct the first intentional overflight of the Soviet Union since December 1956. This mission broke new ground in two respects: it was the first overflight conducted from American soil and the first by the new Detachment C.

Detachment C, the third group of pilots to complete training in the autumn of 1956, officially identified as the Weather Reconnaissance Squadron, Provisional-3. The third detachment needed a new base because of Area 51 becoming the training site for pilots flying the twenty-nine U-2s purchased by the U.S. Air Force. The CIA decided Edwards AFB was the best location for Detachment C and began looking for bases there.

Even without the arrival of the U.S. Air Force pilots, Detachment C could not have stayed much longer. In June 1957, the entire facility evacuated, with all remaining CIA personnel, materiel and aircraft transferring to Edwards AFB in California as Detachment G.

By the fall of 1957, only months after the first deployment of a dirty bird, it became obvious to Bissell and the scientific team that the treatments had only a marginal effect on tracking and they needed a new aircraft with antiradar features to escape detection.

CHAPTER 10

BACK AT THE RANCH

FROM DREAMLAND TO GHOST TOWN

In May 1957, Atomic Energy Commission radiological safety officer Charles Weaver, Oliver R. Placak and Melvin W. Carter participated in two meetings at Area 51, where Weaver revealed and discussed the film *Atomic Tests in Nevada*. The Atomic Energy Commission briefed Watertown personnel on nuclear testing activities, radiation safety and the possibility of radiation hazards from the test series. Before leaving Watertown, the Atomic Energy Commission men met with two air force officers, Colonel Jack Nole and Colonel Schilling, and the CIA commander, Richard Newton, to discuss arrangements for radiation monitors to visit the airbase whenever anticipating the fallout in the Watertown area.

Even before the departure of the U-2s, the Atomic Energy Commission used the Area 51 facility as a test bed for its nuclear tests. In June 1957, two minor atomic blasts occurred in Yucca Flat as CIA pilot classes finished training and the U-2 test operation moved to North Base at Edwards AFB, California, leaving Watertown a virtual ghost town in caretaker status with a site manager, security and minimal complement of personnel present.

For the next few years, the remaining Watertown residents learned to live with their atomic neighbor, evacuating the facility during nuclear tests and returning to repair the damage caused by the atomic detonations. At Watertown, the workers wrapped chicken wire around the fluorescent lights in the mess hall and hangars to catch any bulbs shaken out by the underground tests or the sonic booms from the planes.

On one occasion, Watertown received notification of an underground atomic test in the range to the west. About nine o'clock in the morning, residents felt the earth quake like a shake of the test. A short time later, they learned of the underground test venting and the prevailing winds blowing the radiation toward the CIA's Groom Lake facility.

The Lockheed transport planes evacuated the non-critical people, and everyone else assembled in the metal mess hall for possible evacuation. The authorities informed them of the planes returning from Burbank to evacuate them and instructed them to remain inside. The mess hall remained open twenty-four hours a day with free food.

The Atomic Energy Commission conducted Operation PLUMBBOB as a series of nuclear tests between May 28 and October 7, 1957, following Project 57, the biggest, longest and most controversial test series in the continental United States. The operation consisted of twenty-nine explosions with twenty-one laboratories and government agencies involved.

Outside the Atomic Proving Grounds, the Atomic Energy Commission used the CIA facility as a test bed for monitoring and measuring for radiation exposure inside the evacuated buildings and vehicles. The commission used the Groom Lake facility to study the ability of various materials to shield against fallout. In effect, Watertown was a laboratory to determine the shielding qualities of typical building materials found in any average American small town.

The fallout wasn't the only unwelcome visitor to the inactive facility. In July 1957, security at the CIA facility detained a civilian pilot named Edward K. Current Jr., a Douglas Aircraft Company employee who was flying a cross-country training flight when he became lost and ran low on fuel. He landed at Groom Lake, where the security officers held him overnight for questioning. The Nevada Test Organization (NTO) security officials reported the incident to the Civil Aeronautics Administration (CAA), which administered the air closure over the test site. The following day, the NTO Office of Test Information issued a press release to the news media describing the incident.

In another incident, a flight of three F-105 Thunderchiefs, led by British exchange pilot Anthony "Bugs" Bendell, was on a practice nuclear weapon delivery sortie eighty miles north of Nellis Air Force Base when one aircraft experienced an oil pressure malfunction. One F-105 returned to Nellis, while Bendell led the stricken craft to the airfield at Groom Lake. After making a pass over the field with no response to distress calls, Bendell advised the student pilot to land. At this point, two F-101 Voodoos intercepted Bendell and forced him to land.

At Langley, Bissell and his air force assistant, Colonel Jack Gibbs, continued the overseas U-2 deployments, expecting at any time to lose a U-2 to a Soviet missile. They knew it was simply a matter of time before the Soviet Union would advance its air defenses to take down a U-2. After having a taste of stealth with RAINBOW, they discussed the aircraft and materials manufacturers, as well as various laboratories, to understand what materials and designs could replace the U-2. On December 4, 1957, Bissell conducted a meeting where he summed up the various techniques:

Engines and other metal structures inside the aircraft required shielding by reflection.

Some structural members that are impossible to shield required transparency by using plastic and eliminating metal components inside.

Protecting against S-band and X-band radars required shaping the exterior of the aircraft to reflect the energy away from the radar unit.

To reduce reflections exposed edges would require "softening" to have a gradual change in the impedance of the structure.

Meanwhile, in May 1957, Eisenhower again authorized overflights over certain important Soviet missile and atomic facilities. He continued to authorize each flight, examining maps and sometimes making changes to the flight plan. By 1957, one of the European units was based at Giebelstadt and another at the far eastern unit at the Naval Air Facility in Atsugi, Japan.

Soviet overflights resumed with the CIA flying Operation Soft Touch missions over Russia and China. An August mission provided the first photographs of the Baikonur Cosmodrome near Tyuratam that the CIA was unaware of until then. Other flights examined the Semipalatinsk nuclear test site and the Saryshagan missile test site. These occurred at a time when the U.S. president sought to avoid angering the Soviets as he worked to achieve a nuclear test ban.

The Soviets were by now trying to shoot down even U-2 flights that never entered the Soviet airspace. The details in their diplomatic protests showed that Soviet radar operators could effectively track the aircraft.

By now, the Soviets had developed their overflight aircraft, flying variants of the Yak-25, which, in addition to photographing various parts of the world through the early 1960s, also acted as a target for the new MiG-19 and MiG-21 interceptors to practice for the U-2.

Lockheed attempted to hide the aircraft by painting it in a blue-black color called Sea Blue to blend in against the darkness of space. The weight of the paint robbed the U-2 of 1,500 feet altitude. The CIA countered this and the Soviet threat by powering the aircraft with the more powerful J75-P13 engine, which increased its maximum altitude an additional 2,500 feet, to 74,600 feet.

The Missile Gap

In August 1957, the U.S. had watched as Russia launched the first intercontinental ballistic missile (ICBM). In October that year, the CIA woke up one morning to the beeping sound of the Sputnik 1 in orbit. It became worse. The United States watched Russia place the first man in space. Then, it launched the first woman into space and then the first three cosmonauts into space. The first spacecraft to hit the moon followed.

The United States knows now that this all happened thanks to the anonymous chief designer Sergei Pavlovich Korolev, head of the OKB-1 experimental design bureau #1 and Russia's most senior rocket scientist. The United States had no counterpart in its space exploration program.

In its effort to beat the United States to place a man on the moon, the Russians realized the lack of infrastructure to design a gargantuan engine. Whereas the United States planned using five rocket engines to power its launch vehicle, the Russians designed their N-1 rocket to launch using thirty lesser-powered engines. These engines used a full cycle design that the United States considered too risky.

The successful launch of Sputnik 1 on October 4, 1957, gave credence to Soviet claims about the progress of its ICBM program. The surprise launch began the Sputnik crisis in the United States. In December 1958, Khrushchev boasted that a Soviet missile could deliver a five-megaton warhead eight thousand miles. The United States feared the Soviets' SS-6 Sapwood missile program. The fear that they might have a three-to-one temporary advantage in ICBMs during the early 1960s caused widespread concern in the United States about the existence of a "missile gap." The Russians had better rocket engines capable of doing things that the United States could not do. The space race superiority was a wonderful period for the Russians.

Detachment A, which had earlier deployed to England on a PCS basis (without dependents or household effects) in anticipation of a full tour in England, encountered unforeseen events that necessitated a hurried move to Germany. Before the year was out, the detachment moved to another German base before returning to the ZI after eighteen months overseas.

This experience led to the decision of detachments deploying TDY (temporary duty) rather than PCS (permanent change of station) given the inability to predict the length of stay at a given base. General Cabell approved this change of policy in August 1956 when Detachment B deployed TDY to Adana, Turkey, without dependents or household effects. In March 1957, Detachment C deployed to Japan on the same basis.

On September 25, 1957, the project director wrote to the deputy director, support (DD/S), to advise him of the desired change in policy. With the prospect of continuing Project AQUATONE operations overseas at least through the calendar year 1958, he suggested they make plans to have the dependents of project personnel join them at overseas locations. He pointed how the concept to date centered on maintaining a high degree of mobility for personnel and equipment.

The events of the past eighteen months had shown the political impact of having an AQUATONE unit within the borders of a friendly country less than anticipated, and this consequently shifted them to a fixed-base concept with a forward staging capability. A fixed-base operation made them consistent with the secrecy concerned of including dependents for unit personnel. The concept included the CIA's contract pilots, some of them married with dependents wanting to join them overseas.

The DD/S approved them establishing this policy and initiating a crash program to prepare dependent housing. They accomplished this at Adana by rental and renovation of local economy houses and using trailers shipped from the United States.

In Atsugi, they remodeled existing agency billets and constructed more units through a local builder. This program cost total several hundred thousand dollars in each case. The CIA could not recoup this cost when the two detachments returned to the ZI.

The CIA continued its U-2 flights while developing a replacement. With the failure of the CIA's Project RAINBOW to reduce the radar cross-section of the U-2, preliminary work began at Lockheed in late 1957 to develop a follow-on aircraft to overfly the Soviet Union. Under Project GUSTO, the designs were nicknamed "Archangel," after the U-2 program, which had been known as "Angel."

Virtually every mission flown by the U-2 produced invaluable intelligence on what the Soviet Union was up to with its bomber, missile and nuclear capabilities. Soviet Overflight Mission 4035 located and photographed the Soviet missile test facility at Tyuratam at a distance. Other flights examined the Semipalatinsk nuclear test site and the Saryshagan missile test site. Because of Eisenhower's increasing cautiousness, only five more occurred during the year before the May 1960 incident that stopped all manned overflights of the Soviet Union.

The twelfth and thirteenth Soviet overflights discovered the nuclear weapons testing facility in Semipalatinsk and revealed many of the ground zeros from previous nuclear tests. The U-2 mapped the whole of Tibet, the Soviet missile test center at Kapustin Yar and the Soviet Far East naval aviation bases at Komsomolsk and Khabarovsk.

Toward the end of March 1957, seven U-2s staged from Eielson and returned during an operation code named Congo Maiden, where they photographed the Soviet Northern Siberian coastline to determine the status of upgraded World War II Soviet airfields in this frozen region. They enabled the CIA to evaluate Soviet air defenses in case a preemptive U.S. strike on the Arctic airfields became necessary along the extreme eastern and northern coastlines of Siberia.

Bissell suggested bringing the British into the program to increase the number of overflights. Prime Minister Harold Macmillan agreed with the plan and sent four Royal Air Force officers of Laughlin Air Force Base in Texas for training in May 1958. On July 8, the senior British pilot, Squadron Leader Christopher H. Walker, died when his U-2 malfunctioned and crashed near Wayside, Texas. The CIA did not disclose the circumstances of this first death involving the U-2 for over fifty years. The CIA selected and sent another pilot to replace Walker.

After training, the group of Royal Air Force U-2 pilots arrived in Turkey in November 1958. The United States and the United Kingdom remained jointly involved following the CIA's Detachment B from Adana, which provided valuable intelligence during the 1958 Lebanon crisis.

The CIA and Eisenhower viewed using British pilots as a way of increasing plausible deniability for the flights. The CIA saw British participation as a way of obtaining additional Soviet overflights the president would not authorize. The United Kingdom gained the ability to target flights toward areas of the world of less interest to the United States and to avoid another Suez-like interruption of U-2 photographs.

Although the Royal Air Force unit operated as part of Detachment B, the United Kingdom received title to the U-2s its pilots flew, and Eisenhower wrote about the nations conducting two complementary programs rather than a joint one because of the separate lines of authority.

While most British flights occurred over the Middle East during the two years the United Kingdom program existed, the Brits flew two successful missions over Soviet missile test sites. One overflight occurred in December and another in February 1960. Neither proved nor disproved the missile gap. Nonetheless, the British flights' success contributed to Eisenhower's authorization of one overflight in April. Like Eisenhower, Macmillan approved the Soviet overflights. Direct British involvement in overflights ended after the May 1960 U-2 downing incident. Although four pilots remained stationed in California until 1974, the CIA's official history of the program states no Royal Air Force pilots ever conducted another overflight in an agency U-2. Even though their U-2 experience remained secret, between 1960 and 1961, the first four pilots received the U.S. Air Force Cross.

In April 1958, the CIA source Pyotr Sehisonovich Popov told his handler, George Kisevalter, of a senior KGB official boasting of having "full technical details" of the U-2. Bissell concluded the project to have a leak. However, the CIA never identified the source of the leak. Many speculated it was a radar operator at a U-2 base in Japan, the same Lee Harvey Oswald who assassinated President Kennedy.

On May 15, 1959, Lyle Rudd flew the nineteenth Soviet overflight from NAS Cubi Point in the Philippines, flying nine hours and forty minutes in the air, the longest operational U-2 mission to date, covering 4,200 miles.

Operation Hot Shop on June 9 and 18, 1959, obtained the first telemetry ever of a Soviet R-7 ICBM during the first stage burn—eighty seconds after launch. Three months later, Detachment B overflights of Israel discovered the Dimona nuclear reactor and processing facility under construction.

On December 6, 1959, Squadron Leader Robbie Robinson flew the twenty-first Soviet overflight, Mission 8005, as the first mission flown by the Royal Air Force out of Peshawar. The following flight by the RAF discovered a new Soviet bomber at Kazan. Robinson captured eight Tu-22 BLINDER aircraft on film. From there, he headed south down the Volga over the missile factory at Dnepropetrovsk.

On April 19, 1960, Bob Ericson flew the twenty-third Soviet overflight, Mission 4155, Operation Square Deal, which the Soviet Air Defense organization manually tracked the whole time. Several MiG-19s made unsuccessful attempts to shoot down the aircraft.

Khrushchev claimed in his memoir that a new Soviet surface-to-air missile should have shot down the April flight had the missile crews not reacted too slowly. By this time, the CIA concluded that the Soviet SAMs had "a high probability of a successful intercept at seventy thousand feet, providing they detected the plane in sufficient time to alert the site."

Despite the now much greater risk, the CIA failed to stop the overflights because of overconfidence from the years of successful missions and because of the strong demand for more missile site photos. By this time, the U-2 was the major source of covert intelligence on the Soviet Union; the aircraft photographed 15 percent of the country, resulting in 5,500 separate intelligence reports. Eisenhower authorized one more overflight to occur no later than May 1, 1960, because of the important Paris Summit of the Big Four on May 16.

On September 24, 1959, while conducting a test flight in Article 360 from Detachment C in Atsugi in Japan, Tom Crull encountered problems on a test flight and eventually ran out of fuel. With great skill, he managed to dead-stick the aircraft onto a small civilian airfield in Fujisawa, where curious Japanese civilians promptly surrounded and photographed it.

The CIA shipped the damaged U-2C aircraft back to Lockheed in the United States for repairs. Article 360 returned to Detachment B at Adana in Turkey, where it gained a reputation as a "Hangar Queen" for a variety of reasons. As a matter of fate, Gary Powers drew Article 360 to fly on Mission 4154, Operation Grand Slam.

When the U-2 became operational in June 1956, an official predicted a useful lifetime over the USSR of two years. Its first flight over Soviet territory revealed the Soviet defense warning system detecting and tracking it. The U-2 remained a unique and invaluable source of intelligence information for four years. Everything changed near Sverdlovsk on May Day, May 1, 1960, when Russian missiles shot down Francis Gary Powers in Article 360, the Hangar Queen. All eyes turned on Area 51 and the U-2's proposed replacement, the Mach 3 A-12. The U-2 continued flying, but not over Russia.

The CIA chose for the fateful mission—the twenty-fourth deep-penetration Soviet overflight, Operation Grand Slam—an ambitious flight plan for the first crossing of the Soviet Union from Peshawar, Pakistan, to Bodø, Norway; previous flights always exited in the direction from which they entered. The route permitted visits to Tyuratam, Sverdlovsk, Kotlas, Severodvinsk and Murmansk.

The CIA chose Francis Gary Powers, the most experienced pilot, for the flight. Powers had flown twenty-seven missions at this point. After several delays, the flight, Mission 4154, in a U-2C known as the Hangar Queen, finally occurred on May Day 1960.

Out of 365 days in a year, the CIA could not have picked a worse day to fly over Russia. On May Day each year, the United States and its allies went on military alert because this was an important Soviet holiday. Each May Day, the Soviet Union held massive parades to show off its war equipment. Also, this being a Soviet holiday meant much less air traffic than usual.

Frank Powers's mission that day was to fly over Russia and land at Bodø, Norway, where Marty Knutson was waiting to take the aircraft on its return flight. Knutson was sitting in Norway breathing oxygen and preparing to don his pressurized space suit to take over the aircraft that Powers was flying. At Bodø, they knew something was amiss when the aircraft failed to arrive within the required timeframe.

The Soviet's radar systems detected the Hangar Queen flying fifteen miles outside the Soviet border and tracked it over Sverdlovsk. Four and a half hours into the flight, one of three SA-2 missiles detonated behind the aircraft at 70,500 feet. Another missile hit a Soviet interceptor attempting to reach the American aircraft. Powers survived the near miss.

The CIA did not know the Russians had captured Powers. Nor did the CIA know that the crash had failed to destroy the U-2 and it was in Soviet hands. The conspired cover story went into effect with NASA issuing a press release using the CIA's cover story about a U-2 conducting weather research that may have strayed off course after the pilot "reported difficulties with his oxygen equipment."

The CIA rushed a U-2 from North Base at Edwards AFB to the NASA Dryden hangars to bolster the cover-up. NASA quickly painted NASA markings on it with a fictitious NASA serial number. NASA put the plane on display for the news media photo op at the NASA Flight Research Center at Edwards AFB.

Bissell and other project officials believed it impossible to survive a U-2 accident from above seventy thousand feet. Consequently, they used the preexisting cover story.

On May 3, the National Aeronautics and Space Administration, the successor to NACA, announced one of its aircraft missing while making a high-altitude research flight in Turkey. The government planned to say, if necessary, that the NASA aircraft had drifted with an incapacitated pilot across the Soviet border. NACA director Dr. Hugh L. Dryden's press release stated the U-2 aircraft was conducting weather research for NACA with air force support and had gone missing and was presumed lost while operating overseas.

Khrushchev learned of America's NASA cover story and developed a political trap for Eisenhower. By remaining silent, Khrushchev lured the Americans into reinforcing the cover story. As the saying goes, the Russians gave the Americans enough slack rope to hang themselves. Politically, the United States did exactly that. At this point, Soviet premier Nikita Khrushchev exposed the cover-up by revealing on May 7 that Powers was alive and had confessed to spying on the Soviet Union.

Eisenhower turned down Dulles's offer to resign and publicly took full responsibility for the incident on May 11. By then, the CIA had canceled all overflights. The Paris Summit collapsed after Khrushchev, as the first speaker, demanded an apology from the United States, which Eisenhower refused.

Powers had received little instruction on what to do during an interrogation. Although he said that he could reveal everything since the Soviets could learn what they wanted from the aircraft, Powers did his best to conceal classified information while appearing to cooperate. His trial began on August 17, 1960. Powers, who apologized on the advice of his Soviet defense counsel, received a three-year sentence in prison. However, on February 10, 1962, the USSR exchanged him and American student Frederic Pryor for Rudolf Abel at the Glienicke Bridge between West Berlin and Potsdam, Germany.

Two CIA investigations found that Powers performed well during the interrogation and "complied with his obligations as an American citizen during this period." Nonetheless, the government was reluctant to reinstate him to the USAF because of its statements that the U-2 program was civilian. The CIA promised to do so after his CIA employment ended. Powers resolved the dilemma by choosing to work for Lockheed as a U-2 pilot.

NASA, concerned about the damage to its reputation in the wake of the Powers U-2 affair, disengaged from the CIA and no longer provided it the cover story support needed for its covert U-2 operations.

Four months later, the May Day incident resulted in a cessation of overflight operations. The CIA reduced the number of pilots in Detachments B and C and then returned them to the United States. Other air activities, however, increased, including the U-2 successor program. Satellite activity and clandestine air operations in various areas of the world and the Far East increased as well. So did the staffing of cadres for the detachments at Eglin, Kadena and the new detachment in Taiwan.

The Russians used the debris of Powers's aircraft to design a copy under the name Berijev S-13. They discarded the Berijev S-13 for the MiG-25R and reconnaissance satellites.

From 1956 to 1960, U-2 aircraft flew twenty-four missions over the USSR. Detachment A flew six missions, Detachment C flew four and Detachment B flew fourteen, including Powers's flight.

Unknown to Bissell at the time, the clouds of war were gathering much closer to home with Cuban president Fulgencio Batista fleeing Cuba for the Dominican Republic ahead of the Cuban revolution, making Fidel Castro the leader of Cuba. Although he refrained from declaring that the country was going communist, Cuba inspired guerrilla movements to spring up across Latin America.

Meanwhile, the troops that President Truman had committed to fighting France's war in Vietnam were still there and still engaged in a proxy fight with Russia and the National Front for the Liberation of Vietnam, which was threatening to overthrow the government of South Vietnam.

The CIA's U-2 program conducted eight overflights over communist territory and had not found any Myasishchev M-4 Bison bombers at the nine bases they had visited. The U-2 proved the feared bomber gap did not exist.

Changes to the CIA Program

Immediately after the Soviets announced that Powers was alive, the CIA evacuated the British pilots from Detachment B, as Turkey did not know of their presence in the country. The end of Soviet overflights meant that Detachment B would soon leave Turkey, and in July, Detachment C would leave Japan following a Japanese governmental request.

Both detachments merged into Detachment G at Edwards Air Force Base, California, where the CIA had relocated the U-2 program after nuclear testing forced it to move from Area 51 in 1957.

By the next U-2 flight, in October 1960 over Cuba, the National Security Council Special Group had replaced the previous informal procedure in which the president personally approved or disapproved each flight after discussion with advisors. The expansion of satellite intelligence partly compensated for the overflights' end, but because U-2 photographs remained superior to satellite imagery, future administrations considered resumption at times, such as during the Berlin crisis of 1961.

In November 1960, the deputy director of plans, Dick Bissell, contacted Colonel William Burke, the chief of the development project division.

He notified Burke of his intent to take advantage of the reduction of Detachment B. He hoped to achieve a reduction in the authorized strength of the division, thus reflecting the gradual shift of resources away from the U-2 into new programs.

The staff remained static until February 1962. Bissell left the CIA, and a six-month period of reorganization ensued. In May 1965, the CIA separated its satellite operations from the other activities within OSA under the Special Projects Staff (SPS). Effective September 15, 1965, the CIA established the Office of Special Projects within the CIA's Directorate for Science and Technology (DS&T) to carry on these operations.

In March–April 1963, CIA satellites noted the Russians were building a massive launch pad at the Baikonur Cosmodrome in Kazakhstan. The size of the assembly building had all the earmarks for a very large launch vehicle. With the CIA, it was, "Hello. What is going on here?"

A very large causeway led up to two launch pads side by side. In the analysis, back in Washington, the launch pads were firsthand evidence of the preparations of a huge rocket. The activity could mean only one thing: the United States was in a space race to the moon.

EPILOGUE

Area 51 wasn't meant to be a permanent base. The CIA acquired Area 51 and built the Groom Lake facility in 1955 for test flying the CIA's U-2 reconnaissance plane and abandoned the facility when the U-2s moved out to become operational.

At the time, neither Dick Bissell with the CIA nor Lockheed's Kelly Johnson expected the U-2 reconnaissance plane to be perpetually invulnerable to Soviet counter-countermeasures. Thus, shortly after the operational commitment of the U-2 in June 1956, research had already begun to improve its survivability and extend the program's lifetime. The outgrowth of the early studies became a subproject of AQUATONE called Project RAINBOW. Early estimates showed a high probability of success in U-2 overflights based on the U-2's operating altitude. Its high penetration and operating altitude were expected to diminish the possibility of detection and accurate tracking by hostile defense systems. Unfortunately, the Soviet air defense warning system proved up to the challenge.

The U-2 was not only detected by radar as it penetrated denied territory but was also tracked quite accurately in its earliest flights over satellite and Soviet areas. This state of affairs could only lead to an intensification of Soviet defensive efforts and the consequent shortening of the U-2's usefulness as a reconnaissance aircraft.

The Soviet Union was not the only threat to the CIA's U-2 reconnaissance. From the start, General LeMay had stated his intent to take the U-2s away from the CIA once the agency got them flying.

The CIA accomplished what it was supposed to do: it disputed the existence of the feared bomber gap and the missile gap.

Two years after the U-2s left, the CIA returned, bringing new life to Area 51 following a project code named GUSTO that confirmed the need to replace the U-2. In September 1959, at Area 51, the CIA had returned to begin base construction to support Project OXCART, the Mach 3+, high-flying stealth Lockheed A-12 Archangel to replace the U-2 Angel and resume overflights of the Soviet Union.

In early 1960, following the Cuban revolution, which propelled Fidel Castro to power on January 1, 1959, Castro sought and failed to gain a meeting with U.S. president Eisenhower to get relief from a U.S. economic embargo. Consequently, Cuba turned to Soviet premier Nikita Khrushchev for economic and political aid.

The Soviet Union saw where supporting Cuba gave the Soviet Union an opportunity to spread its threat of communism to within ninety miles of the United States. The CIA responded to this new intelligence-gathering need by modifying the six agency U-2Fs at Edwards AFB, California, to allow in-flight refueling for Detachment G, which was having to make its many overflights of Cuba from Laughlin AFB, Texas.

In April 1961, General LeMay's Strategic Air Command U-2s were operating over Cuba during the aftermath of the failed Bay of Pigs military invasion of Cuba undertaken by Bissell's CIA-sponsored paramilitary group Brigade 2506. On March 17, 1960, the CIA put forward its plan for the overthrow of Castro's administration to the U.S. National Security Council, where President Dwight D. Eisenhower gave his support. On April 4, 1961, President Kennedy approved the Bay of Pigs plan.

The invasion had started when President Kennedy received a telegram from Nikita Khrushchev in Moscow, stating the Russians would not allow the United States to enter Cuba, and implied swift nuclear retribution to the United States heartland if their warnings went unheeded. After a U.S. bombing run against the Cuban air force, a group of 1,500 armed exiles landed at the Bay of Pigs on the southern coast. As the invasion faltered, President John F. Kennedy called off the promised airstrikes, leaving the CIA and the Cuban exiles at the fate of Castro, who executed the CIA-supported exiles, whom he denounced as invaders. Following the failed Bay of Pigs invasion of 1961, Castro declared Cuba a socialist republic.

President Kennedy was deeply dispirited and angered and reportedly said he wanted to "splinter the CIA into a thousand pieces and scatter it to the winds." Later in the month, Russia and East Germany began construction on the Berlin Wall to separate Germany physically.

Sure enough, the end was in sight for the CIA U-2 reconnaissance when President Kennedy ordered the CIA to allow the U.S. Air Force to fly the CIA's better ECM-equipped U-2s during the Cuban crisis in 1962. Major Rudolf Anderson Jr. was the only combat casualty of the Cuban Missile Crisis when killed while flying CIA Article 343 U-2. NASA was also a challenge, already flying CIA aircraft in August 1974 when the CIA's U-2 manned reconnaissance operations ended. The CIA transferred all its U-2 aircraft, equipment and logistical support parts directly to the U.S. Air Force.

With Project OXCART, the CIA would design, build and fly 2,580 flights out of Area 51 in America's first stealth plane, the A-12, a plane that flew up to ninety thousand feet at speeds above Mach 3, the fastest and highest-flying plane ever. The CIA's A-12 would fly twenty-six Operation BLACK SHIELD reconnaissance missions over Southeast Asia during the Vietnam War and three missions over North Korea during the North Korean seizure of the USS *Pueblo* and its crew, held for over a year. The CIA lost two of its project pilots in the A-12. The six BLACK SHIELD pilots earned the CIA's highest award, the Intelligence Star for Valor. One received his award

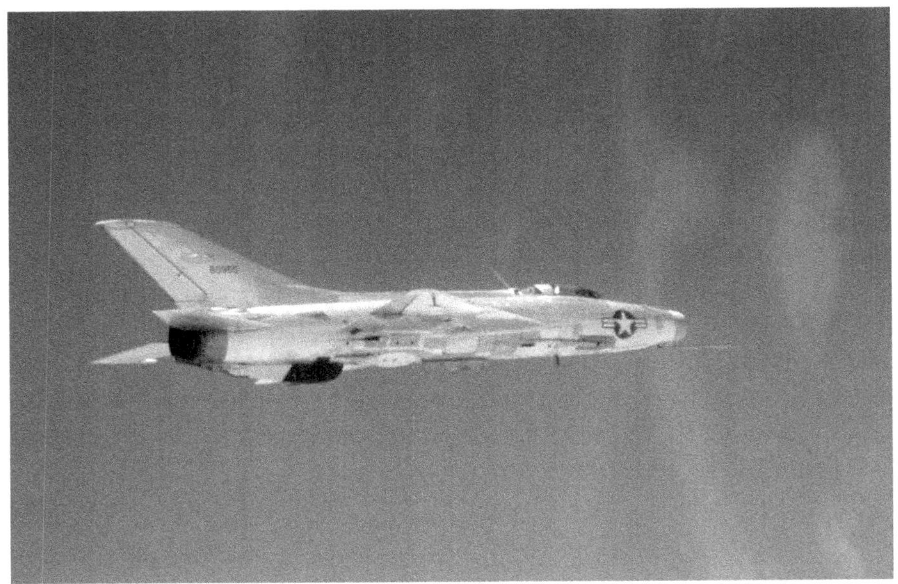

Soviet MiG-21 exploited at Area 51 by the author during Project HAVE DOUGHNUT. *USAF.*

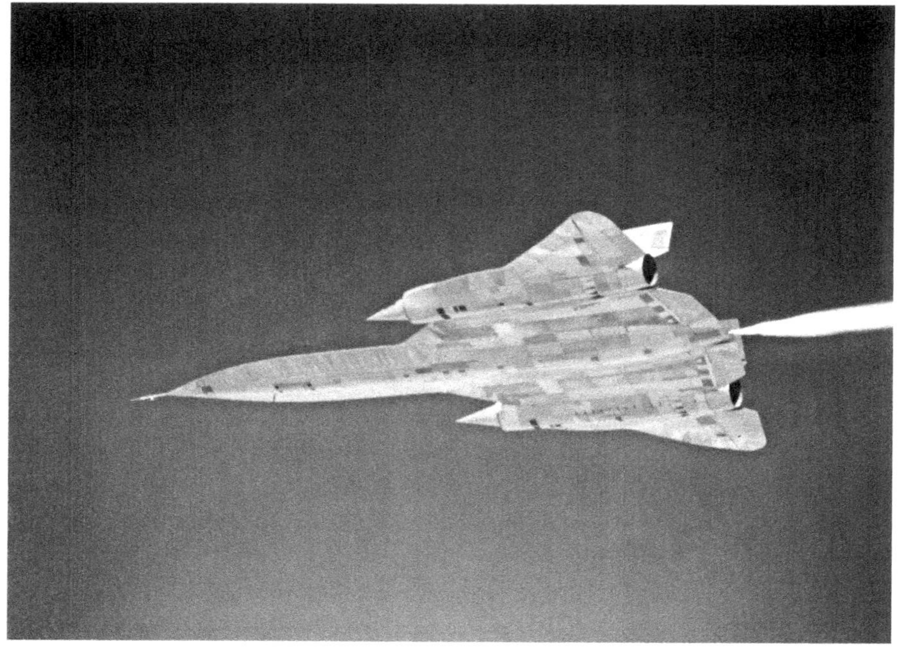

A-12 Archangel jettisoning fuel over Area 51 for landing during Project OXCART. *CIA via TD Barnes Collection.*

posthumously. When the OXCART left Area 51, the CIA stayed for a new line of business: the exploitation of enemy aircraft.

At Area 51, the CIA support in obtaining and exploiting the Soviet MiG-21 Fishbed sparked the U.S. Navy to initiate its Top Gun Weapons School that reversed a 9:1 kill ratio of the navy aircrews fighting in the Vietnam War. The MiG-17 Fresco exploitation projects sparked the U.S. Air Force to initiate its Red Flag Exercises that reversed the 9:1 kill ratio of the U.S. Air Force fighting in Vietnam and every war it has fought since. These and additional exploitation projects maintained U.S. Navy and Air Force air superiority in all wars and enemy engagements since the Vietnam War.

All the credit goes to the CIA for establishing Area 51 as a technology laboratory and business that continues today.

GLOSSARY

AEC: The United States Atomic Energy Commission was an agency of the United States government established after World War II by Congress to foster and control the peacetime development of atomic science and technology.

CAT: Civil Air Transport.

ECCM: electronic counter-countermeasures.

ECM: electronic countermeasures.

NACA: National Advisory Committee for Aeronautics, the institutionalized aeronautical research agency preceeding NASA.

NASA: National Aeronautics and Space Administration, the U.S. federal agency responsible for the civilian space program.

Nevada Test Site: Also known as the Nevada Proving Grounds, the site established in 1951 in Nevada for the testing of nuclear devices.

pogo: Wheeled struts that supported the wings of the U-2 plane during taxi.

Project AQUATONE: Initial program name for CIA-sponsored U-2 reconnaissance plane.

Project BALD EAGLE: USAF counterpart to CIA's AQUATONE; big-wing B-57 Canberra became RB-57D.

Project GUSTO: A 1957 advisory committee selected by the CIA to select a successor to the U-2.

Project OXCART: The CIA project at Groom Lake to design, build and operate the A-12 Blackbird reconnaissance plane to replace the U-2.

RATSCAT: radar target scatter site.

reconnaissance: An overt act of reconnaissance in the field; a search made to produce useful military information to inspect, observe or survey for enemy positions, strengths and intent, etc. No longer just military purposes in this blended technology age.

SCR: signal corps radio #584.

spying: Work for a government or other organization by secretly collecting information about enemies.

TO&E: table of organization and equipment.

Watertown: Name of the Groom Lake facility in Nevada during the CIA U-2 Project AQUATONE.

BIBLIOGRAPHY

Bissell, Richard M., Jr., with Jonathan E. Lewis and Frances T. Pudlo. *Reflections of a Cold Warrior: From Yalta to the Bay of Pigs*. New Haven, CT: Yale University Press, 1996.

Brown, William H. "J58/SR-71 Propulsion Integration." *Center for the Study of Intelligence* 26, no. 2 (Summer 1982): 15–23.

Central Intelligence Agency, Office of Special Activities. "Chronology, 1954–68." Declassified, June 2003. The CIA and the U-2 Program 1954–1974 by Gregory W. Pedlow and Donald E. Weizenbach, History Staff, Center for the Study of Intelligence, CIA, 1998.

CIA BYE 2986–65. Project Oxcart and Operation Black Shield Briefing Notes. October 20, 1965.

Crickmore, Paul F. *Lockheed SR-71: The Secret Missions Exposed.* London: Osprey, 1996.

Drendel, Lou. *SR-71 Blackbird in Action.* Carrollton, TX: Squadron/Signal Publications, 1982.

Goodall, James. *SR-71 Blackbird.* Carrollton, TX: Squadron/Signal Publications, 1995.

Goodall, James, and Jay Miller. *Lockheed's SR-71 "Blackbird" Family: A-12, F-12, M-21, D-21, SR-71*. Hinckley, UK: Midland Publishing, 2002.

Graham, Richard H. *SR-71 Blackbird: Stories, Tales, and Legends*. St. Paul, MN: Zenith Press, 2002.

———. *SR-71 Reveals: The Inside Story*. Osceola, WI: Motorbooks International Publishing, 1996.

Haines, Gerald K. "The CIA's Role in the Study of UFOs, 1947–90." *Center for the Study of Intelligence* 41, no. 1 (1997): 67–84.

Helms, Richard, with William Hood. *A Look Over My Shoulder: A Life in the Central Intelligence Agency*. New York: Random House, 2003.

Jenkins, Dennis R. *Lockheed SR-71/YF-12 Blackbirds*. North Branch, MN: Specialty Press, 1997.

Johnson, Clarence L. "Development of the Lockheed SR-71 Blackbird." *Center for the Study of Intelligence* 26, no. 2 (Summer 1982): 3–14.

———. "Kelly," with Maggie Smith. *Kelly: More than My Share of It All*. Washington, D.C.: Smithsonian Institution Press, 1985.

Landis, Tony R. *Lockheed Blackbird Family: A-12, YF-12, D-21/M-21 and SR-71 Photo Scrapbook*. North Branch, MN: Specialty Press, 2010.

McIninch, Thomas P. "The OXCART Story." *Center for the Study of Intelligence* 15, no. 1 (Winter 1971): 1–25.

Merlin, Peter. *From Archangel to Senior Crown: Design and Development of the Blackbird*. Reston, VA: American Institute of Aeronautics and Astronautics, 2008.

Miller, Jay. *Lockheed Martin's Skunk Works*. Leicester, UK: Midland Publishing, 1995.

Pedlow, Gregory W., and Donald E. Welzenbach. *The Central Intelligence Agency and Overhead Reconnaissance: The U-2 and OXCART Programs, 1954–1974*. Washington, D.C.: Central Intelligence Agency, 1992. Chapter 6 on OXCART declassified October 2004.

Remak, Jeannette, and Joseph Ventolo Jr. *The Archangel and the OXCART: The Lockheed A-12 Blackbirds and the Dawning of Mach III Reconnaissance*. Bloomington, IN: Trafford Publishing Co., 2008.

———. *A-12 Blackbird Declassified*. St. Paul, MN: MBI Publishing Co., 2001.

Rich, Ben R., and Leo Janos. *Skunk Works: A Personal Memoir of My Years at Lockheed*. Boston: Little, Brown, 1994.

Richelson, Jeffrey T. *The Wizards of Langley: Inside the CIA's Directorate of Science and Technology*. Boulder, CO: Westview Press, 2001.

Robarge, David, PhD. *Archangel: CIA's Supersonic A-12 Reconnaissance Aircraft*. 2nd ed. Washington, D.C.: Center for the Study of Intelligence, Central Intelligence Agency, Government Printing Office, January 2012.

Suhler, Paul A. *From Rainbow to GUSTO: Stealth and the Design of the Lockheed Blackbird*. Reston, VA: American Institute of Aeronautics and Astronautics, 2009.

Sweetman, Bill. *Lockheed Stealth*. St. Paul, MN: MBI Publishing, 2001.

Wheelon, Albert D. "And the Truth Shall Keep You Free: Recollections by the First Deputy Director of Science and Technology." *Center for the Study of Intelligence* 39, no. 1 (Spring 1995): 73–78.

Whittenbury, John R. "From Archangel to OXCART: Design Evolution of the Lockheed A-12, First of the Blackbirds." PowerPoint presentation, August 2007.

Wings of Fame. London: Aerospace Publishing, 1997.

Reference Documents

"History of the OXCART Program." Burbank, CA: Lockheed Aircraft Corporation, July 1, 1968. Declassified, August 2007.

Johnson, Clarence L. "Archangel Log." Undated.

Websites

archive.org/stream/HistoryOfTheOfficeOfSpecialActivitiesFromInceptionTo1

area51specialprojects.com

blackbirds.net

roadrunnerinternationale.com

www.habu.org

www.Lockheedmartin.com

INDEX

A

Acheson, Dean 26, 28, 29
Alderman, Ken 157
Allen, Edward L. 34
Allson, Bill 158
Atkins, Dick 157
Atomic Energy Commission 28, 72, 73, 76, 77, 78, 80, 88, 109, 163, 164
Atomic Proving Grounds 74, 80, 82, 164

B

B-57 44, 45, 46, 47
Baird, Walter 71
Baker, Barry 155
Baker, James 32, 46, 70, 71
Barnes, Jim 155
BEACON HILL Report 32, 34, 45
Bell Laboratories 32, 45
Berrli, Colonel Stan 94
Birkhead, Tom 155
Bissell, Richard 65, 86, 90, 104, 114, 136, 137, 138, 139, 142, 160
Boeing 31, 45, 67, 117
Boyd, Warren 157
Byrnes, James 22

C

C-124 97, 147
Campbell, John 157
Carey, Howard 147, 156
Carter, John H. 37
Central Intelligence Group 20, 21, 22, 28
Cherbonneaux, Jim 155
CL-282 33, 37, 39, 40, 46, 47, 48, 53, 56, 58, 64, 98
Cody, Howard 157
Convair 40, 45

Cuban Missile Crisis 71, 177
Culbertson, Colonel Allman 98
Cull, Tom 155
Cunningham, James 91, 114, 123, 128

D

David Clark Co. 121
Davis, Saville 32
Delap, Jack 109
Donovan, Allen 32, 48
Donovan, Bill 15, 17
Douglas Aircraft Company 34, 164
Dowling, David 155
Dragon Lady 64, 98, 158
Dulles, Allen 47, 49, 50, 52, 54, 63, 81, 136, 138, 154
Dunaway, Glendon 147, 154

E

Edens, Buster 155
Edgerton, Germeshausen & Grier 143
Edwards Air Force Base 36, 161, 163, 171, 173, 176
Eielson Air Force Base 161, 168
Eisenhower, President Dwight 33, 43, 49, 50, 63, 65, 74, 111, 133, 134, 135, 140, 158, 176
Emerling, Ed 157
Ericson, Bob 155, 157, 169

F

F-104 37, 39, 106
Fairchild Aircraft 39, 45, 48
Federal Bureau of Investigation 16, 85, 112
Federal Protection Services 74
First Weather Reconnaissance Squadron 142, 145
4070th Special Activities Squadron 110
4028th Squadron 157

G

Gardner, Trevor 47, 48, 51, 58, 74, 96, 137
Garvin, Louis 109, 110, 122
Geary, Colonel Leo P. 90, 98, 111, 117, 123
Gibbs, Colonel Jack 135, 136, 165
Giebelstadt Army Airfield 149, 156, 158, 165
Goldmark, Peter 32
Goudey, Ray 106, 107
Grace, Frank G. 155
Groom Lake 72, 73, 74, 75, 76, 77, 80, 82, 91, 92, 96, 97, 98, 102, 164, 175

H

Hall, Bill 155
Haupt, Ray 157
Heyser, Richard "Steve" 158
Homer, Richard 104

Hycon Manufacturing Company 47, 58, 68, 70, 128, 132

I

Incirlik Air Base 155

J

Jackson, Joe 157
Johnson, Kelly 37, 39, 45, 46, 47, 50, 52, 53, 63, 65, 66, 68, 70, 73, 91, 96, 97, 103, 104, 106, 111, 116, 143, 160, 175
Jones, E.K. 155

K

Kammerer, Dorsey 71, 74
Khrushchev, Nikita 35, 147, 149, 172, 176
Kiefer, Eugene 37
Killian, James 33, 140
King, Joe 157
Knutson, Marty 115, 147, 153, 171
Kodak 32
Koon, Brigadier General Ralph E. 123
Kratt, Jacob 125

L

LaCombe, Bennie 158
Land, Edwin 32, 137, 140
Laughlin Air Force Base 157, 158, 161, 168, 176
Leavitt, Dick 158
Leghorn, Lieutenant Colonel Richard 33
LeMay, General Curtis 14, 31, 35, 39, 40, 44, 47, 54, 55, 56, 57, 64, 94, 110, 175, 176
LeVier, Tony 71, 72, 74, 100, 102, 106
Lien, Lieutenant Colonel Art 109
Lovelace Foundation for Medical Education and Research 112

M

MacArthur, General Douglas A. 28
MacArthur, John 155
March Air Force Base 94, 96, 114, 122, 129, 130
Marshall Plan 14
Martin Aircraft Company 44, 45
Massachusetts Institute of Technology 33, 37, 140
Matye, Bob 75, 104, 106, 109, 123
McCarthy, Senator Joseph 23, 50
McConnell, Colonel Landon 91, 136
McFadden, William 70
McGraw, Richard 157
McMurry, Bill 155
Meierdierck, Hank 110, 121, 129, 140
MiG-15 30, 153
MiG-17 36, 153, 178
Miller, Herbert 71
Miller, Stewart 32
Mills, General John S. 92
Molotov, Vyacheslav 13
Mullin, Major R.E. 109

N

NACA 35, 139, 141, 145, 149, 152, 154, 171
NASA 35, 76, 77, 80, 171, 172, 177
National Security Act 21, 22
National Security Council 48, 49, 50, 176
Nellis Air Force Base 164
Nelson, Colonel Douglas T. 54
Nevada Proving Grounds 74
Nevett, Dick 157
Newton, Richard 96, 97, 109, 163
Nole, Jack 157, 163
Norton Air Force Base 128, 130
Norton, Garrison 47, 104

O

O'Donnell, Lieutenant General Emmett 94
Office of Research and Reports 29, 34
Office of Scientific Intelligence 34, 47, 51, 137, 149
Office of Strategic Services 15, 16, 17, 19, 20, 22, 23, 30, 49
OILSTONE 52, 58, 64, 65, 90, 94
1007th Air Intelligence Service Group 94, 113
Operation Grand Slam 170
Operation Soft Touch 165
Oswald, Lee Harvey 169
Overhage, Carl 32
Overstreet, Carl 147, 150, 151, 152, 154

P

Perkin-Elmer Corperation 32, 68
Perkin, Richard 32, 68
Powers, Gary 136, 155, 170
Pratt & Whitney 40, 52, 67, 117
Project AQUATONE 52, 57, 59, 74, 86, 94, 110, 114, 135, 136, 138, 151, 158, 167
Project GENETRIX 133, 134, 135, 139
Project GUSTO 136, 167
Project LINCOLN 32
Project OARFISH 63
Project OXCART 176, 177
Project RAINBOW 136, 142, 154, 160, 167, 175
Purcell, Edward M. 32
Putt, Lieutenant General Donald L. 39, 52, 57, 58

Q

Quarles, Donald 137

R

Rand, Al 155
RAND Corporation 34, 133
RB-47 31
RB-57D 158
Reynolds Electrical and Engineering Co 78
Ridenour, Louis 32
Ritland, Colonel Osmond 58, 72, 90, 92, 104, 123, 135
Robertson, Colonel Phillip O. 109

Robinson, Robbie 155
Roosevelt, President Franklin D. 13
Root, L. Eugene 37, 45
Rose, Wilburn 147
Roswell, New Mexico 21, 22, 82
Royal Air Force 106, 135, 141, 142, 147, 168, 169
Rudd, Lyle 155, 169

S

Schriever, Brigadier General Bernard 39
Schumacher, Robert 106
Seaberg, Major John 37, 43
Setter, Louis 110, 111
1700th Air Transport Group 128
Shingler, Colonel Herbert 109, 122
Shinn, John 155
Sieker, Robert 106, 160
Skunk Works 39, 44, 56, 65, 71, 117, 128, 160
Smiley, Al 155
Smith, Leo 157
Snyder, Sammy 155
Stalin, Joseph V. 15, 16, 20, 25, 26, 27, 29
Stockman, Hervey 147, 152
Strategic Air Command 35, 40, 157
Strauss, Admiral Lewis 74
Strong, Philip 34, 45
Styer, Mike 157

T

T-33 111, 114, 119, 121
Truman, President Harry S. 13, 25
Turner Air Force Base 94, 110, 150, 157
Twining, General Nathan 54, 57

U

UFO 21, 22

V

Vito, Carmine 147, 152

W

Watertown 80, 81, 97, 109, 110, 111, 115, 121, 123, 128, 129, 132, 133, 136, 138, 142, 145, 147, 157, 163, 164
Wendover Army Air Field 75
White, Colonel Lawrence K. 86
Wienberg, Charles F. 39
Williams, Ernest 91

X

X-16 39, 47, 48

Y

Yancey, Colonel William F. 94, 109

ABOUT THE AUTHOR

Thornton D. "TD" Barnes, author and entrepreneur, grew up on a ranch at Dalhart, Texas. He graduated from Mountain View High School in Oklahoma and embarked on a ten-year military career. He served as an army intelligence specialist in Korea and then continued his education while in the army, attending two and a half years of missile and radar electronics by day and college courses at night. Barnes deployed with the first combat Hawk missile battalion during the Soviet Iron Curtain threat before attending the Artillery Officer Candidate School, where an injury ended his military career.

Barnes's career includes serving as a field engineer at the NASA High Range in Nevada for the X-15, XB-70, lifting bodies and lunar landing vehicles; working on the NERVA project at Jackass Flats, Nevada; and serving in Special Projects at Area 51. Barnes later formed a family oil and gas exploration company, drilling and producing oil and gas and mining uranium and gold.

Barnes currently serves as the CEO of Startel, Inc., a landowner, and is actively mining landscape rock and gold in Nevada. He serves as the president of Roadrunners Internationale, an association of Area 51 veterans, and is the executive director of the Nevada Aerospace Hall of Fame.

Two National Geographic Channel documentaries feature Barnes: *Area 51 Declassified* and *CIA—Secrets of Area 51*. Numerous documentaries on the History Channel, the Discovery Channel, the Travel Channel and others also feature him. The Annie Jacobsen book *Area 51 Declassified* documents his career.

Barnes lives in Henderson, Nevada.

Connect with the Author Online

Facebook: www.facebook.com/ThorntondBarnes
Blog: td-barnes.com/blog
Website: td-barnes. com
LinkedIn: www. LinkedIn.com/profile/edit?trk=tab_pro
Twitter: twitter.com/ThorntonDBarnes

www.ingramcontent.com/pod-product-compliance
Lightning Source LLC
LaVergne TN
LVHW010937100826
845153LV00001B/70
* 9 7 8 1 5 4 0 2 2 6 4 5 7 *